THE RUSTLE
OF A WING
Finding Hope Beyond
Anorexia

Sophia Gore

KARNAC

First published in 2016 by
Karnac Books Ltd
118 Finchley Road
London NW3 5HT

British Library Cataloguing in Publication Data

A C.I.P. for this book is available from the British Library

ISBN-13: 978-1-78220-337-7

Typeset by V Publishing Solutions Pvt Ltd., Chennai, India

Printed in Great Britain by TJ International Ltd, Padstow, Cornwall

www.karnacbooks.com

For the protection of all individuals involved in my treatment and experience as a sufferer of this tragic illness, all names of individuals and places have been changed.

I am using a pen name but not because I am ashamed. Anorexia is an illness and there shouldn't be shame associated with it, but I have to protect the identities of the individuals involved in my story.

FOREWORD

Elizabeth Meakins

One bright Saturday morning *The Rustle of a Wing* arrived in my inbox. I had agreed to read the manuscript, but when it popped up as an attachment I felt torn. Spring birdsong was calling me outside. I didn't want to think about the sadness of a young woman's battle with anorexia nervosa. This was my weekend off. But there was a sad urgency to the task. I knew the author was unlikely to be alive for much longer. I decided to read a couple of chapters to ease my conscience then bolt for the big outdoors.

From the opening pages of Sophia's book I was tugged in and swept along. No longer aware of the morning's birdsong, her immensely sad and raw struggle was the only audible tune. It was the harrowing song of a caged bird who has been tortured and who is dying.

This book is not about why someone develops anorexia nervosa. There is a smattering of hints and guesses about why Sophia went to battle with herself and the world around her as she recalls the early days of the illness, memories of the perverse triumph she felt whenever she succeeded in depriving herself of nourishment. *The Rustle of a Wing* doesn't explain the "why" of this terrible disorder, but it does explore what happened to the illness when Sophia entered the world of hospital treatment.

It is a shocking tale of warfare. The repeated violence of having nasogastric tubes forced down her throat, the bruising on her arms and legs from staff restraint, the injuries to her hands from the tightness of restraining bandaging, the locked doors, the humiliation of having her trousers ripped down for a sedating injection. Unable to control either the tyranny of her illness or the physical and emotional brutality of the treatment she was subjected to, Sophia was, in her own words, "trapped in treatment".

It is a tale well told. Close to death though she is, Sophia has cleverly and subversively used access to her own medical notes to recreate the voices she was surrounded by. Extracts from the doctor's log, nursing entries and discharge summaries are pitted against her own furious and infuriatingly intransigent fight against both herself and what feels to her like the terror of experts. Relentless and interminable, it is a battle seemingly without purpose, progress or end.

Unexpected memories drifted to mind as I read the book: one from recently, an art therapist showing me her work with a Sri Lankan patient who had been imprisoned and tortured in his homeland. One from several decades ago when I was working in one of the vast old psychiatric "bins" that no longer exist and came upon a distressed and confused elderly woman who had been physically tied to her chair. On the plastic tray on her lap was a piece of paper with the words scrawled: "Edith Be Quite."

This book is a shocking reminder of how easy it is to respond to the symptom and not the person. How easy it is to use power for imposition rather than collaboration. How necessary it is to listen to what Sophia is telling us: "The treatment did nothing but grind down my soul" she writes. "It reduced me to feeling I wasn't seen as a person anymore". And elsewhere: "I am mad, and I must not be listened to." Perhaps most problematically of all, it challenges us to think about issues of free will and determinism in the matter of life and death. "They don't have the right to keep me alive if I don't want to be," Sophia writes. "Allow me to go in peace."

INTRODUCTION

"There's nothing wrong with me a little ice cream won't fix."

—*Anonymous*

I wasn't ever much into extracurricular activities. I was incredibly shy at school and didn't enjoy being there in the day let alone once school was over. To me, rounders club was the only extracurricular bore that had any benefit, and that was because there was a very special reward to be had.

During summer term, we would be marched to the local park to play rounders in the summer evenings. I was embarrassingly useless, so I tended to just try and stay as far away from the ball as possible. Week after week I would endure this, reminding myself of the end of the term treat that awaited me. On the last club of the summer term, our sports teacher would take us to the park café and buy us each an ice cream.

I have always loved food and was not a fussy eater. Out of everything, ice cream had to be my favourite food of choice. The difficulty with this reward was that we were only allowed one scoop, which meant that I had a big dilemma.

Vanilla, strawberry, and chocolate flavours were boring—I never understood my classmates who opted for them. My problem was that both the mint choc chip and toffee swirl were equally delicious and to decide between them was a serious challenge. The sweet, creamy coolness of the ice cream after the long summer's day was heaven. I loved the joy that food could bring—if only that had always stayed the case.

AUTHOR'S NOTE

The condition *anorexia nervosa* translates as a loss of appetite for nervous reasons.

In reality, you do not lose your appetite if you have anorexia nervosa. You simply do not allow yourself to satisfy your appetite.

Many anorexics profess that they hate food. They are lying. If they did not love food, why would it be a punishment to deny themselves the right to eat it?

For many years, I stuck my head in the sand about addressing my anorexia nervosa. I wish that I had dealt with it before it had the chance to completely destroy my life.

Writing this book has been a rewarding journey for me. My treatment was challenging for everyone involved and I am relieved I no longer hold the same level of anger towards those who tried to treat me. Having the opportunity of reading my medical notes enabled me to see that those involved in my care thought that they were acting in my best interests. I think it is extremely difficult for doctors to decide when forced treatment is necessary and whether the long-term outcome will justify such treatment.

I would like this book to promote a better understanding of the issues surrounding treatment of anorexia nervosa, and ultimately a better treatment outcome for this debilitating disorder, especially for the chronically unwell.

1. The day my world was turned upside down

January 2012

Without health life is not life; it is only a state of languor and suffering—an image of death.

—*Gautama Buddha*

Monday

Doctor's log: Patient has been transferred to the Eating Disorder Unit from intensive care under restraint. Patient has been reluctant to engage with treatment. Dr. Cole has detained her under section 3 of the Mental Health Act. Patient was combative walking over, trying to trip up staff escorts restraining her.

Nursing entry: Sophia has a long and enduring history of anorexia nervosa, restricting type. She has had numerous admissions to mental health services. Sophia is currently at a very low weight and starved, her body is running on empty.

Sophia is furious—says that we plotted and tricked her to get her onto our ward. Our aim is simply to help Sophia stabilise her eating and weight to be in a safer place. Sophia is in fighting mode—not collaborative in every respect possible. Admission clerking will be completed tomorrow (not able to do today due to high level of distress on admission).

I don't know how anorexia engulfed me—it snuck in through the back door. I never saw it coming and I certainly never thought it could devastate my life in the way it has. I can see how ugly it has made me, the pain it has inflicted and yet I keep starving myself. I don't deny myself food because I like the person anorexia has turned me into—I just don't know how to stop.

Tuesday

Nursing entry: Sophia has been monitored on intensive nursing throughout the night. She was angry with staff checking her physical observations but was explained the importance of these. She refused to be weighed.

Sophia presents as an emaciated young woman. She refuses to interact with the team and lies on her bed in the foetal position with her eyes closed. She appears to be passively aggressive and irritable with low mood.

Sophia was given a half portion of food at dinnertime to eat under nurse supervision in her room. After much hysterics, she ate a small portion but refused most of what was on her plate.

Sophia's blood sugars will be checked four times a day with an additional 4am check. Nurses are to treat with Hypostop to counteract hypoglycaemia if blood sugar is low.

So I've screwed up yet again. Every time I have to be hospitalised, I work for months and months to get my illness under control, to learn to feed myself and build my life again. And every time, some-times straight away, sometimes after months, I start to mess it up all

2

over again. And each time it just gets worse. My weight gets lower, my eating more deranged and the people around me just can't take it anymore. I am becoming more and more alone.

Wednesday

Nursing entry: Sophia has refused to get out of bed to have her vital signs monitored. She said she was too tired and shouted at staff to leave.

A food plan has been prescribed and Sophia must attend the dining room.

I won't do it. They can't make me. I have rules I must live by and they don't understand that. I am fine—I don't need anyone interfering and telling me what to do. I hate this horrible place. All they want is to stuff me with food, fatten me up and pat themselves on the back for "curing" me.

Thursday

Nursing entry: Sophia will be having staged increases of calories to her diet from tomorrow. She remains keeping to herself in her room and does not engage in conversation.

There is no point in communicating with anyone in this hellish place. I won't be staying long and I am not one of them. I don't fit— I never do.

My first couple of years at preparatory school were very difficult. I struggled to socialise with the other children and the form teachers I had felt I was being difficult. When I was four years old, we had a regular paper weaving class that involved weaving bits of paper into a grid to make a placemat. It was a daft exercise but it was a great source of unhappiness for me. All the girls in my class were given pink grids while the boys had blue grids. My form teacher insisted that I had to have a blue grid. I did not want a blue grid and when I asked for a pink one she told me I was not allowed. Looking back on this, I feel angry at the way she treated me, but at the time all I could think about was the shame as the other children looked confused as to why my teacher was labelling me a boy. I wished to be pretty and dainty like the other girls in my class, but I could see I was different—fat and ugly. That became my core belief.

> I am forever engaged in a silent battle in my head over whether or not to lift the fork to my mouth, and when I talk myself into doing so, I taste only shame.
>
> —*Jena Morrow*, Hope for the Hollow, published
> by Lighthouse Publishing of the Carolinas,
> used with permission

My parents tell me that my appetite for food was evident even in my early years. As a toddler, I used to wake up before my parents and go to the kitchen. Dragging a chair over to the fridge, I would climb up to reach the handle and open the fridge. I would then remove all yoghurts within my reach and devour them. My parents would wake up to lots of empty pots scattered over the kitchen floor.

I certainly was never a picky eater—I would eat whatever was put in front of me and I was open to trying new things. Despite being a hearty eater and allowing myself to indulge in food, I cannot remember a time when I didn't feel guilty about it afterwards. I have always seen myself as greedy and felt weak for giving in to my appetite. My anorexia definitely latched on to this—it was the perfect ammunition for my spiral into self-destruction.

Friday

Nursing entry: Sophia had about a spoonful of her breakfast this morning and walked out of the dining room. I followed Sophia and asked her what was wrong. Sophia became very tearful and said that everybody hates her and that she finds it difficult sitting in the dining room with everybody. She was persuaded to return to the dining room but only had 2 more little spoons before leaving again.

Do they not understand that I do not respond well to peer pressure? The impending doom I always felt making my morning trip to school, the dread of being amongst those teenage girls who were all cooler, more attractive and likable than me. The more pressure I feel, the more I want to disappear.

I enter the locker room and the "cool" crowd of girls are always sat in one corner. They whisper and laugh and I am sure they are mocking me. When I walk into school, I feel huge. I just wish I were smaller. Maybe if I were smaller they wouldn't notice me. Yes—the more I can disappear the better. Even fifteen years on, I still can't walk down the road my school was on without feeling sick. The sight of young girls wearing the uniform I used to wear brings all those insecurities flooding back. Despite all the hard times I have been through, I still feel just as vulnerable as that wretched teenager.

You can avoid reality, but you cannot avoid the consequences of avoiding reality.

—*Attributed to Ayn Rand*, philosopher
and novelist, used by permission
of Ayn Rand Institute

Ward round: Blood tests show that Sophia is not eating enough and is dehydrated. Bilateral leg oedema going up to her knees present, which she reports as being very uncomfortable.

Sophia's oedema is unusual. It is not the type of oedema commonly associated with anorexia nervosa and is the consequence of the low levels of albumin in her blood due to malnutrition. We have explained to Sophia that when she eats more, her albumin levels will rise and her oedema should resolve. It is not fully understood but the use of diuretics for this type of oedema is likely to make the situation worse. Therefore, treatment with diuretics would not be appropriate.

Rationally I know that underneath all the water bloating my body, there is a very emaciated woman. But it is hard to keep telling myself that when all I can see is how huge my body is because of all the fluid it is storing. It makes eating even harder for my head to justify, and yet eating is what I need to do in order for the oedema to improve and for my body to start shedding all this water weight. I feel stuck in a miserable trap.

Saturday

Nursing entry: Sophia refused to attend for afternoon snack and was very rude towards staff, swearing at them. Sophia fights to avoid being made a fool of or humiliated.

Maybe if I am as horrible as possible they will hate me enough to not want me around. I think that might be the best tactic at this point. I admit it feels good to take out my anger on them—does that make me horrible? Well, this illness is horrible and so am I.

Sunday

Nursing entry: During the night, Sophia rang her buzzer and reported feeling dizzy and queasy. She had to be assisted to sit up in bed this morning—she is too weak to lift her head.

After lunch, Sophia fell to the floor. The alarm pulled and vital signs were taken. Sophia was aided into a wheelchair, although she was confrontational at this— "I am not a cripple".

I am concerned at the risks related to postural drops and the physical weakness Sophia has, which was notice-able in today's incident.

Oh God, oh God, oh God. The cracks are beginning to show. I can't let them see what is happening. I am sure I am fine really. I just need to go home and sort myself out. Please Sophia, hold it together. They will never let you go if you start to fall apart. You are FINE—it's just this place that's making you sick.

Monday

Nursing entry: Today is Sophia's 26th birthday. She appeared low in mood and did not respond when greeted with "Happy Birthday" by patients or staff.

I am 26. My illness is 13. Many congratulations. How the fuck did I let this illness take so many years from me?

Don't dig your grave with your own knife and fork.

—English proverb

The majority of the patients at the unit at the moment are younger and their eating disorder has been prevalent for a relatively short time. When I was first in treatment, I probably would have fitted in with them. But fifteen years on, I now am very alienated from the rest of the patient group. The reality of having an eating disorder of such severity and duration has taken its toll on me and there is no hiding it. I can't relate to what they chat about in the dining room or the lounge and listening to them talk just makes me feel even more alienated.

There is usually an undercurrent of competitiveness on Eating Disorder Units. I don't judge myself to be sicker than anyone else as I think a lot of sufferers have the potential to become as ill as I am if they do not face up to their problems. It's just a matter of time.

Tuesday

Nursing entry: Sophia was unable to attend the dining room for dinner. She stated that she felt weak and was sat on the side of her bed with her head down towards her chest. There is bruising on her knees and her feet are swollen. Sophia slowly ate her dinner under nursing supervision in her room.

I've tried to hide it but I just can't today. I feel guilty for giving in. The relief is bitter sweet. Tomorrow I'll be strong again. I'll be fit for battle after a rest today.

Today, "fat" has become not a description of size but a
moral category tainted with criticism and contempt.

—Susie Orbach, psychoanalyst and writer,
used by permission

During my childhood, I had frequent bouts of tonsillitis. When
I was twelve, the doctors and my parents agreed that it would
probably be a good idea for me to have a tonsillectomy, as my
bouts of tonsillitis were causing me to miss school and would
probably cause even greater problems in adulthood.

Before the operation, I arrived at the hospital and changed
into a gown. A nurse then led me to the scales to weigh me.
I didn't weigh myself regularly and the numbers displayed
on the scales didn't mean much to me, but the nurse immediately commented "Gosh, that's a lot." That is the last thing
that I remember before the operation. I don't remember being
taken down to theatre. I don't remember being administered
the anaesthetic. All I remember is that comment and a voice in
my head that screamed "YOU ARE FAT".

Sometimes I wonder what would have happened if I had
never had that operation. Would I have developed an eating
disorder anyway? Would not hearing that nurse's comment

have saved me from the torturous depths of anorexia nervosa? I will never know for sure, but when I came round from the anaesthetic something in my head had clicked and after that I never resumed normal eating.

Wednesday

Doctor's log: Patient needed two members of staff to sit up for a chest exam. She is unable to lift or move her head without assistance and has severe muscle wastage.

Her bloods show low phosphate levels indicating she has refeeding syndrome and this is potentially fatal. I also have concerns over cardiac function.

Patient's weight is dropping so her diet needs to be reviewed.

Patient remains very resistant to treatment.

I don't know what is right. I can't think straight. They are making me eat so much food but I just feel worse and worse. Why is my body not working? My muscles won't do what I tell them to. I am scared. All I know is that I really don't need all this food.

Thursday

Nursing entry: Sophia has been very anxious today and struggled through breakfast and lunch. She refuses to come to the dining room so is eating in her room. She thinks the other patients hate her.

Sophia is struggling to complete her diet with her food intake minimal for survival. She has been observed to hide food. It is clear that she lacks the capacity, in the context of heightened anxiety and existing anorexia nervosa, to carry through on decisions regarding her diet. If her phosphate levels do not rise, she will need to be transferred to a medical ward.

Something is very wrong. I don't feel in control anymore. And I don't know that I even care. I am in free fall.

I wake up on the cold bathroom floor. I can hear my mother calling through the door, "Sophia, are you alright?"

I have no idea what happened, but I know I must paper over the cracks. "Yes, fine, just coming."

I slowly get to my feet and I remember I was just about to brush my teeth before feeling dizzy and collapsing.

I know why it happened, which is why I won't tell my mother what's happened. I know I am not eating enough. I know my body is breaking down. I know I am deteriorating. I must eat more.

I come out of the bathroom and my mum has laid out breakfast. I sit down and try to eat, but I can't. My body begs me for food, but I can't break my rules. I will feel so guilty if I eat the delicious Danish pastry in front of me. I have a few mouthfuls of fruit salad, arguing it's better than nothing at all.

Hunger of choice is a painful luxury; hunger of necessity
is terrifying torture"

—*Mike Mullin*, "Ashfall", used by
permission of Peggy Tierney

I have many files containing recipes I have collected from
magazines or photocopied from cookbooks. Most of them I
have never cooked and doubt I ever will. But I love cutting
them out and pasting them to make a patchwork of pretty
pages all carefully organised. I spend hours obsessing over
them and I know this is part of my illness. It gives me a sense
of indulgence that my body is longing for but my mind won't
give in I look at the pictures, I analyse the ingredients, and I
eat all the beautiful looking food with my eyes because I can't
with my mouth.

Friday

Nursing entry: Sophia has been irritable in mood and
makes no interaction with staff or patients. She takes a

long time to start her food and attempts to dispose of it. She refused to scrape her yoghurt lid and left some yoghurt in the pot.

Her phosphate levels have improved so we will continue to treat her on our ward for now. Sophia remains at high risk of death although she does fully acknowledge how ill she is.

I DO NOT NEED ALL THIS FOOD. I do not want to scrape my yoghurt pot. I do not want to eat it at all. Leave me alone and stop going on at me. Nothing I do is ever good enough and I'm sick of it.

Saturday

Nursing entry: Sophia was prompted to take her tablets at medication time. I followed her down the corridor to check she had swallowed them. Sophia spat all the tablets out and threw them on the floor.

Idiots. Take your tablets and shove them up your arse. I will not put things in my body I don't agree with. I don't need to take them and I don't like being told what to do. If they think they are going to make me a zombie, they can think again.

Sunday

Nursing entry: Sophia's oedema is getting worse—it is now present in her lower abdomen. She had to be aided by two staff members to sit up from the toilet.

Great. So now you have to ask them to help you take a piss. Does it get any more humiliating? Next they'll have to wipe your arse for you too. You are pathetic. I bet they laugh about you in staff handover. I have lost any shred of dignity I had left. I am so ashamed I just want to crawl into a hole and die.

Monday

Doctor's log: Patient says she went to the bathroom and felt very weak and fell backwards onto the floor. This can be attributed to the loss of muscle weight and subsequent loss of strength. She hit her head but does not appear to be concussed. Staff must monitor her very closely.

How did I let it get this bad this time? Every relapse gets worse, and the crawl back up harder and harder. I don't think I can face it this time. I am so tired and my head hurts. I'm sure I'd be fine if they let me go home though. I was managing before they forced me into hospital. I certainly felt a lot better than I do now so this place is definitely not helping me.

"If you wish to grow thinner, diminish your dinner."

—*H. S. Leigh*, author

My parents were pretty quick to pick up on my weight loss and declining food intake. They tried as best they could to get me to eat, and I tried as best I could to make it look like I was eating to get them off my back.

I used to set my morning alarm so that I would be awake before they got up. I would rush down to the kitchen, pour a little milk in a bowl and sprinkle some cereal dust into it. I then smeared this around the bowl to make it look like I had eaten. I shook crumbs out of the toaster onto a plate and smeared a knife with some butter. Breakfast complete, I would head to school where I knew I could get away with not eating all day. On return home, I knew I would have to eat supper but at least that was it for the whole day. I'd pick at my meal and say I wasn't hungry because my lunch was "huge".

Starving myself in this way did not make me happy, but I never considered not doing it. For the first time I felt in control of my life and that felt good. The more regimented and strict I was with myself, the better I felt and I hadn't felt good about myself for a very long time.

Tuesday

Nursing entry: Sophia appeared more settled last night. She managed to bring herself to the dining room for her snack and her behaviour was better.

No more energy to think. What a relief. My brain has left the building.

2. Dumped

March 2012

In a disordered mind, as in a disordered body, soundness of health is impossible.

—*Cicero*, Roman philosopher

There is nothing more depressing than waking up to find I don't have the strength to lift my head up off the pillow. With each relapse, my weight drops lower and the physical complications more severe. My organs get smaller as my body eats away at them, and my skeletal muscles are pathetic. I have no option but to wait for someone to come and lift my head up for me. And yet I will still argue that I have too many cornflakes in my bowl at breakfast.

Wednesday

Doctor's log: Patient's worsening oedema and low blood phosphate levels have required transfer of her care to a medical ward. Without phosphate supplementation, she has become notably confused and delusional.

Patient is at very high risk of death, suffering from refeeding syndrome and can be treated under the mental capacity act. It remains crucial her diet plan is adhered to whilst addressing her blood phosphate levels.

Someone keeps touching my feet but they say no one is there. Why can't they see them? My face feels strange and I can't breathe properly. I am aware of nurses around me but I can't see them and what I hear them say doesn't make any sense. I don't like this at all.

May be I should eat something. I don't know. I might not need it. No, I'm just being pathetic—I don't need it.

Thursday

Nursing entry: Sophia has been transferred to an Acute Ward in a general hospital. She had a chest x-ray in A&E and has been given a phosphate drip throughout the night. She is on a cardiac monitor, complains of being cold and her temperature is below 35.

Where am I? I don't understand. All I know is that I am really, really cold. At least I've missed supper—I was dreading that cheesy pasta bake. Why do I have to have some stupid nurse staring at me the whole time? It's ridiculous. The infusion going into my arm really hurts. The doctor's say I am allergic to the phosphate supplementations, which is why my arm is all inflamed and sore. I want to rip out the cannula and stop the infusion, but I know it would be pointless, as they would just reinsert it.

Friday

Nursing entry: Sophia has had a very turbulent day. She refused to eat breakfast and shouted at the doctor when she was told she might have to stay for a week.

I attempted to talk Sophia through this, by outlining the immediate risks, but she remained aroused and distressed. Sophia has abruptly removed her cardiac monitor.

I am NOT staying here. They can't keep me like this. What gives them the right to shove me around like some piece of meat? I don't have any of my things, the food does not feel safe and I don't need to be here. They promised me it would only be a couple of nights—bloody liars. They lie about everything. I don't trust any of them.

My friend Ruth is allowed to come and take me out of the hospital in a wheelchair. She rolls me out the doors and towards a local café. We sit and chat and drink Diet Coke. I love spending time with her, but I feel so bad that she has to take me out in a wheelchair. It shouldn't be like this. It shouldn't be that I am so unwell my friends have to act as my carers.

I'm only twenty-seven years old and I am a cripple. I know this, yet I still can't stop what I am doing to myself. Food feels impossible.

The most violent element in society is ignorance.

—*Emma Goldman*, political activist

When it had become clear to my mother that my weight was plummeting, she turned to the secondary school I was attending for help. I was dragged out of class by the school nurse, much to the interest of my fellow classmates, and frogmarched to the nursing office. She made me get on the scales and scribbled away in her notebook. She demanded to know what I was eating, which of course I didn't answer honestly, and then asked me, "Why are you doing this to yourself? You're not a stupid girl."

From that moment on I knew I could not EVER admit to ANYONE that I had an eating disorder—I didn't want to be thought of as stupid. I returned to my lesson, mortified and ashamed that I would now be the subject of the school gossip of the day.

It never crossed my mind that what the nurse said was ridiculously ignorant, but I wish my ears had never heard it because that was the moment anorexia became my dirty secret.

Saturday

Nursing entry: Sophia was quite difficult to manage on the early part of the shift. The consultant has informed her they are concerned about her heart. Sophia was upset that she had been told she would only be in the medical ward for a couple of nights. She lashed out and laid herself on the floor. Nursing staff assisted her back to the bed. She is not complying with her meal plan and she states that she does not want to return to the Eating Disorder Unit.

Well if they are going to keep me in this dump, I might as well make the most of not being made to eat. And if they think I am going back to that shit hole, they can think again. At least here I can follow my own rules again, even if I do have someone gawping at me 24/7.

Labels are for filing. Labels are for clothing. Labels are not for people.

—*Martina Navratilova*, tennis player, used by permission of Martina Enterprises, Inc.

Treating anorexia nervosa on a medical ward is often problematic. The staff are not experienced with eating disorders and the busy nature of the wards means the level of supervision is often not high enough to prevent anorexic patients from engaging in treatment-sabotaging behaviours.

The first time I was treated in a medical ward, I was being fed through a nasogastric tube that was attached to a pump that allowed the feedbag to slowly drip into my stomach. Being on a ward, I was surrounded by other patients so I would pull the hospital curtains around my bed across to give me the privacy I needed. I would detach my nasogastric tube from the pump and allow the feed being pumped through it to go into an empty plastic bottle I kept hidden under my blanket.

I had been getting away with this undetected for some time until the arrival of a rather unpleasant staff nurse. She sensed something dodgy was going on and ripped my blanket off me. On discovery of my secret, she shouted, "I know what you naughty anorexics are like—you won't get away with it with me!"

From then on, my feed was administered via syringe under the supervision of the nurses. Not only was I devastated I could no longer prevent the feed going into me, I also felt ashamed about my pathetic behaviour. That nurse labelled me as a "naughty anorexic" and, as much as I hated that, I knew she was right.

Sunday

Nursing entry: During the afternoon, Sophia was distressed and tearful regarding her fears that she would be force fed through a nasogastric tube, which has always been a traumatic experience in previous admissions. She was encouraged to complete her prescribed diet to avoid this from happening. She agreed to sip her energy drink in small amounts throughout the evening.

Sophia has reported a pressure sore on her back, which was observed to be red and painful. She declined to use the commode as suggested by the doctor however she agreed to use the wheelchair to the bathroom under staff supervision.

Sophia seems much weaker today and has been tearful over her physical state.

This is awful. I hate the doctor—yet another person popping up to dictate what I put into my body. I've got a nurse on my back the whole time and those stupid Ensure energy drinks are loaded with calories. They always pull out the trump card—they can always "help" me with a wonderful nasogastric tube rammed into my nose. To me, that is the ultimate violation. They've done that too many times before for me to be fooled into thinking it could be remotely easier for me.

And if that wanker of a doctor thinks I am using a commode he can think again.

Nursing entry: Sophia is struggling to eat small amounts even. She became agitated and distressed, tipping her Ensure onto her bed. She declines to eat at allocated meal times.

The consultant gastroenterologist is keen to pass a nasogastric tube and restrain Sophia to ensure feeding, however we feel this is unlikely to help Sophia long term, as it will make Sophia react with even greater anorexic will power. We have decided as a team to give Sophia one last chance to feed herself orally on the medical ward.

Oh fuck. I've really got to make some kind of effort now. Relaxing my rules a little is worth it if it means I can retain some level of control about what happens. I have a strategy to try to get some calories into me. I sip my Ensure gradually while I do a Sudoku or any other available distraction technique. Every couple of minutes I take a small sip while my mind is busy and the anorexic thoughts are subdued.

It takes me a long time, but eventually I get through the bottle. The staff are impatient, but this is the only way I can allow myself to get the calories in. To drink the Ensure fast, it feels even more out of control and frightening. I wish the staff could understand that I am not just trying to be purposefully irritating.

I always eat slowly. I do this because eating fast feels more out of control and because at times when I have restricted my intake to a pitiful amount, making it last as long as possible allows me to savour each mouthful. This is greatly challenged in treatment, where you are expected to eat relatively enormous amounts of food in a fixed time period that carries a threat of an Ensure on top of what you have just eaten if you don't finish in time.

See what it is to play unfair! Where cheating is, there's mischief there.

—*William Blake*, painter, poet, and printmaker

Tuesday

Nursing entry: Sophia is complying with a dietary plan devised by a dietician in the main hospital. Her phosphate, calcium and albumin levels remain low.

Sophia's mood is low but that is to be expected. We are trying to allow her to retain control of her care as previous loss of this has led her to becoming even more resistant to treatment. However, if she stops complying with dietary intake, we will need to reassess.

It's great when you get away with things. I know I should have those horrible energy drinks, but I just can't tolerate them. Do I feel bad for cheating them? Not really. It serves them right. Who are they to keep me a prisoner? The nurses watching me don't have a clue. It's easy to make them think I am eating what I am supposed to be. I spit my Ensure into my mug of "tea" and everyone is happy.

My anorexia has developed a very devious streak in me. I have committed some bizarre acts in my quest to fight treatment and weight gain. I have watered down supplement drinks, I have shoved various bits of food in various places and I have done everything I can think of in order to avoid calories. I don't feel pleased with myself for this kind of behaviour and looking back I am not proud of the pathetic attempts to fool everyone around me when they are trying desperately to help me. But I can't help but find some of my behaviour amusing.

One of my most devious acts carried a high level of risk. The clinic I was in at the time had a dining room with a small hatch that connected it with the kitchen. Our meals were passed through this hatch. The kitchen contained a large folder with all the meal plans for each patient, but the door was locked at all times to prevent patients from entering.

At about 3am one night, I quietly made my way from my room to the dining room. Staff regularly checked patients during the night but I had time in-between checks to sneak out of my room. I crawled through the hatch into the kitchen and crept over to the meal plan folder. I was shaking with nerves but I managed to find my meal plan and alter it so that all my hot desserts were replaced with yoghurts. I came very close to being caught. As I came out of the dining room, a member of staff was walking down the corridor and asked why I wasn't in bed. I said I had a headache and wanted some Paracetamol.

I was worried my crime would be discovered, but right up to the day I was discharged, no one ever noticed. Everyone just assumed the dietician had amended my meal plan and the dietician remained none the wiser. I took great relish in informing the dietician what I had done on my day of discharge. We had not seen eye to eye throughout my admission.

Wednesday

Nursing entry: Sophia remains in the medical ward. At morning handover, the nurse in charge has stated that

Sophia has been unable to eat anything since breakfast as the nurse observing her couldn't prepare her food.

I talked to Sophia—she was extremely stressed and anxious. I prepared her morning snack for her. She had a bowl of soup for lunch, which is not part of her care plan. I prepared the lunch prescribed on her meal plan but she would not eat it. She says, "I just want to give up". I have spoken to the nurse and discussed what Sophia needs to eat and at what times to avoid further miscommunication. I have noticed that Sophia is moving her meal times later and later.

Okay so the problem with anorexia is that once you start, you can't stop. Things don't stay still, because the voice always gets stronger. One day it's leaving a few crumbs, the next it will be half a biscuit discretely pocketed and before you know it the whole biscuit is spat out and allowed to sink to the bottom of your cup of tea. The cup of tea is then left to go cold, and then whisked away by the trolley lady while the nurse gawping at me is blissfully ignorant. The relief is euphoric.

Guilt is a destructive and ultimately pointless emotion.

—*"Hope with Eating Disorders"*, used
with permission of Lynn Crilly

When I was younger, my grandparents had a beautiful English setter called Lucy. One Christmas, we went to stay with them in their home in Dorset. I loved being there—the garden was huge and even in the cold winter it was a magical place.

On Christmas Day, my siblings and I were each given a large chocolate reindeer. Being Christmas, and therefore a day of indulgence, I wolfed mine down for breakfast. I was on a chocolate high but I craved more. When the rest of the family were safely downstairs enjoying a leisurely breakfast, I snuck into the bedroom my siblings were sharing and swiped their reindeers. I ripped off the foil and shoved the chocolate into my mouth, barely giving myself enough time to swallow before the next mouthful. When no more chocolate remained, it began to sink in what I had done and I felt horribly guilty. The shreds of foil lay all over the floor and I couldn't bear to look at it. I ran back to my bedroom to hide.

To my great relief, on discovery of the crime, the adults of the family came to the conclusion that the culprit was Lucy, who fortunately for me had a tendency to steal food when given the opportunity. Poor Lucy. I let her take the blame and she was in disgrace the whole day.

Although it was a relief to have avoided the shame of being caught, the feelings of guilt ruined that Christmas for me. I felt so bad about the chocolate that I didn't feel I deserved any of my presents. Guilt and food were linked in my head many years before anorexia sunk its claws into me.

Before I became anorexic, I would indulge in desserts and then feel awful afterwards. In my head I would wish that I were thinner so that I didn't have to feel guilty about eating a lovely slice of chocolate gateau. The irony is, the thinner I got the guiltier I felt about eating. Now I know that, however much weight I lose, I will never feel deserving of that delicious slice of chocolate cake.

Thursday

Nursing entry: At snack time, Sophia was due to have a cereal bar however there were none in the kitchen. When I told Sophia, she insisted on coming to the kitchen and said she had three cereal bars put in the kitchen yesterday. When she could not find them, she started screaming and shouting that someone had stolen them.

Sophia started throwing her belongings across the ward, including her tablets. She started punching the walls and saying she "just wants to die". I was able to calm her down and bring her back to her bed.

I am FURIOUS. The rage is overwhelming. Those cereal bars were my special food. They are one of the few things that are safe for me to eat and now I can't have anything because nothing else is right. It has to be that exact thing. Someone has done this on purpose to wind me up. I am so angry I don't know what to do with myself. Those cereal bars are gone and I can't bear it. I even put labels on them so whoever took them knew that they belonged to me. *This is the worst day ever.*

Christ, how did I become this pathetic?

I can't even imagine a life that doesn't revolve around food. I miss being that girl who loved eating ice cream and got excited about going to restaurants. My eating disorder has made it impossible for me to be part of life in so many ways. I can't cope with food so I have to avoid any situations where it might be sprung on me. I can't be with my family or friends because it's just too hard.

But despite my frustrations with my anorexia, I don't know how I would exist without it. How can you just be "normal" again?

Friday

Nursing entry: It has been agreed with the team that a further 2 weeks on the medical ward is needed. When I relayed this to Sophia she became very irate and screamed at me to get out. She told me not to come back and if I do she will have me removed from the ward. She attempted to throw her plate at me.

My body is repulsive. My legs are so full of fluid the skin feels like it is going to burst. I can't stand for more than two minutes before the pain becomes unbearable. I am a swollen blob. My body is too heavy for me to move. I can't do anything. I am stuck with the same tormented thoughts and there is no escape. For years my mind has punished my body, and now my body is torturing my mind. I feel desperate for someone to do something and take all of this misery away, but I don't believe that eating will make things better. I think they are just saying that to get me to eat more. I can't trust anyone at the moment.

Saturday

Nursing entry: Today Sophia told me she did not want to see me. When I asked how she was, she said

34

"wonderful". She said I had better leave now or she would put in a complaint about me. She says the advantage of being in a medical ward was that she didn't have to tolerate the staff from the eating disorder unit. After telling me to "piss off", I asked her not to be verbally abusive towards me. She told me to leave the ward or she would ring the alarm bell and ask for me to be removed. I left the ward.

Everyone is just a source of irritation. They get in the way and they interfere. Everything they say is stupid and I am too exhausted to be nice to people. When the nurses come in, I just snap and scowl at them. I am fed up and miserable. I am resentful of everyone and I don't hide it. If I am challenged, I swear and shout at people. My language is obscene and if that isn't enough to keep people away, I will start throwing anything within my reach at them.

This is not who I am. I was brought up to be a decent person. But my behaviour is far from decent now. I am ugly in every way possible.

The hatred I feel towards myself, towards life, comes out in bitterness towards anyone who comes into the crossfire.

Does being ill excuse this? No, but I was never this spiteful before anorexia came into play. The anorexia nervosa, the depression, and my desperate frustration have made me more and more spiteful. Over the years, I've become a withered, warped, and wicked witch.

Thou shouldst eat to live, not live to eat.

—*Cicero*, Roman philosopher

When your mind is in starvation mode, you can't help but become obsessed with food. It's impossible not to think about food when you are denying yourself it. I won't eat anything I don't know the nutrition of. This makes it pretty impossible to go to restaurants or pop round to a friend for dinner. I feel sad about that, but I know that even if I were to go, I wouldn't enjoy it because I would be so stressed out about the food. So instead it is easier to stay at home where my only company is anorexia nervosa and I can have the limited foods I feel safe with.

Sunday

Nursing entry: Sophia remains in the medical ward and continues to be hostile towards staff visiting her. She appears to be adhering to the diet plan but we need to be looking out for evidence that she is not.

Each day is the same battle. Each day is about being jabbed with needles, stuck on drips, plonked on the scales and facing the next meal. All there is to think about is food. I am sad this is what my life has come to. My brain used to be filled with creativity and knowledge. I would have finished my veterinary medicine training by now— I would be a qualified vet. I would be respected, successful and hard working. Now my brain just rots as I become more and more obsessed with food.

That's the catch when you stop eating—food starts to eat you.

Monday

Doctor's log: The plan was for the patient to return to the eating disorder clinic today or tomorrow. However she now requires further phosphate drips following the low phosphate levels in the bloods taken from her yesterday. This was discussed with the patient. She remains hostile towards me "I hate you more than words can say". She would not reply to me when I asked if she would consent to returning to the eating disorder clinic.

I pray my bloods don't get better. I don't want to go back to the Eating Disorders Unit. Things here are bad, but there they will be even worse. And I can't bear the thought of giving the horrible unit doctor the satisfaction of dragging me back. I am protected from people like him here. I prefer the medical staff. They don't play mind games with me.

The mind is its own place, and in itself, can make heaven of Hell and a hell of Heaven.

—*John Milton*, English poet

After a while, you adapt to being on a medical ward. Your ears eventually stop hearing the constant bleeping of machines. The majority of the other patients on the ward are elderly and confused. I spent a month on a ward next to an old lady who did nothing but repeatedly call "Help me" all day and sometimes all night. When new patients were admitted, they were initially very upset that this lady was calling for help and the nurses were not attending to her. After a while they realised it was just something she said the whole time so it was best just to ignore it.

As much as I thought I had blocked her voice out of my head, at times I can still hear her saying those two words again and again. She never had any visitors and I was told that she passed away about two weeks after I left, which was probably the kindest thing for her.

Tuesday

Nursing entry: Sophia confided in me today that she is not managing her prescribed diet. Her food chart has been amended to reflect missed meals. She has been portioning her own food and thus the portion size has progressively decreased. She has not been fully supervised during her meals.

Sophia did speak today regarding the arguments she is having with unit staff. She feels unable to manage her anxiety and fear and therefore becomes abusive.

I like Anne. I can't tolerate most of the poor individuals that have to gawp at me 24 hours a day, but she is the exception to the rule. There is something about her that makes me feel able to talk. She speaks to me like I am still a person. She sees beyond the disorder and reminds me that I still exist somewhere within its clutches. After speaking with her, I feel hopeful that life could be good again one day. But when her shift is over and she leaves, the hope goes and everything looks bleak again.

You may force a horse to water, but you cannot make
it drink.

—Danish proverb

During one of my more successful episodes of treatment, my
weight had improved to the point where I no longer fit my
"skinny" clothes. The occupational therapist suggested that
she accompany me to buy some new clothes as she appreci-
ated that this would be difficult for me.

It was harder than I imagined. We went into a high street
store and I selected a few things to try on. Looking at myself
in the long mirrors in the fitting room made me feel fatter than
ever. I tried on everything but the only item I felt vaguely
comfortable in was a pretty top. It was short sleeved with a
plunge neckline and had a dainty cherry blossom print. I liked
the print and that was my only justification for buying it. The
occupational therapist insisted on seeing me wear it so I came
out of the changing cubicle. Both the occupational therapist
and the girl working in the shop fitting room expressed that it
looked beautiful. For a few minutes, I believed them and that
was enough to get me to buy the top.

That was eight years ago. I still have that top. I have never worn it.

Wednesday

Doctor's log: Handover from the staff at the medical ward reported that the patient has not had her prescribed diet this morning and has not been weighed. Patient was abusive towards me and told me to "Piss off". As a result, I did not stay long.

I'm not taking any more of this crap. Why should I do what they want? They are making me suffer day after day. See how they like it when I subject them to my abuse.

Thursday

Doctor's log: Patient has stated that she does not want staff from the eating disorder clinic to visit her in the medical ward. She feels they have disrespected her throughout her admission. She has been particularly upset since being informed that our staff have moved her belongings into a different room in our unit and is extremely angry that she was not asked and that this happened without her consent. She reports visits from our staff are making her frustrated and distressed. She attempted to leave the medical ward saying she was going home. She had to be brought back to her bed.

The medical ward feel it is best staff from our unit do not visit her for the time being. They will do their best to monitor her until she returns to our unit.

HOW FUCKING DARE THEY? Just to make it clear that I am no longer a person, they not only treat me like a caged animal but they

*also have the disrespect to interfere with my property. The thought
of them touching my things and moving them around repulses me.
I have to keep my belongings in a certain position. They have to be
aligned. And now I know they are all messed up and there is nothing I can do about it because I am stuck here. I feel sick. These little
things are all I have left to make me feel safe and slowly they are taking them away. I am certain they spend staff meetings brainstorming
the next idea to torture me. Well they really hit the nail on the head
with this one.*

If my home isn't clean, I can't rest. Every day the floors must be
hoovered and mopped regardless of whether they need to be
or not. If I don't do it, I can't trust it isn't clean and I feel guilty
for "letting myself off" a chore. The chores become rituals that
I must do in order to allow myself whatever meagre amount
of food I have earned. If things aren't in order, if things aren't
tidy and clean, then I can't eat or drink without feeling guilty.
I don't know how I got into this way of thinking and I don't
enjoy existing in this way, but it doesn't feel like a choice. I am
compelled by my thoughts, however exhausted I am of them.

3. Back to hell

April 2012

If we could see the miracle of a single flower clearly our whole lives would change.

—*Gautama Buddha*

I have not yet met one person suffering with anorexia nervosa who does not find change terrifying. You are convinced that doing things differently will make you gain weight or something equally terrible. Even changing the times you allow yourself food is hard, let alone being made to eat foods you don't usually allow yourself in the required quantities. Rational thinking is impossible—an extra pea on your plate can be enough to push you over the edge.

Monday

Doctor's log: Patient has been transferred back from the medical ward. She remains angry with staff and feels she has not been treated with respect. It was difficult to conduct an interview with her. She shouted at me and then closed her eyes and would not answer my questions.

It has been agreed that she will eat in her room for the time being. A member of staff must supervise during meal times, as there is likely to be a high risk of non-compliance with eating.

I can't believe I am back here. I am devastated. I don't want to be a part of this regime where everything is about stuffing patients with food and piling on the pounds. This type of treatment never helps me. All I can think about is fighting back. Having someone watch me eat feels so awkward and makes it harder to hide the fact I am disposing of food.

Tuesday

Nursing entry: I have noticed to my own error that Sophia's protein sachet was omitted from her snack last night. I have offered her the choice of the two flavours available this evening. She has refused.

Stupid woman. Does she really think it's possible for me to add back calories I missed yesterday? And it's her fault not mine. If she didn't think I needed it yesterday, then I don't need it today and I won't need it tomorrow or ever again as far as I am concerned.

As you make your bed, so you must lie in it.

—*Czech proverb*

It breaks my heart to know my parents are constantly living with the fear I will die. I can remember during the first years of my illness I would wake up in the night and my mother would be lying beside me. She said she was terrified of coming into my bedroom in the morning and finding me dead.

Wednesday

Review with Dr. Cole: Sophia remains angry and says that I don't understand how to help her. She has significantly reduced her intake over the weekend in despair and response to perceived lack of care for her. She says she does not want to be a part of this place—she just wants to function away from this world.

Sophia's thinking is biased by terror of weight gain, disgust at weight increase and confused anorexic beliefs about not needing much food to survive. She is at very high risk of death from starvation.

I spoke briefly to her parents yesterday—they are well aware that Sophia is in a precarious medical state and could die.

I really wish Dr. Cole would stop talking crap. I don't want her filling my parents' heads with rubbish about me dying. I am eating loads now. They are just trying to scare me into eating even more.

Thursday

Nursing entry: Staff were alerted to Sophia shouting from her room. She was found lying on the floor, very tearful and upset. She stated that she had tried to get up from her bed and her legs went from under her. She was assisted to sitting on her chair and put to bed. Sophia is to remain on complete bed rest—she is only to mobilise when staff are present.

I am so humiliated. Have I really done this to myself? I've wasted myself away so bad this time. Perhaps I should try to eat a bit more. Yes, I'll try a bit more food.

But not today, maybe tomorrow. Or maybe at the weekend.

Actually, I think the start of a new week would be better. Yes—I'll definitely do that at some point.

Just not today.

It is best to stay on the safe side.

—Danish proverb

One of the clinics I received treatment in was situated next to an empty house. This empty house had a beautiful garden that I occasionally snuck into to enjoy some peace and tranquillity. Unfortunately, at this time I was severely underweight and the muscles in my legs were very wasted. En route to my "secret garden", I stumbled and fell. However hard I tried, I could not get myself up off the ground. I would summon all my energy and could just about get halfway up but then my knees would collapse and I ended up on the ground again. As time went on, I became more and more distressed.

I was stuck for two hours before one of the nurses heard me shouting. When they found me I felt so humiliated—there was no hiding what a cripple I had become. They banned me from visiting my "secret garden" ever again, not that I wanted to after that experience.

Friday

Nursing entry: Sophia has had a very difficult morning. Initially she refused to speak with all three of the staff members on duty. During the night shift, she had become tearful and communicated her frustration at her current physical health and confinement to her bedroom to the staff on duty. We have encouraged her to comply with treatment as much as possible as this will help her reach a healthier physical state.

It's been a while since I've felt this wretched. What I don't get is that I know I am miserable and I want to change, but I can't let myself do it. I can't let my guard down. I can't let them in. I don't trust people not to hurt me or let me down. Anorexia nervosa might be killing me, but at least I can trust it to always be there.

Saturday

Nursing entry: Sophia refused food this morning and complained of the discomfort she is experiencing in relation to her oedema. She was offered the choice of a nasogastric tube to help her nutritional intake, but dismissed this saying "don't threaten me". She put her outdoor clothes on and said that she was discharging herself. Dr. Cole has spoken with her and she has been persuaded to go back to her bed.

I AM SO FED UP. I scream and shout but nothing changes anything. The oedema will never go—I'll always be a cripple. Eating isn't helping and I am sick of people telling me it will get better when things only get worse. And why do they think shoving a tube down me will make things easier? It might be easier for them, but it would be my worst nightmares coming true again.

> Do they not see the birds above them with wings outspread and [sometimes] folded in? None holds them [aloft] except the Most Merciful.

—*The Qur'an*, chapter 67:19

The hospital admissions I have had where I have been fed through a tube have all been deeply traumatic. Possibly one of the worst experiences of treatment for me was when the day staff did not hand over to the night staff that I had already been administered my last feed of the day. The night staff would not believe me when I said that I had already had the feed, and called in reinforcements to hold me down and administer the feed as I screamed my head off. I therefore was given twice the amount of calories prescribed and I was beside myself. I spent the entire night running up and down the corridors to burn off the extra calories. By the time the day staff came on shift again, I was too exhausted to speak but I have a vague recollection of an apology for the miscommunication.

Telling the truth and not being believed is a horrible feeling. When you are an anorexic in treatment, those treating you do not trust a word you say. You are constantly under suspicion and everything you say or do is seen to carry some kind of manipulative motive. Often, this is justified. But on the occasions it isn't, you feel like total shite.

Sunday

Nursing entry: Sophia is calmer and less aroused today than yesterday. She is frustrated with her slow progress and has a plan to make small increases to her diet. The team agrees that as long as there is evidence of improvement, however slow, we will continue to collaborate. Compelling Sophia to treatment is likely to result in Sophia putting all her effort into resistance. If however, Sophia remains critical, we will need to intervene and tube feed.

Okay so I guess I've accepted there is no other option. I can't stay the way I am—I can't take being a cripple anymore. I have to make some changes. There must be a way to do this that is bearable. I'll speak to my nurse and try to cut the bullshit. If I don't start being more honest with them and myself, I am going to stay stuck like this forever. It's not letting them win; I am just finding a way to get out of this mess.

Monday

Nursing entry: Sophia has completed all meals and snacks today without too much issue, although still eating very slowly. She refused to have her yoghurt at lunchtime as we did not have the "correct" flavour. Staff tried to persuade Sophia to have a different flavour but she continued to refuse. She has refused to have her weight checked and remains on bed rest.

The strawberry flavour is 10 calories more than the cherry flavour, which really isn't acceptable to me. And now that I've not had my yoghurt today, even if they do have the cherry flavour tomorrow,

I can't have it because I am not having it today. Why is that so hard for people to understand?

All day my head is buzzing with numbers. Constantly adding calories, constantly calculating my exact intake and constantly running nutritional content through my thoughts. There is no escape. Sometimes I am even looking at the back of food packets in my sleep. I yearn for the days when my brain was concerned with more interesting things. I am sick of the compulsion to examine and research food, but I can't help myself. Every calorie, every gram of fat has to be analysed.

Tuesday

Nursing entry: The dietician has added a further 100 calories to Sophia's diet plan. Sophia is reluctant to work with this, but I have explained to her that it would not be in her best interest if her diet were not constantly reviewed to ensure she gains nutrition and this is the goal she needs to focus on.

ANOTHER 100 CALORIES! Why are they doing this to me? Every day it is getting more and more out of control. I am so scared. I will have to find a way to compensate. If I don't, I'll pile on the weight and things will get totally out of control. I am sure I'll still gain weight even if I skip a couple of hundred calories. They'll never even know and it's a fair compromise. The dietician is an idiot.

I don't have a great track record with dieticians. Generally, the relationship between the dietician and an anorexic patient is not good. It's hard not to resent and disagree with someone who is prescribing a meal plan you find deeply challenging. I am a particularly difficult patient for a dietician, as I don't hold back in letting them know how much misery they are putting me through. I don't show them any respect for their expertise because I have been anorexic for so long and therefore have a wealth of knowledge about food and nutrition. I often feel dieticians patronise me and speak to me like I am clueless. If only they knew about the many hours I have spent poring over nutrition manuals and my endless research sessions on the internet. My brain is a library of nutritional content—thousands of products etched into my memory.

Stubbornness does have its helpful features. You always know what you are going to be thinking tomorrow.

—*Attributed to Glen Beaman*, author

I have to admit that I think I have always been very stubborn. Even as a child, I had particular ways of doing things and I did not accept change easily. This is one of the core aspects of my eating disorder and certainly makes me a nightmare patient to treat. If my regime is challenged by the regulations of the staff, I become angry and abusive. I refuse to see that I need to change and the more pressure I am under the more stubborn I become.

Wednesday

Ward round: Sophia initially declined to attend, but subsequently entered and then left saying "that's not going to happen" when informed of further calorie increases to her diet.

Sophia remains in critical condition. Given her very low weight, all leave from the unit in future will be dependent on her sticking to her meal plan. She will be allowed a couple of hours to go home at the weekend if she completes everything on her meal plan.

Nursing entry: Following the ward round Sophia stated to nursing staff that she wished to leave the ward and began kicking the ward door. She was assessed by Dr. Cole and considered unsafe to be allowed to leave. She is refusing food and physical monitoring and remains lying on her bedroom floor.

Sophia continues to feel punished by the team, but we are only concerned about her critical medical condition. The dietician has made further increases to her diet plan. Sophia has been informed of this.

No, no, no, no, no. This is not happening. Please don't do this. I don't need to be locked up. If I could stop hiding food they won't have to keep adding more. I know this but I can't help myself. I can't put this much food in me. What am I going to do? I can't cope with what they are already giving me to eat. How am I going to manage even more?

I wish I could turn off my brain. Please stop thinking. The thoughts in my head are unbearable. Each day the struggle gets harder and I lose more and more sight of why it is worth being alive.

I am broken. I don't know how to fix me, and nor does anyone else.

Ward rounds often spell disaster for me. All the people involved in my care come together to review my progress and brainstorm ways to "help" me. It's supposed to be collaborative, but it never feels that way to me. Most of the time I disagree with the decisions made and I take my anger out on the staff or myself.

After one particularly difficult ward round, I worked myself up into a complete state of despair. One of the nurses asked if she could do anything so I asked her for a cup of tea and "please could it be very hot". When she returned with the tea, I took the mug in my hands and then threw the scorching tea down myself. It was piping hot and burnt my skin, but it did dissipate some of my anger, which was a welcome relief, however brief.

Mirrors should think longer before they reflect.

—Jean Cocteau, poet, novelist and dramatist,
with permission of Jean Cocteau Comité

Before I even started down the path of anorexia nervosa, I was demonstrating some abnormal behaviour that my mother found particularly frustrating. Despite having a wardrobe full of clothes, the only thing I would agree to wear was the same pair of tracksuit bottoms and a baggy jumper. I would spend hours in front of the mirror putting on different trousers and tops in a desperate attempt to find an outfit that felt acceptable, but everything I wore made me feel fat. The tracksuit bottoms and baggy jumper hid my figure. I felt bearable in them. Even though I still felt fat, at least they hid my "fatness" from other people. I didn't want to draw attention to myself by wearing colour, so the only colour I would wear was black or navy blue. I don't think I ever confided in anyone about these feelings—I just wanted to hide them just like I was hiding my body.

Thursday

Nursing entry: At lunch Sophia portioned out some chicken. I noted that the calories for the pack were under

55

what she was due to have. I discussed this with her and she became tearful, stated that she doesn't feel she can do any better and feels constantly under pressure.

We have agreed to go through her entire meal plan to work out quantities and discuss increase options. Sophia completed her lunch.

Okay, maybe I can sort this out. I just need to wipe the slate clean and stop cutting corners. It's just food for fucks sake—cut the bullshit Sophia and start taking some responsibility for your survival. You are giving in to the anorexia nervosa and it's killing you. Things are not "fine" so stop pretending they are.

Friday

Doctor's log: Patient has made small superficial cuts on skin. Patient stated that this was done to release the liquid in her legs and drain off the fluid. Informed her that by doing so it would increase the risk of infection, which could potentially cause even further swelling. The scissors she used have been removed from her.

I am disgusting. I thought I could drain the water out so my legs would be normal again. I am desperate for some kind of relief. With every cut, fluid oozed out and I just couldn't stop. If I weren't so loaded up with fluid my body would look less fat and it would be easier to see I need to eat. I can't give myself more food when I am this huge.

Saturday

Nursing entry: I spent time with Sophia this morning to discuss her meal plan, her actions of self-harm and how she is generally finding things. We have identified that her calorie intake is much less than estimated because she rounds up numbers and chooses brands with less calories than others. A new plan with an accurate calorie content has been made.

Sophia has admitted to hiding food and cutting corners. I have advised staff to confront her when she is observed hiding food and asked Sophia to think about her response to this and that staff are only trying to help her.

Sophia regrets cutting her legs to release fluid but she is feeling desperate to release the pressure and pain she is in due to her oedema. Sophia says she will talk to staff if she has the urge to do this again. Seepage of clear fluid continues to be evident from the wounds.

Water keeps leaking out but my body just makes more. My trousers just get immediately soaked so I have to wear shorts and then all the skinny patients can see my fat legs. I am disgusting so I avoid leaving my room as much as possible. The dressings around the wounds are pointless—they just get saturated and fall off. I am so tired of all this.

Sunday

Nursing entry: Sophia was in a bad mood this morning. It all started with the hot water in the shower not working which made her late starting her breakfast. She then reported her worries regarding her treatment and says she has had enough and cannot carry on like this. Her legs are not getting any better despite poking them to get the fluid out. She was tearful as she talked about feeling stuck and drained of motivation.

However frustrated I am, it doesn't make that voice in my head go away. I can't stop hearing it. It's always there. Some days it's not as loud, but it's always there. After 15 years of being there, it's part of me now. I don't want it to be, but it is.

> Every experience, no matter how bad it seems, holds within it a blessing of some kind. The goal is to find it.
>
> —*Gautama Buddha*

Despite my physical state, if I am behaving, the doctors sometimes mercifully grant me a couple of hours of leave from the unit to go home.

My parents have to support me to walk to the car. I manage to get into the car, but I need help to pull myself out. My mum or dad would grip me as I lift each leg up to climb the steps to the front door. My mum would set up the sofa with various cushions to reduce the pain from my pressure sores, lie me down and cover me with blankets. It's so nice to lie there and just sit watching television with my parents. I don't use the toilet though as I would have needed help to lift myself up off the toilet seat and I was too embarrassed to put my parents in that position. It was bad enough already that they had to come to terms that my illness had reached a point that I was completely crippled by it. When the time comes to go back to the hospital, I need help to lift me off the sofa and get into the car.

I guess a lot of people would think it was crazy that I was being allowed visits home when I was so severely unwell, but it was these trips that reminded me that home still existed and gave me some respite from my daily struggles and misery at the unit.

Monday

Nursing entry: At 11am this morning, staff nurse Peter and I went to Sophia's room to discuss her leave from the ward this week. I informed Sophia that her leave had been suspended. She became very angry with this and told us to "fuck off". I informed Sophia that she was not to speak to us that way and she then left her bedroom and went into the bathroom. She declined support back to her bed, saying that she wanted to remain on the bathroom floor, as it was "the pits" which is how she felt.

I hate them. Why bother being alive when I am confined to this miserable dump? What do they care—they can piss off home at the end of their shift. I don't ever get a break from this battle.

He fought because he actually felt safer fighting than running.

—*Richard Adams*, Watership Down, used with permission of Oneworld publications

Tuesday

Ward round: Sophia attended but would not sit down and remained standing.

Bed rest has been recommended but Sophia is not compliant. She remains absolutely reluctant to engage with the programme on the ward despite numerous attempts and encouragement from staff.

Sophia's oedema is worsening and her low levels of phosphate and albumin are a concern.

Sophia told us that she does not want to be here. She left the room after 20 minutes, when we started to discuss food portions.

Dr. Cole is concerned about her slow progress and feels that Sophia is not well enough to spend time with her family at home.

Staff must portion food and then give it to Sophia. Sophia is to be encouraged to attend the dining room.

Nursing entry: Sophia remains in bed all morning. She has refused all food and states she is having a bad day. Staff were able to persuade her to eat lunch but she struggled to eat it because she was certain we had given her too much.

Unless Sophia starts to complete her meal plan, we will have no choice but to insert a nasogastric tube. This is likely to be very difficult and Sophia will require sedation.

I can't eat something I haven't measured. I don't trust them not to give me too much. I'll just have to get rid of bits here and there if it looks too big. The problem is, everything looks too big, even when I've measured it. I don't even trust myself anymore—how the hell am I going to trust any of them?

When I am at home, my kitchen weighing scales are my way of making eating feel safe. I wouldn't be able to eat without them. I weigh everything and it has to be to the exact gram. That is why I find eating in hospital so difficult. I don't trust the nurses; I have to weigh it myself. I have to see the numbers on the scales in order to feel reassured it is the right amount. Sometimes even when I have weighed something, halfway through eating it I become convinced that it is bigger than usual and the scales must be wrong. Paranoia takes over and I throw the food in the bin. Eventually, anorexia nervosa takes away your trust in everything. It wants to make eating harder and harder.

Wednesday

Nursing entry: Sophia could not finish her dinner last night and spat out her food into the bin. I asked her what was going on and her response was that she couldn't do it anymore. Her family have given up and she appears confused—she keeps claiming she can't find things in her room and expressing distress. Sophia is clearly deteriorating and her current care plan is not working.

I have completely lost sight of what is important to me. The things I used to care about—my animals, my education, my ambitions, they have faded away. I don't know who I am anymore. I am incapable of thinking about anything except my illness and feeling completely trapped in the world of my anorexia nervosa. There is no escape.

Food, food, food. It's the last thought in my head when I go to sleep, and it's the first thought in my head when I wake up. I have nothing to show for myself anymore.

I'm no longer a person. Anorexia nervosa has eradicated me.

4. The tables turn

May 2012

We must build dikes of courage to hold back the flood of fear.

—Martin Luther King, Jr., civil rights activist

My first day at school has remained clear in my mind despite being only four years old at the time. On arrival in the classroom, I refused to let go of my mother's hand. I was terrified by the other children and not knowing where I was. As my mother was trying to persuade me to go and sit with the other children, my new teacher lost her patience. She wrenched my hand out of my mother's and instructed my mother to leave. I screamed my head off as my mother backed out of the room. I was embarrassed because my behaviour meant all the other children were staring at me. I sat at the back of the room and did not speak a word to anyone for weeks. I have found the world a frightening place for as long as I can remember.

Thursday

Care Plan Approach meeting: We have tried doing things Sophia's way and there has been no change in medical state. It is time to change the approach to treatment.

We discussed Sophia's isolation, which leads to hostile relationships with staff.

She is now expected to have the standard clinic food with all leave from the clinic contingent on progress. She is likely to need nasogastric feeding.

Nursing entry: Sophia attended her Care Plan Approach meeting this afternoon and left crying. She sat on the floor in the corridor and was unable to get up. Staff took her back to her room in a wheelchair.

This is my worst nightmare. They can't do this. My head feels like it's going to explode with panic. I can't breathe. Oh God, oh God, oh God. No, no, no.

Friday

Nursing entry: Sophia continues to protest against her new plan. At snack time, she threw her milk at staff. Clearly she lacks capacity for decisions about treatment and food. Presumption of capacity has been pushed aside because of her high level of distress and challenging behaviour. Her lack of insight impairs her ability to weigh up the relevant information rationally.

Since her Care Plan Approach meeting, Sophia has refused meals and snacks. Today she was expected to start her new care plan with meals prescribed from the standard menu and meals taken in the dining room. Sophia has refused to attend the dining room. Sophia was given the choice of completing meals orally or we will help with giving her the calories through a nasogastric tube. Sophia refused her snack, throwing it at staff. She has been given her snack via the nasogastric route.

If Sophia does not complete her meals within the usual time frame, she will be fed via the nasogastric route. We must avoid sedation if possible given her lack of muscle

and her physical frailty. Staff may use physical support
and holds as and when deemed essential by the person
in charge.

I try to fight back but there are too many of them. I scream for help but no one comes. I beg them to stop but they won't even look at me. It hurts to resist them holding me down, but I have to make them stop.

My skin rips and my bones tear through it as their hands restrain me. They hold my head and I desperately try to break free but it's useless. I twist and turn but that only makes them hold me harder and hurt me more.

The tube goes down. I feel that familiar discomfort as it moves further and further down my throat. Then there is cold as the calories rush into my stomach. The despair hits me so hard I can barely breathe.

And then they leave.

I rip the tube out, my stomach acid stinging my nostril. I curl up on my floor and sob.

I am in complete darkness.

I was first sectioned at the age of sixteen. I was being detained in an adolescent eating disorder unit and my care plan involved force-feeding via nasogastric tube. On the more difficult days, I would become highly distressed when I was due to be fed through the tube. The staff dealt with this by gathering a team of six staff members, invading my room, ripping my trousers down and stabbing a needle into my backside.

That would be the last thing I remember. I would wake up in a dark room with no idea of how much time had passed. My body would still feel heavy and my head fogged with whatever they had shot into me. All I knew was that my stomach was groaning under the strain of being pumped full of Ensure. I would lie in the darkness and sob.

Having my trousers ripped down like that left me feeling totally violated. Did they really need to resort to such dramatic measures to manage an emaciated sixteen year old? Maybe it was the quickest way to get what they needed to do done, but it came at the cost of damaging me in ways I would never be able to forget.

Saturday

Nursing entry: This afternoon, staff nurse Mandy and I went into Sophia's room to offer an Ensure as Sophia had refused to attend lunch. She was told she had 20 minutes to complete it or we would have to help her by putting it down a nasogastric tube. Sophia started to cry and shout at staff that this was unfair and that she couldn't do it in 20 minutes.

After 20 minutes, Sophia was still drinking the drink. Mandy prompted Sophia and reminded her that she needed to finish now or we would have to help her. She completed the drink after a further 10 minutes.

Sophia was then required to have her snack. She shouted, "You've got to be joking. I've just had an Ensure". I explained she still had to have the snack in the next 20 minutes. Sophia lay down on her bed and shouted at us to "fuck off". I took her milk snack and attempted to hand it to her but she refused to take it. I put her mug of milk on her bedside table and reminded her that I had started counting down her 20 minutes. She then picked up the milk and threw it at me. I sounded the alarm and the ward matron told Sophia this was unacceptable behaviour. At 5pm, five staff members entered Sophia's room to feed her via nasogastric route.

It's official—this is war.

66

There are some remedies worse than the disease.

—*Publilius Syrus*, Roman writer

Looking at my treatment history, the occasions when eating and weight gain have been forced upon me have never had a positive long-term outcome. Despite this, currently the doctors still consider force-feeding as an appropriate avenue of treatment for me. I understand they have a duty to keep me alive, but where do you draw the line? Surely there must be a point where the endless brutality of force-feeding is no longer justified? They should be putting NHS resources into the treatment of patients that have a better prognosis than I do.

Sunday

Nursing entry: Sophia's mood was low and withdrawn last night. I spoke to her briefly and she says she feels violated by staff and that she cannot work with the team because they have disrespected her and treated her like an animal. Sophia feels punished and de-humanised. Sophia views being restrained in an attempt to assist feeding as barbaric.

I have noticed that Sophia has increased her activity to compensate for being force-fed.

I pace my tiny room. Each step eases the anxiety a little. But it's useless. However much I try to make the feelings of revulsion go away, nothing gets rid of the feeling of the Ensure sitting in my stomach and the calories my body is soaking up. I make myself sick, but I know I haven't managed to get rid of it all.

More than anything, I can't let go of how violated I feel. Their hands seize my body and the cuts and sores grow in size and number every day. I don't understand—how can they think that this is helping me?

Monday

Nursing entry: Sophia refused to go into the dining room for lunch. Staff brought her an Ensure drink to drink in 20 minutes. She completed the drink in the time given but immediately stood up afterwards to do some ironing. She says, "You have taken everything else away from me, all my safety. I have nothing left."

I have spoken with the doctor about Sophia's increase in activity. The team will consider prescribing Olanzapine to help reduce her anxiety and activity levels. Sophia is not willing to take it, but it must be given anyway as she is now being treated under the Mental Health Act.

So stuffing me with food isn't enough. Now they are going to stuff me with drugs so I can't fight back. No drug is going to beat me though. I won't allow them to turn me into a zombie.

From the age of fourteen I have been pumped with sedative drugs in order to make me more "manageable". Through the years, different psychiatrists have prescribed a whole variety of pills. At times, I know that the drugs have helped lessen my anxiety, but I have to question whether it was for my benefit or to make life easier for those around me. When I have been on particularly high doses of these drugs, I feel scared by how slow my thinking becomes and whether my brain will be permanently stunted. Everything is dulled. My thoughts are numbed and I am not able to focus on anything. The drugs can render you completely defenceless and useless.

Tuesday

Nursing entry: Sophia refused to take her prescribed Olanzapine last night. I tried to encourage her to comply but she was adamant and fears it will make her "a zombie".

Doctor's log: Called by nursing team who wanted to insert a nasogastric tube as the patient was refusing oral feeding. When the patient was informed that we were planning to insert a tube, she drank the Ensure drink. She expressed her annoyance that we were "making her put things into her body she did not want". She threw the empty bottle across the room towards us.

Shortly afterwards, her vital signs were recorded and her pulse was notably high. Patient is highly distressed which probably precipitated her tachycardia.

No shit Sherlock—"it's probably due to stress". Every moment of each day I am overwhelmed by panic. It suffocates me at all times, except when I manage to close my eyes and fall into a restless sleep. I look in the mirror but I don't recognise myself anymore. My eyes are dead, my hair has thinned and I am becoming more and more bloated with water. I am bruised and battered. I feel revolting—I am revolting. At least I am locked away from the world so no one can see how repulsive I've become.

> Humour is the weapon of unarmed people: it helps people who are oppressed to smile at the situation that pains them.
>
> —*Simon Wiesenthal*, writer and Nazi hunter, with permission of Paulinka Kreisberg

Even in the early stages of my eating disorder, my behaviour could be pretty spiteful. During one episode of treatment, I was not allowed out of bed. The nurse brought in my breakfast and sat down to supervise me eating it. I asked for a cup of tea so the nurse went to the kitchen to fetch me one. As soon as she left the room, my breakfast went out the window—quite literally.

"Where's your breakfast?"

"I've eaten it of course. I was desperately hungry."

"Now we know that isn't true. What have you done with it?"

"Hmm … well I guess you'll never know."

The nurse fumed as I gave her an evil smile. The nurses didn't leave me with the food anymore, however many times I requested a cup of tea.

Wednesday

Review with Dr. Cole: Sophia appears to be unable to hear the information about Olanzapine because she is so preoccupied, aroused and distressed about food. She does not believe the information from studies that it helps reduce preoccupation, arousal and distress associated with food in anorexia nervosa. Sophia currently therefore lacks capacity because she is unable to weigh up the information.

I suspect that part of Sophia's refusal is motivated by a fear that it will help her treatment and aid weight gain. If she refuses to take it, a preparation of Olanzapine should now be administered through the nasogastric route whilst Sophia is restrained.

It's 5pm and I know what that means. Any minute they'll all come in. I want to run but there is no escape.

At 5:30pm they arrive. It's the same procedure—they don't make eye contact, they say nothing, they just move like robots. This time, Dr. Cole comes in to watch. They hold my head and the tablet and water are shoved down me. When they're satisfied it's gone, they release me.

The beaker of water sits in front of me. Should I? What will the consequences be? Sod it. I pick up the beaker and drench Dr. Cole. Ha! You didn't like that did you? Now you know it's not nice when you're disrespected.

Thursday

Doctor's log: I have been asked to review the patient as she has been banging her head against a wall. Patient is now sat on her bed with her head down. She refuses to look up and keeps saying "get me out of this place".

Bang, bang, bang. Bang, bang, bang. Maybe if I do it hard enough I can knock these thoughts out of my head. I can't take them anymore. I already have a headache and this will make it worse but I can't stop. Bang, bang, bang. Bang, bang, bang. I must not let the drugs disarm me.

I object to violence because when it appears to do good, the good is only temporary; the evil it does is permanent.

—*Mahatma Gandhi*, leader and activist
for India's independence

Friday

Ward round: Sophia has bruising on her arms and legs from staff restraint. She has also had episodes of high pulse.

Dietician has reviewed the diet plan. We aim to increase this week and increases will be regular over the course of the next few weeks until she is on the full weight gaining diet.

No leave granted.

If Sophia has not completed her meal within the allocated time, staff are to inform her the time limit has lapsed and encourage her to focus on the meal with no verbal conversation. She is to be repeatedly reminded she needs to finish her meal.

As I have already stated, I was not a fussy eater as a child. There was little I wouldn't eat, but one thing I couldn't stand was the vile tinned fruit cocktail salad we were served at my preparatory school on a weekly basis. On one occasion, I was adamant I did not want to eat it. My teacher decided that I needed to finish my food and that the whole school would wait in the lunch hall, cutting into the time we had in the playground, until I finished everything.

As desperate as I was to defy my teacher and dig my heels in, I could not bear all the pupils sat there waiting, getting more and more impatient and angry with me. I forced each piece of slimy fruit cubes down me, including the bright red glace cherries that I particularly detested. Each mouthful made me angry. I didn't know it then, but this situation would be constantly repeated later in life. Treatment for my anorexia nervosa has required constant bullying and peer pressure to get me to eat.

> **Nursing entry:** Sophia has appeared quiet throughout the day. She says she does not want to go into the dining room because she will feel humiliated when staff have to help her to stand up from the table because she is too weak to stand from sitting without assistance. She feels embarrassed that it will attract the attention of other patients and hates being seen as a cripple.

It's a horrible feeling. The meal is over and everyone gets up and leaves but I am stuck. I can't pull my body up. It's too heavy with all the oedema and my muscles are too weak. I have to wait for them to come and help me. I can't bear this shame.

Life must be understood backwards, but it must be lived forwards.

—Søren Kierkegaard, Danish philosopher

Being the centre of attention is something I have always avoided at all costs. At primary school, each day began with morning assembly. At the end of the assembly, any pupils that had a birthday that day would be called to the front of the hall and the rest of the school would sing happy birthday to you before you were expected to tell everyone how you were celebrating and what presents you hoped to get.

I absolutely dreaded this happening to the point that I actually dreaded my birthday. Of course, I loved having presents and a cake, but this did not seem worth the ordeal of having to stand up in front of everyone with hundreds of eyes set on you.

Looking back, I wish I had had the courage to refuse to do it. I guess my rebellious streak had yet to show its face.

Saturday

Nursing entry: This afternoon Sophia was found with an empty sheet of tablets in her hand. Staff remained with Sophia, who screamed when we tried to remove the medicine sheet from her. She put herself underneath her bed and declined repeatedly to emerge. Staff forcibly removed Sophia and she was taken to A&E in an ambulance. Her mother confirms that medicine had been taken from her handbag when she visited Sophia today.

I do feel guilty. I shouldn't have done that to my mother. It was awful to root through her handbag like that. But I knew those pills would be there and I can't be alive like this anymore. Frustratingly, I doubt there are enough pills to kill me, but hopefully enough to at least render me unconscious for a while. I need a break—some respite from the fighting.

Doctor's log: On my way out of the building I have been informed by nursing staff that a patient has taken an overdose. An ambulance has been called to transfer her to the main hospital.

Given the patient's extremely low body weight, rigid anorexic thinking, impulsivity and self harm, I do not believe that she is able to weigh in the balance any decisions in respect of her medical treatment, diet or whether to receive treatment for this overdose. If she declines to cooperate with treatment in A&E, this may be performed in her best interests using restraint or tranquilisation.

Even though I feel really sick and drowsy, I can still feel the relief of just being out of that building. There is still a nurse with me, but at least it is only one of them and they can't gang up on me. God, I feel really sick. However much I deserve it, I hope my mum doesn't hate me.

Nothing can harm you as much as your own thoughts unguarded.

—*Gautama Buddha*

Sunday

Nursing entry: Sophia remains in the main hospital. I spoke with her about her current situation. She expressed that she did not want to come back to the eating disorder unit.

Sophia had her breakfast, although the portion size was smaller than prescribed. We discussed how combative she is in her approach to the nursing staff, and how difficult it makes it for us to help her.

Sophia was transferred back to the eating disorder unit at lunchtime. She is now being nursed intensively on one to one observations.

It was stupid of me to hope I might not have to go back. It's going to be even worse now because I've got some stupid nurse staring at me the whole time as a punishment for what I did.

Monday

Nursing entry: Sophia is angry to be back on the unit. She has wished to be dead for a long time and said that she feels she has no other option now staff are enforcing food and treatment. I advised Sophia although she is frustrated at present, she needs to give her new care plan approach a chance to work.

The more they bully me into complying with my care plan, the more anxious about it I feel. If there is one thing in life I have learnt, is people will walk all over you if you let them. I am not living a life I've had no say about. I make my own rules.

Tuesday

Nursing entry: Sophia agreed to attend the dining room at dinner. However, she later left and was tearful, saying she just wanted to give up. She doesn't know how she is going to cope with her meal increases due this week.

Sophia is becoming increasingly resistant and more difficult to manage. Despite the change in approach to her care, she has not made any progress or signs of improvement.

Get up. Get on the scales. Eat this. Drink that. Hurry up. Take these. Swallow. Sit here. Stop pacing.
Blood sugar. Pulse. Temperature. Blood pressure.
Again, again and again.
JUST LEAVE ME ALONE.

To keep the body in good health is a duty ... otherwise we shall not be able to keep our mind strong and clear.

—*Gautama Buddha*

When I've finished my meal I feel so disgusting. I go to the bathroom and turn the shower onto its coldest setting. I make myself stand in the freezing water, refusing to give in to the feelings of being cold. I scrub and scrub and scrub until my skin is raw. I desperately try to wash the calories away before I have to eat again. I must punish myself for eating all that food. I constantly feel dirty and disgusting, but no amount of washing can take those feelings away completely.

Wednesday

Nursing entry: Sophia has appeared angry and reluctant to complete her diet throughout the morning. She came into the dining room at breakfast and ate her cereal with a lot of prompting from staff. She completed her morning snack but went to the toilet afterwards and refused to have supervision. She possibly vomited before returning to her room and throwing her belongings in the direction of staff.

Get out. This is my room and I don't want you in here. I hate the lot of you. None of you understand and you've stripped everything away so all I have now is anorexia. I wish I were still a person.

On one occasion when I was food shopping, I was inspecting the nutritional information on a box of cereal when I felt a tap on my arm. An elderly woman was standing next to me and she quietly lent towards me and said she really thought I should buy it because I clearly needed to eat more.

I was conspicuously underweight at the time but it came as a shock to me that a stranger would actually notice and say something like that to me. I wanted to be angry and defensive, but her manner was so kind and her face full of concern. I said thank you and put the cereal in my basket. I walked towards the checkout and turned around. When I was certain she could no longer see me, I dumped my basket and left the shop as quickly as possible, feeling overwhelming shame.

I hate knowing that strangers can identify my illness—something so deeply personal, without even knowing me. It's ironic that at the start of my illness, I thought being smaller would make me less noticeable. The reality is anorexia nervosa has made me a freak show and makes me stand out in an extreme way. People don't see a person anymore—they see an anorexic. I'm not "Sophia"; I am "the anorexic girl". I hate knowing this because I don't feel able to anything about it—it doesn't make eating any easier.

I now prefer to do my food shopping online where I can analyse the food I am buying away from watchful eyes and in the privacy of my own home.

No man can think clearly when his fists are clenched.

—*George Jean Nathan*, drama critic and editor,
used with permission of Patricia Angelin,
literary executrix, the George Jean Nathan Estate

I think forming relationships with the staff is essential for an anorexic in treatment in order for the treatment to be effective. The only times I have been able to move forward in recovery have been when I have become close to the staff and trust them. It is only working together that genuine change can be made. Change that comes from pressure or dishonesty never lasts long.

Thursday

Ward round: Sophia is to be intensively nursed during the day and evening shift. No leave granted. Continue current plans to support weight gain.

Nursing entry: At afternoon snack, Sophia became distressed and annoyed when staff asked her not to cover her mug of milk with a saucer. She left the dining room.

We approached Sophia as a team in her room. She became angry and shouted because she felt threatened by the number of staff in the room. It was explained to her that this was the course of action if she refuses to complete her food. Boundaries were held. Sophia attempted to leave her room on several occasions and was brought back by staff. She eventually completed her snack.

I spoke with Sophia about the events that transpired. She stated she felt things were ruined with regards to her care. I advised her that it is about recovering from incidents like this and moving forward.

Sophia must come for meals on time. If she is unable to finish within the specified meal times, staff are to verbally disengage with her.

I have to cover my mug with a saucer because otherwise the milk doesn't stay hot enough. If it's not hot enough, I can't drink it because it has to be perfect. If it's not perfect, I don't want it in my body. If I even bother to try to explain this to them, it's a waste of breath. They will never understand.

I guess working with eating disorder patients can be very frustrating. I can appreciate that watching us slowly consume bits of food must be pretty tedious and require patience that not everyone possesses.

One of the nurses lumped with me was incredibly lazy. She loved watching her soap operas and resented having to sit with me while I slowly tried to get through my meal. Regularly, she got fed up and she would snatch my plate and scrape the food into the bin. She would tell me not to tell anyone before rushing through to the lounge to watch her programmes.

My initial reaction was shock, and then huge relief that I could "get away" with not eating. But the problem was, the next time it would be a different nurse who certainly would not be binning my meal. If I hadn't eaten it the day before,

I could not simply eat it the next day. My head doesn't work like that. Anorexia nervosa dictates that if I eat more on one day than I did the day before, I would gain weight. I didn't want to tell anyone what this nurse was doing because I now knew she would let me not eat which was the best present my anorexia nervosa could ever hope for. So I was stuck in a miserable cycle of euphoria at having my meal binned, only to feel horrendous the next day when I had to eat it.

Envy is thin because it bites but never eats.

—*Spanish proverb*

Friday

Nursing entry: This evening I asked Sophia how her day had been and she replied "awful". She explained that this was because she had "someone in her face all day", referring to the intensive nursing level. I acknowledged her frustrations but reassured her that whatever approach is now being used, it is considered to be in her best interests.

I am so jealous of the other patients. They can all go out this weekend. Some of them even get to go home. I miss home. I would give anything just to have some time out of this place, a break from the world of anorexia nervosa and treatment. I know there is so much more to life than this, but I am completely stuck.

We are not born with feelings of envy. Babies aren't envious. We become envious. For as long as I can remember, I have felt envy of others. Everyone is happier, more confident, and generally a better person than me. The feeling of envy does not make me feel good about myself and I feel it is something I should not admit to. It is undeniable that anorexia nervosa is riddled with envy—especially in treatment.

Some patients are more competitive than others, but nearly all at some stage of their illness or treatment harbour at least some envy and resentment over weight, food, and any eating disorder behaviour. Despite this, it is still possible for genuine friendship to blossom in the environment of an eating disorder unit.

Saturday

Nursing entry: Sophia had a fall in the bathroom today. She was struggling to open the door and fell backwards. She has grazed her back and her left elbow.

Sophia has a number of pressure sores on the left side of her body (left hip and sacrum). She has bilateral leg and foot oedema. Blisters of fluid are present on the upper right and upper left feet.

Dressings have been applied using aseptic technique. A pressure mattress has been ordered for her bed.

My body hurts all over. I still can't stand up without help. I am a battered cripple and I can't bear it. When I wake up in the morning, my face is so puffy with oedema that I can't open my eyes properly. My feet are swollen to the point that little blisters of fluid are breaking out on them. The wounds don't heal because my body doesn't have the resources to form new skin tissue. My bones poke through my skin and my hair is falling out. I can't lift my head up from my pillow because the muscles in my neck have wasted away. My body has eaten up all its external fat and muscle, now it is eating my organs. I can't use the toilet without two people to help me. I can't wash properly which makes me feel even more disgusting.

So, is anorexia glamorous?

Do I deny myself food because I believe it makes me look nicer to be skinny?

NO. I don't do this because I am a stupid woman who has gone on some faddy diet. I love food, what would be the point of denying myself of it if I didn't? I don't eat to punish myself because I hate who I am. And the more anorexic I have become, the more hatred towards myself I feel. It's a horrible trap.

Diseases of the soul are more dangerous and more numerous than those of the body.

—*Cicero*, Roman philosopher

The hardest thing about coming to terms with my anorexia nervosa is that I feel such a sense of shame about it. I try to tell myself it is an illness like any other, but a lot of the time "normal" people make scathing comments and think I am an idiot for not being able to feed myself. I am mortified when I notice complete strangers staring at me in horror at my appearance, or whispering, "Look at her". Once, I was walking into the Tube station and some guy shouted, "Eat something!" at me. I was so embarrassed I wanted the ground to swallow me up.

Sometimes I feel angry that people don't understand or have any compassion for anorexics, but then I remember that I didn't before I got ill. I thought eating disorders were something that vain supermodels got because they had to be really skinny. I didn't appreciate the psychological aspect of the disorder.

It's not as simple as just making yourself eat and gain weight. Eating disorders are so much more than that. They infiltrate every aspect of you, they twist and contort your

87

identity, they alter every relationship you have, and they stunt your thoughts and drain you of every shred of self-worth. They devastate your life and alter it to the point of it being completely unrecognisable. And it's not just your life that's burdened—everyone around you suffers too. An eating disorder is not something you would wish on your worst enemy.

Sunday

Nursing entry: Sophia had low blood sugar during the night. She was asked to drink some fruit juice, which she refused. She told staff to get out of her room and tucked her head under her blankets. She remains distressed that staff are checking her blood sugars every 15 minutes. I informed her that her blood sugars are running dangerously low.

Sophia's night snack has been increased to counteract her low blood sugars during the night.

I am glad my blood sugars are low. I hope I slip into a coma and die. It would be a peaceful way to go, and I don't want to be alive like this anymore.

Monday

Doctor's log: Nurse Sally has informed me that she has witnessed Sophia swapping her full mug of milk with an empty one that she keeps in a hollowed out tissue box. We will address this as a team.

It's amazing how long it takes them to catch on. Over the years I've built up quite a talent of making food magically disappear. Anorexia nervosa is unbelievably cunning and deceptive when it wants to be. It convinces you there must be a way around this eating lark. You can get better and leave hospital without having to eat those potatoes. Eating them and feeling disgustingly guilty is not essential. You don't have to put yourself through that.

It's not denial. I'm just selective about the reality I accept.

—*Bill Watterson*, artist and author, used with
permission of Universal Uclick

Denial prevails in anorexia nervosa. I will convince myself that I am fine and people are just overreacting. Even at times when I have been severely ill, I cannot see how bad things have got. So what if I don't drink or eat all day? I'll have something before I go to bed—that will be enough. Sometimes when my weight goes down I refuse to accept that it is the reality—the scales are obviously wrong. Dieticians will tell me how many calories I need to consume and I think they are being ridiculous. As if I would need that much!

In treatment, I will take every option I can to cut corners on my food intake. I do not recognise what I am doing. What's the big deal if I hide a bit of my butter? At least I am eating my toast. A bit of butter is not going to make any difference when I am piling all this food into me. A bit of biscuit at snack time isn't going to matter either. And a potato at lunchtime is not a big deal when I've eaten two of them already. A whole chocolate bar is unnecessary—half of it can go up my sleeve (where, unfortunately, it begins to melt and I have to wash my cardigan afterwards). If I've got a pie at supper, eating the pastry would just be excessive when I've got chips next to it. So the pastry goes into my pocket. And the chips are too many so a few of those can go too. I'll eat everything at night snack, unless my mug looks like it's got more milk in it than usual (which is most nights). Hmm … so it probably does add up to quite a bit. But I don't need to worry—I'll still gain loads of weight on what I am eating.

And so denial rules—it's so much easier to stick your head in the sand. I don't want to address what I am doing because I am too scared not to hide the food. So it's easier just to pretend it isn't happening. Even when I am too weak to stand up, my head will not accept that I need to change.

Tuesday

Nursing entry: Sophia has been very abusive towards staff today. She was confronted regarding the milk she has been disposing of. She is adamant that she will not drink it.

A nurse must sit alongside her for closer observation during snack times. If Sophia refuses to drink the milk, we will have to give it to her via the nasogastric route.

Oh piss off. I haven't been drinking my milk for ages and I'm not going to start now just because you've stopped being idiots and noticed one of my tricks. There are so many ways I can get around my stupid care plan. I don't agree with any of it so I am not going to be a good girl and take my "medicine".

Wednesday

Nursing entry: Sophia refused to drink her milk. I told her we would have to help her by putting a tube down her. She started to shout and then wedged herself

underneath her bed. She eventually calmed but it took
some manoeuvring to get her out from under the bed.

*You have repeatedly violated and abused me. I will not allow you to
do it anymore. The way I have been manhandled is unacceptable. You
cannot justify this as treatment when all it is achieving is damage.
I need to start asserting myself more—I am ill but I know right from
wrong. And you are very, very wrong.*

An insincere and evil friend is more to be feared than a wild beast; a wild beast may wound your body, but an evil friend will wound your mind.

—*Gautama Buddha*

Not all the treatment I have received for my anorexia nervosa has been traumatic and distressing. There have been some clinics where I have had good days. The best Christmas I have ever had was in an eating disorder clinic. Although I was far from home and family, the day was spent with staff and patients I had come to love and respect.

In the afternoon, a nurse I had formed a very close bond with and a patient who had become a dear friend went on a long car ride to the coast. The roads were empty and we sped along as the countryside flew past us. The evening sun was setting and casting a beautiful light over everything. We reached the coast and watched the grey waves crashing against the shore. I felt so at peace.

I have had many times of laughter and joy in treatment, but over the years that has become harder and harder to achieve. I am more miserable with each admission and I don't want to interact with those around me because I know that after discharge you go back to being alone again. It's easier to stay alone all the time so you don't have to go through getting used to it again.

Thursday

Nursing entry: Sophia struggled with supper, picking parts out. She accepted the Ensure replacement drink and is being assisted to drink this following boundaries that it will be prescribed via the nasogastric route if she is unable to drink it.

I don't care whether I take this orally or you shove a tube down me. I can make myself sick as soon as you're satisfied enough to piss off and leave me alone.

Be as a bird perched on a frail branch that she feels bending beneath her, still she sings away all the same, knowing she has wings.

—*Victor Hugo*, poet, novelist, and dramatist

Friday

Ward round: Sophia is now on the full weight gaining diet. We suspect that she is vomiting as a response to feeling controlled by us. She must remain on intensive nursing with full supervision in the bathroom. Any food refused must be administered by nasogastric route. No leave from the ward granted.

Nursing entry: Sophia attempted to complete lunch but refused to have her yoghurt. She crawled under the table in tears because she was so full from completing the main meal. The team assisted her with restraint and she was taken to her room in a wheelchair.

Following team discussion, we agreed to maintain the boundaries of her diet plan, which is that a full

Ensure must be taken either orally or through nasogastric route.

On entering her room, Sophia was found on the floor screaming "don't do this to me". She appeared so aroused by this encounter that we do not believe that she has the capacity to consent or refuse intervention and she was assisted from the floor.

She was subsequently offered the option of consuming Ensure orally or of being assisted to do so with a nasogastric tube. We were forced to use the nasogastric route. Sophia repeatedly said, "I will never trust any of you again" and likened nasogastric feeding to being "violated". She then vomited on the floor. Her pulse was high (140 bpm) and she was tearful and swearing throughout.

The team must continue to maintain boundaries around food. Sophia has been returned to her bed. She is tearful and largely silent.

Sophia has had a distressing day in response to the care plan boundaries being enforced. She remains on enhanced nursing support: eyesight observations at mealtimes and extended supervision after meals to reduce opportunity to harm herself or purge.

I am so racked with despair all I can do is sob. I am exhausted from fighting them. My body is so weak that being restrained and dragged by them wipes everything out of me. I try not to but eventually I fall asleep. When I wake up I briefly forget what has happened. And then I smell vomited Ensure in my hair and on my face and I remember everything. My face is caked with sick but I don't even care. Today has damaged me in a way I won't ever be able to forget.

Despite this, I can take a small comfort. I managed to replace half the Ensure with water before it was put in the fridge earlier. Sometimes you lose a battle, but mischief always wins the war.

Those unfortunate professionals that have had the task of trying to get me to eat know that I am notoriously mischievous when it comes to food. Food goes in pockets, up sleeves, in socks, into secret napkins or cups and wherever it can possibly be secreted. I even resort to packing food into the sides of my mouth and disposing of it when I leave the dining room. Often nurses do spot that my cheeks are bulging, hamster style, and I am made to swallow.

When I "get away" with something, I feel elated. However relieved I am to have managed to get rid of food, deep down I know that I am only cheating myself. I can lie and trick the staff, but I keep myself stuck by doing so.

Saturday

Doctor's log: Patient has sustained injuries on her right knee and right shoulder from yesterday's restraint. Staff administered Olanzapine as prescribed.

Patient's foot is still seeping with water from the blisters present. We are changing the dressing up to 6 times per day.

There is a new tear to her right upper leg. Swabs and a crepe bandage have been applied.

The oedema makes my skin like paper. There are rips and tears all over me from their hands clutching at me. It hurts but I don't care. I am glad it hurts. At least the misery on the inside is being reflected on the outside too.

The bandages they apply saturate with water that oozes from every sore and fall off. And yet all they do is tell me off because they are convinced I am doing it on purpose. Why would I do it on purpose? I really don't get the way they think.

I go to sleep with towels wrapped round me. I wake up in the night and the towels are soaking. I want to replace them with dry ones, but

I am too weak to get up. I lie in bed and dread the day ahead, praying morning will never come.

Sunday

Nursing entry: Following discussion with Sophia about the promethazine, she threw her prescribed dose at staff nurse Jackie.

With much persuasion, Sophia came to the dining room for supper. She firstly refused her meal, then spent time pressing food onto the plate. Staff explained that she needed to scrape her plate. Sophia was observed spitting food into a napkin. Staff explained that this would have to be replaced. Sophia became angry and threw her fork and then her plate. Staff removed all utensils.

Eventually Sophia complied with her care plan and completed her meal once it was replaced.

I fucking hate the lot of you. I am so angry I don't care how rude or abusive I am. You deserve my hatred—you treat me like shit. I am going to behave like a complete brat so you all hate me so much you'll leave me alone.

> But when the time comes that a man has had his dinner,
> then the true man comes to the surface.

> —*Mark Twain*, author

Having been subjected to different treatment programmes in a variety of eating disorder clinics, I have experienced a variety of regimes and regulations around food and behaviour in the dining room.

I think a dining room in an eating disorder clinic has to rank pretty highly in a list of the most miserable places in the world. Occasionally, someone makes small talk (usually a staff member desperately trying to "jolly" things up). Some eating disorder units allow the radio to be on, although no one is really listening to it. Most patients will be in their own little world of torment.

Everyone has their own way of coping—their own way of making the act of eating feel "safer". Personally, I choose to eat the vegetables first in the hope that if a miracle were to happen I would not have to progress on to the rest of the meal. Everything is separated out into food groups, divided, ordered, chopped into tiny pieces and dissected. This could go on for hours, which is why there is almost always a time limit.

The time limit varies in different clinics, but the consequence of exceeding the time limit is fairly universal—your meal is replaced with some form of high calorie drink, such as Ensure. This is generally something to be avoided at all costs, even if it means choking yourself as you stuff the last of the contents of your plate down your throat.

Some staff members take it upon themselves to count down the minutes of the time limit left, yelling "10 minutes to go!" and so on. I find this tends to make the atmosphere even more tense because it feels like you are in a race to finish.

Hiding of food is common and if spotted is confronted and your meal replaced. Attempts to dispose of food can be highly imaginative so staff members have to be pretty sharp to spot it. Often other patients pick up on someone else hiding food and the resulting confrontations can get pretty ugly.

Sometimes patients cry and scream, sometimes everyone is just shut down and trying their best not to think about the fact they are eating. Occasionally things will explode—someone will freak out and throw something or storm out of the dining room.

After the mealtime has drawn to a close, patients have a period of supervision to prevent them from engaging in purging behaviours. Throughout this time, the atmosphere continues to be tense. Some patients will sit and jiggle their legs in a desperate attempt to burn off the calories they have just consumed. In some units, you are forced to talk about how you are feeling after eating, which usually just makes everyone even more depressed. You count down the seconds and then when supervision is over, you think, "OK, so just a couple of hours to go before I get to do this all over again. Lucky me."

I've spent too long in these dining rooms and I don't find it helpful to be sat around others struggling to eat. Therefore, I avoid the dining room at all costs and prefer to eat in the privacy of my room. Unfortunately for me, the staff have now decided that they will drag me to the dining room by my arms and legs if I refuse to attend.

Monday

Nursing entry: This evening Sophia has shown staff her knees. Both are swollen and one knee has a large split in the skin that is oozing water. The doctor has recommended she lie down and elevate her legs. Sophia refuses to comply with this and remains standing. She then walked to the shower and had a shower against staff advice. Eventually, the duty doctor arrived and put Steristrips across the split.

I can't change my routine just because my knee has burst. I need to have my shower. I am not allowed to lie down and rest until later—I have to do all my rituals first. My rituals are the only way I can cope with all this. As long as I do my routines, I am safe. I can breathe. I am still in control. All this stupid water—my body is exploding with it. I am not going to let anything get in the way of my rituals though, however much pain I am in.

Tuesday

Nursing entry: Intensive nursing is continuing throughout the day. Patient remains aloof with the occasional comment "You are a vile witch".

I can be pretty spiteful and horrible. I have a sharp tongue and a sadistic sense of humour. Sometimes I don't like myself for it and it pushes people away. But it's my way of coping with the shit in life and I don't think I could have lived for so long with this illness without it. I am able to laugh at the stupidity of it all. I am a fighter and that can be both good and bad. I don't give up. I don't know if that personality trait keeps me alive or keeps me ill—perhaps a bit of both.

You wouldn't believe it if you met me when my anorexia nervosa is not being challenged, but I can be a monster. I will be violent, I will swear, but worst of all I will make the most of my sharp tongue. If I can pick up on an insecurity that someone involved in my care may have, I will use it to hurt whoever they are. I will say anything I know will hurt them the most. I am not a nice person when anorexia nervosa is ruling the show. I am a skeletal demon.

Wednesday

Nursing entry: I attempted to dress Sophia's knee mid morning. She declined and stated that I was incompetent.

Sophia has discussed the recent episode of force-feeding and restraint. She feels hugely punished and betrayed, and felt that staff were unfair to her. We discussed the physical restraint aspect of the event. She felt purposely intimidated by staff.

A team of people bursting into your room and pouncing on you— who the hell wouldn't feel intimidated? Why do they think my feelings are not a normal reaction to that?

I would like to do it to them and see how they react. I bet they would shout and scream and beg for it to stop. I bet they would try to break free. I bet they would lash out because it hurts. I bet they would weep hopelessly after, when everyone has gone and it's all over. Rip the tube out and breathe. Thank God, I can curl up in the darkness again.

Attachment there leads to suffering.

—*Gautama Buddha*

I do not remember a time when I didn't feel fearful about the world. Even as a toddler, I didn't like my parents going out at night because "they would get all covered with dark". When we attended social gatherings with other families, I hated being sent to play with the other children. All I wanted was to be with my mum. Sometimes when my mum insisted I go play so she could have some "grown up time", I would go and hide in our car instead. I've always felt scared about things—it just took a while for that to turn to food.

Thursday

Doctor's log: Patient's right foot looks worse and she reports that it is very painful. The laceration below her knee is alarming and water continues to ooze out of it. The sores on her back constantly need to be dressed. The graze on the left side of her back that is a result of being restrained looks red and sore.

Nursing entry: Sophia has voiced her unhappiness at being on the unit and how barbaric her treatment has become. As a team, there is great concern among us that Sophia is becoming more and more difficult to manage. We can't restrain her for feeding without hurting her because she is so underweight and frail.

I can see it sometimes. I can see in their faces they don't like what they are doing. They are afraid of looking at me when I beg for it to stop. Sometimes one of them starts to well up and has to leave—the situation is distressing for them as well as me.

They come back a little later and try to make me feel better. They can't say it but I think they feel uncomfortable about what is happening. They don't necessarily make the decisions—they accept what the doctors say because it's their job. But the more brutal things get, the more cracks in the team appear. Chinks in the armour—it's only a matter of time before something snaps.

Since my school days, I have become braver in standing up to those that intimidate others. In one of the eating disorder units where I was receiving treatment, there was a patient who was particularly difficult to be around. She was very set in her ways and quite unpleasant towards other patients and staff if challenged. She had a particular seat in the dining room that she had to sit in, and all the patients just accepted that and were too afraid to put themselves in the firing line.

One particular day, I decided I had had enough of her threatening behaviour. At lunch, I collected my meal on a tray from the kitchen and sat down in her "place" at the dining table. The other patients looked on aghast and horrified as we waited. When she walked into the room, she looked completely thrown. I was prepared for a violent attack although I was not giving that away in my behaviour and I carried on eating as if everything was normal. She stood staring at me for a while, but then just took a seat at the opposite side of the dining room.

The patient group were very surprised by this, but I guess sometimes others give bullies power too easily. I wish I had been this brave at school. I allowed myself to stay scared because I didn't have the confidence to face the people that I feared.

Friday

Ward round: Dr. Cole is concerned about Sophia's physical health and the risks of transfer. In light of her challenging behaviour, treatment resistance, low weight, skin wounds and oedema she is at extremely high risk.

Past experience has demonstrated that effective feeding orally cannot be sustained in a medical setting. Sedation is dangerous and there is a high risk of infection on a medical ward.

There are also risks in changing the treatment team, but also potential benefit as Sophia would have the opportunity to back down her resistance and have a fresh start.

Avery Lodge have offered a 4–6 weeks respite admission and the commissioners have agreed to fund this. They have a ward that is more medically equipped to address Sophia's physical problems. The team confer that if physical health deteriorates, Sophia will have to be sedated and entirely fed via the nasogastric route.

SOPHIA IS NOT AWARE OF THE OPTION TO TRANSFER HER TREATMENT TO AVERY LODGE AND SHE SHOULD NOT BE TOLD.

Nursing entry: At supper, Sophia tried to hide a handful of omelette in her cardigan pocket. Staff challenged her on this and she took it out. Sophia completed her meal but took an extra 30 minutes.

When I get caught hiding food I feel so embarrassed. All the other patients look at me and I know they will bitch about me later when I am not around. However bad this makes me feel, I still have to take the chance I will get away with it. The relief of not having to eat it gives me the only comfort I have left. Right now, pleasing the anorexia nervosa feels more important than any feelings of humiliation.

You're entirely bonkers. But I'll tell you a secret. All the best people are.

—*Lewis Carroll*, Alice in Wonderland

As well as struggling to feed myself, I also suffer from obsessions about cleanliness and tidiness. I feel extremely panicked if things are dirty or out of place. My room is arranged in a specific way and everything has an order. If something is out of place I can't concentrate on anything until I have put it back in the right place again.

One of the more quirky aspects of my eating disorder includes the collection of special cutlery. I have particular teaspoons that I like the shape of. They are precious to me and I get very upset if I can't find them—to the point where I am unable to eat because I can't without that particular spoon. I won't use normal size spoons—they would be too big for the small mouthfuls I take. I also like to use a particular fork that is quite small and slender. I don't have special knives though. I don't know why I don't have a special knife; perhaps I just haven't found the "perfect" one yet. I like having my special cutlery. I feel a lot safer eating something when I am able to use my favourite utensils.

Saturday

Nursing entry: Sophia delayed in coming to breakfast and was distraught that she could not find her tea-spoon. When she opened her packet of Weetabix she was observed trying to hide a portion of it. She was confronted and the portion was replaced. Sophia sat for around 5 minutes staring at the breakfast but eventually started and completed the meal.

At lunch, Sophia became very upset and anxious. She stated that she could not eat and blamed staff for how she was feeling. She eventually agreed to come to the dining room but was unable to eat the meal and had an Ensure replacement drink instead. Sophia expressed that she is really struggling and does not see any point in carrying on.

This evening Sophia reported that she was experiencing pain in her right foot. The doctor removed the dressing and the foot appeared extremely red. The doctor has redressed it and advised Sophia to elevate it. This will be handed over to the medical team for further assessment.

God, I am so sick of being in pain. It's just one thing after another. I hate my body—it's a constant source of irritation. At least that distracts me from thinking about all the calories I am consuming.

Envy lurks at the bottom of the human heart like a viper in its hole.

—*Honoré de Balzac*, novelist and playwright

Every morning I check social media. I don't ever post updates about myself and I am careful to keep my shameful life as private as possible. I don't really know why I have to check because when I do it makes me miserable. I look at all the amazing things people I have known have achieved with their lives. They are getting married, starting new jobs, having children, going on amazing holidays, eating delicious food, having a drunk night out, and generally living life to the full. This is all documented in their status updates and endless photos.

I feel pathetic for the fact my life has amounted to so little and I long so desperately to have what they have. I am sure they all have their fair share of problems, but it would be nice for me to feel that there was some happiness in my life that I wanted to share with people. I long to feel proud of something I have achieved instead of this constant feeling of shame. Jealousy eats you up and drags you deeper into that black hole.

Sunday

Nursing entry: Sophia was prompted to attend lunch. She struggled with the meal and kept putting her head between her hands and glancing to see if I was watching her. When she realised I wasn't going to take my eyes off her she started getting very anxious and shaking. She spent 10 minutes cutting up her food, which made the plate look even fuller, and then started eating little bits.

After a few mouthfuls she regurgitated the food into her hands. I told Sophia that I could see she was really struggling and asked if an Ensure would be easier. She said she would rather stick with the meal as she had already started. She became tearful. I encouraged her to keep going but told her she couldn't keep spitting her food out. She persisted with her meal for about an hour and managed to complete it.

Staff have observed Sophia regurgitating and smearing food into her clothes throughout the weekend.

I am utterly repulsive. The things I do are disgusting. I am not an unhygienic person—I am obsessive about cleanliness. Even as a child my room was always tidy and I didn't like it when things got dirty. But the fear of food has become so huge that when I swallow I can't bear it. I bring it back up and then I don't know what else to do because I can't swallow it again. So I spit it out and smear it anywhere I can in the hope no one notices. It's a relief not to have the food inside me, but I know I am gross.

Gosh, how did I become such a revolting creature?

5. A nasty surprise

May 2012

The cruelest lies are often told in silence.

—*Robert Louis Stevenson*, novelist and poet

Monday

Nursing entry: Sophia has been very low in mood this morning and continues to struggle with her meals. She regurgitated most of her breakfast and was given a replacement but then regurgitated that on returning to her room. She was also sick after her morning snack and refused her lunch.

Sophia clearly states that what we are asking her to do is "impossible" and continues to exhibit challenging behaviour when treatment is imposed. She recklessly sabotages herself and this reflects her anorexic drive to fight treatment. There is a clear pattern of escalating non-compliance.

Doctor's log: Patient tearful throughout physical assessment and complains of nausea. Staff are having difficulty in managing wounds.

All wounds have been assessed.

Right foot:	tension blister covering half of upper foot with large amounts of watery exudate
Right knee:	traumatic wound, pink, yellow and white in colour, excessive amount of watery exudate
Left hip:	pressure ulcer grade 2
Sacrum:	pressure ulcer grade 2
Back:	4 traumatic wounds of various size

Transfer to Avery Lodge to be arranged for 1pm tomorrow.

PATIENT MUST NOT BE INFORMED UNTIL JUST BEFORE TRANSFER TO MINIMISE HER OPPURTU-NITY TO EXERT REACTIVE BEHAVIOUR ON OUR UNIT.

I just can't do it. Even when I manage to get the food down, the panic overwhelms me and I can't keep it down. Nothing is acceptable anymore. I won't allow myself anything without feeling unbearable guilt.

Surely things can end now? My anorexia nervosa has won—there is nothing anyone can do at this point. My body will not tolerate food.

6. Do or die

14 days later

Bad is never good until worse happens.

—*Danish proverb*

I guess they had to admit defeat. They were failing to manage me. I was just getting worse. So they gave up.

I was furious when they staff revealed I was being transferred. For some time, I have wanted to be sent somewhere else, but I thought that if that were to happen it would be planned and at least discussed with my family. I had an hour's notice in which I frantically packed my belongings whilst trying to get my head around the fact I was being forced to go somewhere I had never been before and was a lot further away from home.

I was bundled off in an ambulance and on arrival I waited for four hours to be admitted. There didn't seem to be much of a handover, particularly in terms of my meal plan and expectations around food. The rug had been swiftly pulled from under my feet, and I was pretty certain my illness could take control of the situation to its advantage.

The standard of care at Avery Lodge was pretty diabolical, but it was a relief for the battle to be so easy. For the most part, my anorexia nervosa could get away with whatever it wanted. Sometimes staff noticed and they told me off, but they didn't force feed me. The boundaries were gone and each day more and more food went down the side of my bed. I was too weak to walk so I couldn't dispose of it any other way.

I would press my alarm button to call someone to help me to the toilet, but they didn't come so I wet the bed. The muscles in my bladder were getting weaker so I couldn't hold it in. I would lie in my own piss and wonder how long I would be lying there before someone would come and help. The nurses would get annoyed with me because eventually they would have to clean it up, but then they would also get angry with me when they struggled to lift me on or off the toilet so I couldn't win either way. I was just a constant source of irritation for them and they certainly did everything they could to make me aware that was how they felt towards me.

The doctors forbid me from using the shower and said the nurses would bathe me at my bed. When I asked to be washed, the nurses would just walk away and ignore me. The only time I washed was when my mother visited. She helped me sit up, undressed me and wiped me with a soaked flannel. I felt so much better just for being cleaner, but I couldn't stop thinking no mother should have to do this for her adult daughter.

Avery Lodge didn't ever restrain me so I stopped getting new sores and bruises, but the sores I already had were unbearably itchy and smelt horrible. At least that helped to disguise the smell of rotting food under my bed.

My oedema got worse with every day. The water seeped further and further up my body and breathing started to hurt. I knew what was coming and I hoped it could be as peaceful as possible. And after being so ripped apart, dying comparably felt a much more gentle experience than the brutal fight life had become. I hoped that I would just drift into unconsciousness and be ignorant of death creeping closer and closer. I never asked to be transferred elsewhere and I hoped that I could stay at Avery Lodge. Death was all I wanted at that stage and I felt relieved that no one was going to stand in the way of that anymore.

Dr. Cole: Liaison with Avery Lodge team.

Unfortunately, I have been informed that Sophia has deteriorated rapidly over the two weeks she has been at Avery Lodge. They report that Sophia is poorly compliant with phosphate supplements because they give her diarrhoea. On admission, the wounds on her back sustained from restraint on our unit were infected and required antibiotics.

Sophia's phosphate levels have dropped. Avery Lodge do not feel they can safely force feed her as she is too ill for restraint and needs cardiac monitoring if sedated. They feel they are making little progress. Because of her critical condition, her nutritional status needs to improve more rapidly than Avery Lodge can manage.

Given her perilous medical state, it has been agreed that Sophia will now be transferred to a medical ward for nasogastric feeding with sedation and monitoring. It is recognised that whatever the setting for treatment, Sophia's prognosis is extremely poor. Feeding is such an urgent priority that risks of delays through Sophia's removal of the nasogastric tube must be avoided.

Sedation with benzodiazepines and olanzapine prescribed. Sophia will have to have her hands bound to prevent her from removing the tube.

7. Grasping to keep me alive

June 2012

> Rabbits live close to death and when death comes closer than usual, thinking about survival leaves little room for anything else.
>
> —*Richard Adams*, Watership Down, used with permission of Oneworld publications

I've been on my feet all day. I started work at 9am, only getting home at 6pm and then having to go to various houses to feed various cats whilst their owners are away. Now I am back home I am desperate to sit down and eat but I can't allow myself.

First I have to clean out and feed all my animals and then I have to hoover and mop the entire house.

Then I have to have a shower. After that I can allow myself to sit down. But I am not allowed to eat or drink until 11pm. I don't know why this is my rule, but it is my rule.

I am parched and weak with lack of food, but all I can do is watch the clock slowly tick. When it reaches 11pm, I get up to go to the fridge. But then I remember I can't because last night I didn't get round to eating until 11:15pm, so I have to wait another fifteen minutes. I sit back down again.

Why can't I stand up to this voice in my head? Why can't I just be like normal people and eat or drink when I want to?

It's all driven by fear. If I break the rules, something bad will happen and I won't enjoy eating anyway because I will feel too guilty that I've broken the rules.

This existence is misery. But I will keep going. I must.

Monday

Nursing entry: Sophia is now in a medical bed in the main hospital. Dr. Cole and gastroenterologist Dr. Pace have reviewed her this afternoon. It has been explained to Sophia that she is too ill to continue negotiating food at present and that she will be fed entirely by nasogastric tube. She will be kept on bed rest in a side room of the Acute Assessment Unit and has been given a commode, which she must use.

Dr. Pace is the only person who is authorised to make changes to the diet plan. Sophia is not to be seen by a dietician. Staff are not to enter into discussions about food with Sophia and a member of staff will nurse her at all times.

Sophia and her parents understand that Sophia will die unless she complies with feeding as a matter of urgency.

I'm too cold and tired to feel scared. I hear what they are saying to me and I know my worst nightmare is coming true, but I can't scream and shout—I don't have enough strength left in me. May be it would be better to leave me to die. I can't come back from this.

Tuesday

Nursing entry: Sophia was asleep when I arrived and stayed so for the first hour of my shift. The ward nurse in charge today looked at the sores on Sophia and we gave her a bed bath. Sophia then fell back asleep. The nurse passed Ensure through her nasogastric tube.

In the afternoon, we tried to change Sophia's position to prevent further bedsores. She woke up from her sedation and said she felt sick. The nurse passed her a bowl and proceeded to pass Ensure through the nasogastric tube. After she did this, Sophia was sick.

It took four members of staff to help her get onto the commode this morning so the nurse has provided a bedpan instead. Sophia felt terribly embarrassed and distressed about the situation.

Sophia's mum came to visit Sophia and we changed her bed sheet. Sophia asked if she could get up and wash her face. We agreed and assisted her to the sink, but I reminded Sophia that she was very weak. During this task, Sophia became very tired, panicked at feeling so weak and asked to be taken back to her bed. She was too weak to sit up and be moved up the bed so her mum moved her legs to the foetal position and we put the barriers up so she wouldn't fall.

The commode was depressing in itself, but now I am even beyond being able to use that. I was very unhappy when they said they would be moving me from Avery Lodge, but hopefully it's too late anyway. I am glad. At least mum is here. I don't want to die with just strangers around me.

Childhood is a promise that is never kept.

—*Ken Hill*, playwright, used with
permission of Rachel Daniels

When I was younger I just assumed that one day I would be married and have my own family. After many years of anorexia, I have come to terms with the fact that this is highly unlikely to happen. It saddens me when I see mothers with their children. Yet another joy in life that anorexia nervosa has robbed from me. There will never be a child calling me "mummy". It's probably a blessing—all I would do is fuck up being a mother like I do with everything else.

Wednesday

Doctor's log: Albumin dropping, phosphate dropping, and greater oedema evident—this suggests the patient was getting virtually no calories whilst at Avery Lodge.

ECGs show cardiac abnormalities. Patient must wear a heart monitor at all times.

Nursing entry: Sophia has been trying to negotiate with staff about how much feed she has been prescribed. She is begging to be allowed to take it orally rather than down the nasogastric tube. This is not to be agreed.

Because Sophia is too weak to pass urine, the nurse has catheterised her.

Oh God, my brain is starting to wake up again. This is not happening—I won't let this happen. This tube is coming out. They are not going to stuff me with calories. I don't know how much they are putting in me—no one will tell me anything. I feel completely out of control. I don't want this—why won't anyone listen to what I am saying? It should be my decision, not theirs.

Thursday

Nursing entry: Sophia has had very loose bowel movements. After using the commode, she moved her bowels again without warning when returned to her bed. She is very embarrassed and upset about this but calmed down when staff spoke to her. She is drowsy and dropping in and out of sleep. The sedation she has been receiving has been effective—she is considerably easier to feed.

I am so disgusting. I can't bear people seeing me like this, even if they are nurses and used to it. I don't want anyone to see me in this pathetic state. I feel filthy and I desperately want to wash myself but I am too tired to do anything. I drift in and out of sleep, but I still feel the cold rush of calories running down the tube when the nurse feeds me. It's misery.

Friday

Nursing entry: Sophia was asleep when I arrived. She was fed through the tube and woke up when we washed

121

her and changed her clothes and dressings on her legs.

Sophia was low in mood and says she wants to die.

I am being pumped full of poison. I spend every minute trying to think of something I could do to put an end to all this but there is nothing I can think of. I just have to wait until I get the chance. They don't have the right to keep me alive if I don't want to be.

A forced kindness deserves no thanks.

—Italian proverb

In whatever treatment setting, aggressive force-feeding has always incurred a huge cost to me psychologically that I feel outweighs any physiological gains, which are likely to be short-lived anyway. Making me gain weight and overloading my body with calories is something I experience as physically and psychologically abusive. They might justify it by saying they are stopping me from dying, but I will be the one reliving this trauma over and over.

Whichever restraint technique the staff use, it is impossible for them not to cause me injury because I am so frail. The rips in my skin are painful and the sores become infected.

How can they justify this treatment when the long-term prognosis with force-feeding is so poor? I so wish the violence would stop. I think that for someone who has been as severely ill for as long as I have, it is justifiable that the kindest thing to do is to let nature runs its course.

Saturday

Nursing entry: It was handed over that Sophia has a very disturbed night and was refusing the nasogastric tube whilst awake. She was fed when she was asleep for about two hours.

Sophia is requesting to see the dietician. She says she wants to eat breakfast this morning and is going to refuse to be fed through the tube today. She refused the antibiotics for her leg and her antipsychotic medication. The nurse in charge says she will get the doctors to speak to her.

This afternoon Sophia was very sedated and unable to communicate much at all. She is complaining about the feeding regime and expresses a wish to die rather than be fed.

Sophia has been more difficult to manage today but staff are being firm and giving prescribed calories and medication.

Sophia removed the nasogastric tube and staff rapidly reinserted it. Sophia had got hold of a syringe to remove the feed from her stomach via the nasogastric tube and Ensure has been found in a juice carton by her bed. Her hands need to be bound and the nurse with her must be able to see the end of the nasogastric tube at all times.

You can't do this to me. STOP, STOP, STOP. Get this fucking tube out of me you BASTARDS. I am not allowing this to happen. This isn't happening. THIS IS NOT HAPPENING. You can't. I won't. Please no, JUST STOP.

The problem in defense is how far you can go without destroying from within what you are trying to defend from without.

—*Dwight D. Eisenhower*, 34th president of United States,
used with permission of John S. D. Eisenhower

I am so desperate to get rid of what they have just put in me. I know it's disgusting but I don't care—I do it anyway. I only have a few minutes. The nurse has stepped out of my room to take a phone call. She's not supposed to but she leaves me on my own.

I manage to get up and make it to the sink as quietly and quickly as possible. I feel so weak but the adrenalin spurs me into action. I take the cap of the end of the tube and I suck as hard as I can. I manage to get a mouthful of my stomach contents up and spit it out. The taste is disgusting but I've got to get rid of as much as I can.

I can hear the nurse coming back so I grab my toothbrush and pretend to be brushing my teeth. She is cross that I am out of bed but of course she's not able to report that to the doctors because she shouldn't have left the room in the first place.

I wish I had had longer so I could have got rid of more. Now I have to go back to the bed and sit with the torment of knowing all those calories are in my stomach still and slowly being absorbed into me. I feel so revolted that I want to rip my stomach out.

Sunday

Nursing entry: When arrived to take over from nurse Patrick, Sophia's mum was holding one of Sophia's hands and nurse Patrick was holding the other as Sophia was attempting to remove her tube. She managed to struggle free, remove the bandages around her hands and pull the tube out whilst feed was being administered. She was sedated and the tube was reinserted after much of a struggle.

Extraordinarily, Sophia then managed to push the tube out through her mouth using her tongue. Sophia was screaming as her hands were rebound and the tube reinserted.

If you think crushing my fingers together is going to stop me then you are very wrong. I don't care how much it hurts—this tube is going to be ripped out every time you shove it back down me. You can blast my brain with sedatives all you like but you are not putting food in me. I will not tolerate it. I don't care if I am disturbing the other patients, I am going to scream and scream and scream until someone hears me and stops what you are doing.

Monday

Nursing entry: Sophia has been emotional and combative with nursing staff. Her hands remain bound but Sophia needs to be restrained to prevent her from biting at the bandages. Sophia has been fed milk and water through the tube but has vomited three times.

Let go of my arms. These stupid bandages are coming off. Get the fuck off me. Why can't you see how pointless this is? My body has had enough—just let me go. This can't be ethical.

Tuesday

Nursing entry: Sophia has struggled for the full two hours that I was with her, trying to pull off the bandages on her hands and knock the nasogastric tube out of place. I had to hold her in restraint for the entire shift. Sophia states that she will fight staff and that she will win.

I am so tired but I will not rest until this tube is out. You can't hold me down like this forever. My mind can only focus on getting out the tube. Even the pain of ripping it out doesn't stop me, nor the discomfort as it is rammed back down. I twist and turn but I've got hands tightly pinning me down. I try to move my head away from the tube but they hold it still and I am too weak to overcome the restraint. The tube is thrust into my nostril and I am told to swallow but I don't. I fight the tube as it dives deeper and deeper down my oesophagus, which makes the whole procedure even more painful. I am beside myself with distress as they administer the Ensure down the tube. I scream and scream. Even once it is over, they continue to hold me down until they can get enough sedatives in me to render me senseless.

I assure you; while I look like a ghost, I'm no spirit or demon. I'm nothing but a girl struggling to make her way in an intolerant world. I bleed, I love, and someday, I'll die.

—*Leanna Renee Hieber*, The Strangely Beautiful Tale of Miss Percy Parker, used with author's permission

Before my first admission to hospital, I initially tried to get well at home. My consultant at that time advised my mother that she should prepare my meals and bring them to my room for me to eat. My mother dutifully prepared small meals for me to consume at various times throughout the day. At first my intentions were good and I tried to eat. But after a few days more and more of the food that my mother bought was shoved into my bedroom cupboard.

While the rest of the family were asleep during the night, I would try to get rid of the food in the bathroom but that just blocked the pipes. So the mound of food in my cupboard grew and began to smell. Eventually my mother discovered it and was rightfully and heartbreakingly disappointed by me.

My failure to get well at home quickly resulted in my bags being packed and admission to an eating disorder unit—where hiding food in my cupboard was certainly not an option.

Wednesday

Ward round: Patient is demonstrating highly agitated behaviour and keeps removing her nasogastric tube. She has also been managing to aspirate her stomach contents.

Patient complains of being "treated like a barbarian" and remains resistant to accept treatment. She is clearly lacking capacity to make decisions at present regarding her care.

A high level of vigilance is required to prevent the patient from aspirating her stomach contents. All syringes must be removed and the nasogastric tube must be fully visible at all times.

Nursing entry: Sophia struggled to remove her bandages last night until she eventually fell asleep. She had been shouting at staff, calling "help" repeatedly and trying to use her hands to knock the nasogastric tube.

This morning Sophia woke up crying and called for help. She appeared confused as to where she was. She briefly tried to remove her bandages but did not resist when I asked her to place her arms down.

Eventually Sophia fell asleep and was fed milk and Ensure through the tube.

I'm getting more and more tired. I am failing. I thought they would have given up by now. I am so tired. I should keep fighting, but I can't. I'm too tired.

He who eats alone chokes alone.

—*Arabian proverb*

Sometimes arriving home from school we would get such a lovely treat. On days where my mother had been to the supermarket, she would occasionally buy a pack of delicious raspberry iced buns. My siblings and I would each sit with our bun and devour this delicious, sugary treat. The best part was the juicy pocket of raspberry jam in the middle of the doughy bread. I liked saving the super sweet slither of pink icing on the top of the bun until last.

On one of these special occasions, one bun was simply not enough for me. As soon as my mother and siblings left the kitchen, I snuck up to the bread bin and stole a second iced bun. I had to eat it quickly to avoid being caught red handed. I almost started to choke as I gobbled it down.

My hope was that it would go unnoticed but of course later that evening my mother clocked on to the missing bun and knew there could be only one culprit as my brother and sister were too small to reach the bread bin.

As a punishment, she decided I didn't deserve to go swimming tomorrow. I was furious and announced I was running away. I went up to my bedroom to get my jumper but when I returned downstairs and went to the front door my mother had double locked it so I couldn't get out. Frustrated, I returned to my bedroom and put away my jumper.

I decided I probably shouldn't steal an iced bun again—especially as I didn't really enjoy it when I had to eat it so quickly anyway.

I wish I didn't like food so much.

Thursday

Nursing entry: Sophia has been pleading for her hand bandages to be removed so that she can read a book. I informed her that I was not able to make that decision.

Sophia's lips have been observed to be very dry. I offered to clean them with sponges and water and she allowed me to fix her hair back from her face. When I was distracted doing this, Sophia managed to remove her left hand bandage. Whilst waiting for it to be reinstated, Sophia dug her nails into my hand whilst I prevented her from taking out her tube. Sophia tried to pull her blanket over her head but was informed that we need to be able to see her face and hands at all times. Sophia shouted at me to leave and hit out at me. She eventually calmed down enough for me to release her hands and she fell asleep.

I don't recognise myself anymore. I don't care who I hurt. I would kill them if I could. I would scratch, bite and beat them if I weren't so weak.

When I am in combat, I stop seeing the staff as human beings. They are objects that are getting in the way of my anorexia nervosa. I have no respect for them and I don't think about my actions. My anorexia nervosa takes over and manifests itself in violence towards anything it can—including myself. I will

131

hit others and if I am stopped I try to hit myself. My anorexia nervosa is in full swing and its deep ugliness is undeniable. Despite the fact that all my muscles are eaten away and even my vital organs are being broken down, the anorexia propels my body to fight with a force that is fairly remarkable for someone so emaciated. But eventually a point is reached when my feeble body is too weak to be much of a weapon for the anorexia. The staff are stronger than me and I am forced to surrender until my body is not so weak and pathetic.

Friday

Nursing entry: Sophia remains verbally resistant to her hand bandages and attempts (sometimes successfully) to remove them. She remains at high risk of death. Sophia has expressed that she would like to be transferred to a hospice to die.

If someone doesn't want to live with their illness anymore, they shouldn't have to. Treatment has failed. Why won't they just accept that and stop all this unnecessary distress? Allow me to go in peace.

Saturday

Nursing entry: I checked Sophia's catheter, as she was in pain and her bladder felt full. She was very disorientated and kept asking what day it was, what time it was and if her parents had been to visit her. A few moments later she asked the same questions again.

Dr. Pace came to speak to her. Sophia asked him how much longer she would have to stay like this and he told her she would be kept like this until he feels she is more stable. He explained that she has to go along with this care plan, as he is the expert. Sophia expressed she is not comfortable with him as her consultant and would like to be moved to a different consultant as he does not know what he is doing. Dr. Pace calmly asked if there was anything else she wanted to talk about. Sophia became irate so Dr. Pace left.

Dickhead. Who the fuck does he think he is? What gives him the right to dictate to me? I don't give a shit about his expertise. He can shove his treatment up his arse. I am feeling even angrier now—I will fight harder.

Sunday

Nursing entry: Sophia was sleeping when I arrived but woke after about 30 minutes when she had her bloods taken. She put the cover over her head so I asked her to remove it so I could see her face. She refused and told me repeatedly to "fuck off" whilst hitting out at me.

Dr. Pace arrived and asked her to remove the covers from her hands. Sophia refused. When we removed the cover, Sophia did not have the bandaging on her right hand anymore. We have removed her cover so that she cannot hide her hands and the bandage has been reapplied.

I think I hate Dr. Pace more than any of the rest of them put together. He speaks to me like I am nothing. In his eyes, I am not a person and he is far superior than I am. He doesn't have a clue about me.

> They cannot take away our self-respect if we do not give
> it to them.

> —*Mahatma Gandhi*

In order to secure my place to study veterinary medicine at university, I needed to do as much work experience as possible. I spent a number of weeks in different veterinary clinics during my school holidays. In one such clinic, I spent two weeks doing all the jobs no one wanted to do—cleaning surgical equipment, cleaning out animal crates, hoovering, etc. Despite these tasks being somewhat tedious, I still put all my energies into my work and I did enjoy some of it.

At the end of the two weeks, the head vet at the practice called me into the consultation room and just announced I shouldn't bother applying to veterinary school, as I didn't have the people skills to be a good vet. I was so upset that I was unable to speak. I just nodded and left. I sobbed the whole way home. Rationally I knew that he had no right to pass that judgement on me—he barely even knew me. But what he said was yet another knock to my already fragile self-esteem.

Monday

Nursing entry: Whilst the staff nurse was administering Sophia's feed, Sophia managed to rip out her nasogastric tube and stated that Dr. Pace can't treat her like this. She started screaming and trying to roll off the bed. Another nurse came in and we began to restrain Sophia.

The doctor was called to reinsert the nasogastric tube. Sophia asked for her phone to speak to her mum to calm herself down. After I had handed her the phone, she rang the police. When I realised what she was doing, I removed the phone and explained the situation to the police.

At this point, the doctor arrived and three members of staff restrained Sophia while the tube was reinserted. Sophia was shouting and tilting her head back. The doctor told Sophia to calm down and that screaming was preventing her from breathing properly. When we let go of her hands, Sophia tried to bite and scratch at staff. She proceeded to bang her head.

Dr. Pace arrived and checked her vital signs. Sophia shouted at him to get out and called him a "shit". When he left, Sophia cried and I tried to calm her down. She asked to speak to her parents but I said she had to wait until she had calmed down.

Midmorning, Sophia's parents arrived to visit her and Sophia complained that they had forced a bigger tube down brutally. Her mum asked me why they have used such a big tube and was worried that it had been done to punish Sophia. Her father became aroused at seeing Sophia in such a state and demanded to see Dr. Pace. The nurse said she had passed on the message but Dr. Pace was unavailable at this time. Sophia's parents then saw Dr. Pace running down the stairs. Sophia's mum said he was trying to get away and Sophia's dad ran after him. Dr. Pace has explained to Sophia's parents that the larger tube is the standard tube used and that the staff member able to insert the thinner type of tube is not on duty today.

Bang, bang, bang. Make the pain go away.

Bang, bang, bang. It hurts so much I can't breathe.

Bang, bang, bang. This is what Dr. Pace has done because you are bad.

Bang, bang, bang. You won't take your medicine like a good girl.

Bang, bang, bang. Keep banging until you knock the pain away.

Police report: The police have contacted staff about the incident with Sophia. I explained why Sophia was so distressed and that she is under section 3 of the Mental Health Act.

Tuesday

Nursing entry: Sophia has spent the entire day arguing with staff about the larger tube and the hand bandages. She says she is in excruciating pain and the bandages are too tight. I tried to slightly loosen them and Sophia expressed a lot of hopeless feelings. She states that she cannot continue fighting anymore and she feels that "the world is better off without her".

Sophia was given her Ensure through the tube but towards the end of the feed she vomited clotted blood. Dr. Pace was informed and he examined the position of the nasogastric tube. Sophia has continued to vomit blood three times.

The nurse in charge agreed to remove the hand bandages briefly to relieve Sophia's hands. Sophia became much calmer and relaxed, reading a newspaper. Her hands were bandaged again before the start of night duty as the nurses said the doctors are insistent on this despite

Sophia demonstrating she has not removed the tube whilst not wearing the bandages.

No more punishments please—I can't take the pain. I promise to be good. Just free my hands. The bandages are so tight I can't even feel my fingers anymore. The pain is excruciating and I am helpless to reduce it. The bandages have been tied so tight now—there is no way I can squeeze my hands out. I promise I won't try to take out the tube, just free my hands please. Take away the pain.

What's the vomiting blood about? Something's not right. What they are doing isn't right. I can see some of the nurses aren't comfortable. They can see I am in genuine pain because of the way they are treating me.

Wednesday

Nursing entry: Sophia continues to say she is in pain. She is aroused and irritable. She has attempted to bite her right shoulder and has managed to remove her bandages. She keeps saying, "I want to die".

The medical team have stated that Sophia is resistive to the degree that she needs ongoing restraint and that this will need two nurses with her at all times. An additional nurse has been organised from tomorrow.

The dietician has decided that Sophia is now on 1500 kcal per day.

SOPHIA MUST NOT BE INFORMED OF THIS AND SHE IS NOT TO BE GIVEN ANY FOOD OR FLUIDS TO TAKE ORALLY.

Great. So now I've got two people gawping at me. Yet another set of eyes to witness my suffering and doing nothing to make it stop. There is nothing I can do to distract myself from the pain. I know I am a bad person, but do I deserve all of this? Death would be so much kinder than this.

Hell is empty, and all the devils are here.

—*William Shakespeare*, poet, playwright, and actor

Thursday

Nursing entry: It has been agreed that Sophia can have her nasogastric tube replaced with a thinner one this afternoon. Sophia is very relieved and has asked for this to be done when her father is present during his visit later.

I don't think I have ever felt more relieved to have that huge tube pulled out. After being in so much pain, I almost forget how miserable everything is. The thinner one goes down—I don't fight it. I am a grateful for even the smallest act of kindness.

As much as staff deny their actions as being punitive, I don't understand why it took four days for them to replace the large nasogastric tube with a thinner one.

I guess Dr. Pace has made his point—if I don't play ball, he can make me suffer more than I ever imagined possible.

Friday

Nursing entry: This morning Sophia was helped to wash and clean her teeth. It is still very difficult for Sophia to move even with aid due to the fluid trapped in her body. She seems quite down compared to yesterday and keeps saying she thinks she is going to die. Reassurance was given but Sophia remained quiet.

I can feel the fluid creeping up and up and up. It swells and pushes against my organs. It makes me feel more and more tired. I wish I could just go to sleep forever. It's getting harder and harder to breathe. It could be because I am stuck in the claustrophobic room, but I feel like my lungs are too heavy to inhale air.

The soul has illusions as the bird has wings: it is supported by them.

—*Victor Hugo*, poet, novelist and dramatist

The thought that death could be imminent is a relief. But there is still a part of me that doesn't want the end to be like this. I don't want to die fighting with everyone around me. I don't want to die knowing my parents are witness to the current state I am in. If I am to lose my life to anorexia nervosa, I want it to be as peaceful as possible. And this is most certainly not peaceful.

Saturday

Ward round: Sophia remains at high risk of death from medical complications of starvation. She needs further increases in calories urgently if blood biochemistry allows.

Sophia has a urinary infection from her catheter and requires on-going cardiac monitoring. She remains significantly unwell with unstable electrolytes.

Nursing entry: Last night the nurse gave Sophia some water because she complained of extreme thirst. It has been clarified that Sophia MUST NOT BE GIVEN ANY WATER.

Myself and the other nurse observing Sophia today have washed her hair and changed her bed sheets. She has been given feed through her tube and has a phosphate drip running. Sophia is mostly asleep and remains on a cardiac monitor.

My mouth is so dry. It's the height of summer, the windows don't open and it's unbearably stuffy. I would give anything for just the tiniest bit of cold water—just a taste to loosen my tongue and cool me off. That nurse last night was so kind. Being able to drink just a small beaker of water sent me into ecstasy.

Your heart has been sore wounded too. Dear Light, love shall cherish you, till you again look on life with happy eyes.

—*Byron Caldwell Smith*, professor of Greek language, in a letter to Kate Stephens

My parents are very adventurous individuals so I was lucky in that I saw a lot of the world and had many holidays abroad during my childhood. The holiday that holds the best memories for me was a trip to the Seychelles when I was around the age of ten.

We stayed in a beautiful hotel and took many excursions to particular areas that were good for snorkelling. On one such trip we spent the morning swimming with turtles and fish displaying a riot of exotic colours. We then feasted on a lunch prepared by our boat driver. He grilled fresh tuna steaks on an impromptu barbeque. It was possibly the best thing I have ever eaten in my life. I devoured my tuna steak and relished the sweetness of the meat that was balanced by a squeeze of sour lime. I almost wept with disappointment when there was not enough tuna for a second serving.

It's so bizarre to think of this memory—how warped my attitude to food has become. The thoughts of seconds would send me into a complete terror now, even if it were the most delicious thing I had ever eaten.

Sunday

Nursing entry: Sophia has been very low in mood today. She is frustrated and desperate at not being able to move herself properly. She was visited by her parents and was tearful throughout this time. We assisted Sophia to change her position in bed and she was fed through her nasogastric tube. Sophia is demonstrating less combative behaviour and has not attempted to remove her nasogastric tube.

Oh mum and dad, I have put you through so much. You don't deserve any of this. You gave me such a good life and look what I have done to myself.

Monday

Nursing entry: Sophia is experiencing shortness of breath. The doctor listened to her chest and said that she has fluid around her lungs. An x-ray has been ordered. Sophia became very tired and went to sleep.

I try to let the air in, but my lungs won't work properly. I wheeze and fight to fill my lungs, but it's pointless. All I can do is drift off to sleep and pray that death will creep through my exhausted body.

Tuesday

Nursing entry: Sophia has had her x-ray and is now experiencing chest pains and palpitations. The shortness of breath has got worse and her oxygen saturation is dropping. She now has an oxygen mask. The doctor listened to her chest and examined the wounds on her legs. Sophia reports discomfort and pain around her stomach. Dr. Pace has ordered a CT scan so that the fluid from her chest can be drained. Staff must ensure the oxygen mask is fitted at all times.

At least I am in so much pain that I am distracted from the calories they are pouring into me. Every cloud has a silver lining I suppose.

8. Rock bottom

July 2012

In the night of death, hope sees a star, and listening love can hear the rustle of a wing.

—*Robert Green Ingersoll*, lawyer and
political leader

It's funny how you can think you've hit rock bottom, only to discover there is a further level of misery illness can inflict. I don't think it could be much worse than this though. Surely this is the final stage before death?

Strangely, I don't feel scared at all. I am in pain and it's hard to breathe, but otherwise I feel less tormented. My thoughts are drifting away and I am too exhausted to obsess about food or rituals. Time slips past and I don't even know what time of day it is. My brain has switched off and my anxiety and obsessions are gone. It's bliss.

Wednesday

Ward round: Pleural effusion likely, secondary of ascites.
Oxygen saturation low and chest drain now in situ.
Ascites drain also to be sited.

There is a very high risk that Sophia will not survive this degree of physiological compromise.

Remains for resuscitation—will be transferred to intensive care if needed. It may then be necessary to assess whether treatment has become futile.

If it is necessary to consider futility of treatment, or resuscitation decisions, Dr. Pace will consult with family.

Sophia remains emaciated and frail, with shortness of breath. She is on oxygen and barely able to talk.

Nursing entry: Sophia is experiencing pain in her abdomen. Dr. Pace has inserted a stomach drain to drain out fluid, and she has a drain in her right lung. Her parents have visited and Sophia remains very drowsy. Sophia has an oxygen mask. If it is removed she quickly becomes very breathless.

The drains hurt but at last the fluid is coming out. Bag after bag is filled with my tissue fluid as it rushes through the drains and out of my pathetic body. The months spent dragging myself around under the weight of all that water is coming to an end. Suddenly I can see a light at the end of this dark tunnel. I want to weep with relief, but I am too exhausted.

But if the while I think on thee, dear friend,
All losses are restored and sorrows end.

—*William Shakespeare*

Thursday

I don't remember much about the last few days, but I remember my friend Bella visited. I was so happy to see her but I couldn't get my breath back to allow me to chat to her. That made me sad.

I met Bella in treatment and we have remained close for a number of years now. Sometimes both being ill puts a strain on our friendship, but we manage that fairly well. She has been deeply caring for me and continued to visit throughout the darkest times, when most of my friends had given up on me.

However bad I am feeling, seeing her always helps. She sits with me and we watch the DVDs she's brought with her to cheer me up. Usually it's some chick flick that doesn't involve too much effort to concentrate. My sleepy brain can't take anything more intellectual at the moment.

We talk about the future—where we would like to travel and the beauty the world has to offer us. It's helpful to be reminded that the world exists beyond this wretched room. She suggests when I am a bit stronger we will be able to do the things we enjoyed doing together again. We can go to the cinema or take a wander around Covent Garden. It is hard to imagine that happening at the moment but I try to believe it can be a possibility again. Life still has more to give me if I fight for it.

In a long day of misery, she is a shining star. I just wish she could be free of her demons too. So many wonderful people suffer with eating disorders and it saddens me to see their struggles as much as my own.

A healthy body is the guest-chamber of the soul; a sick, its prison.

—*Attributed to Francis Bacon*, artist

When you are chronically anorexic, it's easy to get so engrossed in it that you lose sight of who you are. This isn't just the case for the patient—those around you get drawn into the illness too. They start to relate to you as an ill person and behave differently around you. This reinforces the feeling that the illness has taken you over—you are no longer your former self and the illness becomes an increasingly large part of your identity.

Friday

Ward round: 12 litres of fluid have been drained from Sophia's body.

Sophia continues to feel hopeless and says that she would like to die. She is sick of treatment and does not believe things can get better. She continues to be preoccupied with concerns about calorie intake and demands to be given water.

Phosphate levels are still low but stable. Sophia's calorie intake is to be increased today to 1650 and then to 1800 next week. SOPHIA MUST NOT BE INFORMED OF THIS.

Blood tests show the platelets are high and haemoglobin low—we are concerned there may be a bleed. Doctors to discuss possibility of a blood transfusion.

Sophia remains reliant on intravenous electrolytes in addition to feed. She continues to express frustration that she is not allowed to consume calories orally.

Doctor's log: Patient has been calm but remains very weak. Her nurses have washed her hair and she was able to mobilise to the commode with a lot of assistance.

Patient has complained about the environment in her room. The windows don't open, it's hot, the TV doesn't work and there is no Internet access.

Patient reports she would "rather be dead" than continue in her current state. She does not feel she is getting any benefit from sedation—"it's not touching me anymore".

The patient will be given a blood transfusion to address her low levels of haemoglobin.

I can just about move my legs now. They were too heavy with the water before. I look down at them. Within just a few days they are half the size of what they were. I take comfort in this because everything else is so bleak.

It's the height of summer and the room is hot and stuffy. I have never experienced claustrophobia like this before—this takes being locked up to a whole new level. I just stare into space. I wish those sedatives would knock me out like they used to. I didn't want them before but I have realised they block out the misery. I am desperate to be a zombie now.

Saturday

Nursing entry: Sophia's mood has been stable. Her first blood transfusion has finished going through and she is due another unit in the morning. Sophia states the she wished staff would "just knock her out and feed her up without being witness to it".

I hate watching someone else's blood drip into me. It really freaks me out. I said I didn't want it, but like everything, it is not my decision. They decide what goes into my body. My body is not mine anymore.

Imagination is the only weapon in the war against reality.

—*Lewis Carroll*, Alice in Wonderland

For the past few years I have had a regular habit. Every day, I allow myself to indulge in a little fantasy. I have always loved travelling but being ill and in hospital for so much of my life have made it impossible in recent years. On a day when I was feeling particularly low, I came across the website of a beautiful hotel in Bali. I don't know why, but I felt an immediate connection with this hotel. It seemed more like a sanctuary than a hotel and I pledged to myself that one day I would get there.

I promise myself that I will survive this and when I am no longer being held in hospital against my wishes, I will go there and allow myself to heal. Perhaps being somewhere so tranquil can heal the damage that has been done. Perhaps.

Sunday

Nursing entry: Sophia was asleep when I arrived to take over from the night staff. It was handed over that Sophia has had an unsettled night and constantly needs to pass urine.

The nurse in charge attempted to administer her first feed of Ensure for the day, but Sophia kept moving her head so that she was lying on the nasogastric tube and the feed could not be passed through. We gently held her head to one side but Sophia woke up and started to panic. Her arms had to be held down because she was banging them against the sidebars of the bed. Her head also had to be held down because she was banging it against the back of the bed. She kept shouting but eventually calmed down. We washed her and changed her bed sheets. After her wash she became really tired again and fell asleep.

Bang, bang, bang. Here I go again.

Bang, bang, bang. I feel like I could keep banging forever and then I just collapse. The banging drowns out the thoughts that torment me, until I am too exhausted to hear them.

Monday

Nursing entry: Sophia woke around midday but was very drowsy. She removed her covers and tried to get up, stating that she wanted to leave and was sick and fed up with being in hospital. Staff were required to hold her down and she made several attempts to remove her nasogastric tube.

It comes in waves. At times, I am too exhausted to fight. And then the voice grips me again and I summon every ounce of energy left in me to put a stop to all this torture. My anxiety bubbles and swells every time those syringes of feed are brought into my room. It seems to me that every day the number of syringes increases, but they won't tell me how much they are putting into me—I am not allowed to know. That makes it even more frightening. I am totally out of control.

In one of my episodes of treatment, I had a consultant who was keen to challenge me with insisting on a meal plan that included lots of foods my anorexia nervosa wanted to avoid. Despite being fifteen years ago, I can still remember one meal that was one of the biggest challenges I have had to face in treatment. It consisted of two large spring rolls with a mountain of rice, followed by a large lemon tart with cream.

Before I became ill, I probably would have enjoyed the meal. But pastry and rice were both massive fear foods for me at the time. Each mouthful was terrifying. I couldn't look at my plate so I shut my eyes as I shovelled fork after fork into me. It felt like I was throwing myself off a cliff edge. The hardest thing is that even once the food is finished, you are tormented for hours and even days afterwards with anorexic thoughts screaming in your head.

Despite food being incredibly frightening at times during treatment, I would still rather eat than have the calories syringed into me through a tube. Some anorexics prefer to be tube fed because it lessens the guilt they feel about allowing their body nutrition, but that is not the case for me. I find nasogastric feeding much more repulsive than the act of eating—even if you have to face the foods you fear the most.

Tuesday

Nursing entry: Sophia was woken this morning to have her vitals taken. She tried to refuse and started to thrash around. She says she has had enough of being treated like an animal and wants to die at home. She kept trying to raise her bed sheet over her head and I explained that I needed to see her face. Sophia started to hit me so her hands had to be held by her sides. When we released her hands, Sophia tried to pull out her nasogastric tube. We again held her hands down. After around thirty minutes of trying to fight us, Sophia was exhausted and fell asleep.

You bastards. Let go of me. I've had enough. I am getting out of here—away from you, away from this nightmare. I'll never forgive any of you for this. What you are doing is wrong. You can't keep me like this.

I need to get out of this room. I want some fresh air instead of the stale air in this miserable room. I want to have a cold drink and wet my dry mouth. I want to have a shower to wash away the dirt. I want to see the sky and get away from the bleeping of machines. I want to go home and sit in the summer sunshine in our garden. I need to be reminded of the good things in life because they have been lacking for a very long time and I've lost all hope.

My episodes of inpatient treatment have ranged in duration from three months up to two years. I have had periods where I have not been allowed outside for months, and I have had times when I haven't been able to go home for over a year.

Long spells in treatment have made me lose sight of who I am and what matters to me. I forget that life can be good because all that surrounds me day after day is misery and dreariness.

I still remember happy times, but thinking of them makes me sad because they feel so out of reach now. When I am stuck in hospital month after month, my life becomes just the same shit, different day.

Too few people understand a really good sandwich.

—*James Beard*, cookbook author,
used with permission of the
James Beard Foundation

In my early twenties, I was lucky enough to receive treatment in an excellent eating disorder clinic outside London. There was a lot of effort put in to therapeutic activities for patients and this included an annual summer trip to a beach hut on the coast.

The first year I was there I was not well enough to go, but the second year I was granted permission. It was a lovely day but marred somewhat by lunch. It had been agreed that the chef would prepare sandwiches for the trip.

At lunchtime, the occupational therapist unwrapped these sandwiches to discover that they were absolutely caked with butter. I don't know if this was an intentional and unkind thing that the chef did, or maybe he just wasn't thinking. The therapist tried to scrape some of the butter out, but we still sobbed through our sandwiches. I feel sad that my biggest memory from that day was those sandwiches. Food has the power to ruin everything when you have an eating disorder.

Wednesday

Nursing entry: Sophia remained asleep for the majority of my shift. When I attempted to interact with Sophia she said she just wanted to sleep. She put her hands up to her nasogastric tube a few times but resisted very little when her hands were removed from her face. She appears confused and low in mood.

If you think I am just going to sit and make small talk with you then you are very wrong. No matter how much you try to gloss over it, you are one of them. I am not going to pretend to be nice. You are violating me so don't act like you care how I am. Just shut up and read your magazine. It must be nice to be paid for doing fuck all. I am so angry, I can't even speak to you so I am just going to play being too out of my mind to comprehend any stupid rubbish you talk about. I realise I have become as ugly inside as I am on the outside. My brain is pickled with hatred.

Thursday

Nursing entry: Sophia was visited by her father but had very little interaction with him. Sophia simply lay with her eyes closed while her father read her a book. Once he had left, Sophia attempted to pull the blankets above her head. She was advised to keep the blankets below her head area so that we could see the nasogastric tube at all times.

Sophia started to shout foul language at staff, slapping our hands and digging her nails into our skin. We tried to calm her. She remained low and snapping at staff. She called us "fucking insolent idiots" but stopped trying to cover her face.

Sorry dad, I can't even speak to you anymore. I know I am behaving horribly, but if they insist on making me suffer in this way, they can damn well suffer with me.

After all, when a stone is dropped into a pond, the water continues quivering even after the stone has sunk to the bottom.

—*Arthur Golden*, Memoirs of a Geisha,
with permission

Sophia's father writes

I first noticed that something was amiss when Sophia's mother pointed it out to me. Sophia's weight noticeably deteriorated after she had her tonsils taken out and it was apparent when we spent time together as a family that she was not eating properly. I consulted a friend who was a GP and she said that the only person who can make an anorexic get well was the patient himself or herself.

The coping mechanisms I have used have changed over the years. My first reaction was to try to ignore the problem and hope it would go away. Then when it was clear that it wasn't doing so and that Sophia was blanking me, I tried to support her mother, as it was clear it was taking a toll on her. She was the person who was doing most to facilitate

Sophia's recovery. I tried to help Sophia in terms of trying to find the right treatment and rebuilding her confidence in me. As far as possible, I have tried throughout to ensure that some sort of normality continued in our family life and in my personal life as I think I sensed that in order to be strong enough to do something to help Sophia we had to look after ourselves.

Fairly early on in Sophia's illness, her first consultant psychiatrist told us he thought her case was a lot more difficult than it had seemed at first. He effectively warned us that her condition would be tough to treat and that she might never fully recover. As her illness progressed, I can remember feeling shocked when a doctor first asked her how she felt about dying. This was the first time anyone had come out with this home truth in Sophia's treatment and it was hard to hear but perhaps helped us all in the longer term.

It is important in my view to listen to what professionals tell you, to reflect on it (amidst a lot of noise that inevitably occurs when things go so catastrophically wrong) and to be realistic. The toughest part is when things appear that they might be turning for the better (as they sometimes did) only to go into reverse again. You have to learn to protect yourself against false hopes while clinging to some sense of optimism.

We have been open and transparent with people about Sophia's illness and for the most part they have responded in a supporting way. Unfortunately, a few people have little understanding of anorexia nervosa and think it is a temporary teenage issue. Some reveal very old-fashioned prejudices towards mental illness. Notwithstanding that, we adopted the right approach as it has meant that a lot of good friends have been able to support us through what is a truly miserable experience for patient and parents alike.

Reflecting back on it, the most distress I experienced arose when treatment strayed into cruelty, as I believe it did in the hand tying and insertion of large nasogastric tubes. Force-feeding is horrible to contemplate, even at times when without resorting to it Sophia would have quite quickly died.

Overall, I am left with the tough question of whether, if we had done things differently, Sophia would never have become ill or would have been able to break the addiction's terrible hold. Obviously we will never know, but it doesn't stop the question being any less painful.

In the practice of tolerance, one's enemy is the best teacher.

—*Dalai Lama*, founder of Gelug
Tibetan Buddhism

Friday

Nursing entry: Sophia presented as very low in mood and expressed hopelessness at her current situation. Despite encouragement and support, Sophia remained very despondent. She has asked how long she will be on the medical ward. The doctors have informed her that she will be here for a significant period longer and that she will need to return to the eating disorder unit before she can be discharged home. Sophia states she does not trust any of the staff at the eating disorder unit and she wishes to avoid going back.

I really should stop asking questions. The answers just depress me.

Saturday

Nursing entry: Sophia remains drowsy and low in mood. She says it is easier being drowsy as it passes the time quicker. The ward doctor has told her she is making progress. Her oedema is improving but her weight is decreasing because her body is shedding the fluid it has been storing.

I constantly need to pee. Now it's started shedding the fluid, my body won't stop. More and more comes out, the smaller and smaller I get. I don't think anyone realised just how much fluid I was holding. No wonder I couldn't move. I just feel so angry that I nearly died before they did anything about it. The doctors say that it is unusual to have this type of oedema with anorexia nervosa, so it is difficult to know how to treat it. They said they were concerned about the risk of infection, but I still think that the drains should have been put in much earlier than they were.

Sunday

Nursing entry: Sophia said she needed to pass urine so the other nurse went to fetch the commode. However, Sophia began to get out of bed saying she doesn't want to do it in her room and wants to use the toilet. I explained that she is still too weak but Sophia ignored me. I stood in front of the bed to try and block her from getting up and she tried to hit and kick me. We persuaded her to use the commode.

Sophia appears to have far more energy and strength with getting up from the bed and moving around.

Wow—this is incredible. I can move. My body is small enough now that my feeble muscles actually work. Despite being locked up in this dreadful room, I almost feel free. I've longed for the oedema to go for so many months, I can't believe it's finally happening. Those drains may have been unpleasant, but the relief of the fluid seeping out of my body is euphoric.

Faith without works is like a bird without wings; though she may hop with her companions on earth, yet she will never fly with them to heaven.

—*Francis Beaumont*, dramatist

I am particularly scathing of professionals trying to treat me if I feel they are being patronising or talk to me like I am an idiot. I might be anorexic, but I also studied hard and made the grades in science I needed in order to be accepted onto a veterinary medicine course. I find it insulting when professionals assume I am clueless and speak down to me. It has the unfortunate effect of making me even more resistant towards treatment.

Monday

Nursing entry: Sophia was verbally aggressive towards staff and tried to cover her face up with the bed sheet. She states that she wants to hide and pretend she is not in this "shit hole".

The doctors feel she needs another blood transfusion, as her haemoglobin is low again.

Not another one. Please, no more transfusions. Feeding and medicating me against my wishes is horrendous enough, don't do this to me too.

I am so sick of not having a voice. These should be my choices to make, not theirs. The doctors don't even have the decency to come and tell me I am going to have another transfusion. The nurses just show up with the bag of blood ready to hook up and drip slowly into my body.

I feel angry with the staff. Why did I have to endure so many months of misery before they did anything about my oedema? Were they punishing me for being a difficult patient? I don't know what to think anymore.

The fluid continues to gush out of my body. I have stopped feeling like my skin is going to burst and the bulges of liquid on my feet, legs and stomach are getting smaller and smaller. The drains that lead out of my lungs and abdomen are attached to bags that quickly fill up with the fluid and constantly need to be emptied. I have an albumin infusion into my veins and my bladder feels like it is going to burst. Despite all this, the relief of the water coming off me is blissful.

Tuesday

Nursing entry: Sophia refused to get up to be weighed. She then covered her face with the sheet. Myself and the other nurse approached her and asked her to remove the sheet. She refused and hit out.

The nurse in charge came to speak with Sophia. Sophia expressed how fed up she feels. After a short time, she took the cover off her face and went back to sleep.

Every day I am plonked on the scales. They hide the reading because I am not allowed to know. I am not "well" enough to handle such information. Well, if I can't know my weight, then nor will you. Bastards.

If you really want to be depressed, weigh yourself in grams.

—*Jason Love*, used with comedian's permission

The bathroom scales and I have a love/hate relationship. At times, they have comforted me and at others they have ripped my world apart and sent me into a massive breakdown.

I have spent periods where I have weighed myself up to ten times a day, desperately seeking reassurance and satisfying the obsessive thoughts running through my mind. At other times, I have avoided the scales at all costs—terrified of the numbers that they will present and the destructive potential those numbers have.

Whether I am weighing myself obsessively or not at all, the scales can control and influence every aspect of my existence.

Wednesday

Nursing entry: Sophia was asleep throughout my shift. Her blood results show that her haemoglobin is down to 6.6. She is to have another two units of blood this afternoon. Her weight continues to drop (BMI 9.4) and her oedema is significantly reduced. Her calorie intake continues to be increased, although Sophia is not to be made aware of this.

Yet more of someone else's blood being slowly dripped into me. Why do I find this so disturbing? It's been a long time since I have been able to call my body my own, but I am scared of the nutrients that are in the blood they are giving me and I hate that I have no choice about it. They don't force people to have blood transfusions if they don't agree with it. Why do I not have a choice like they do? Save the blood for someone who wants it, don't waste it on me.

Thursday

Review with Dr. Cole: Sophia appears drowsy with slowed thinking and quiet speech. She says she does not feel the sedatives help and she feels she is being treated like an animal. She is adamant that she could manage to take her nutrition orally and does not see that past experience demonstrates she cannot manage to eat satisfactorily.

My impression from the limited conversation we were able to have is that Sophia lacks capacity for decisions about all her psychotropic medication and food. This is in part because she is sedated and therefore struggles to think and in part because she continues to lack insight into the severity of her disorder—both the medical risks and the degree to which she sabotages treatment when not sedated.

Sophia's weight is still declining and we are concerned she is still finding a way to sabotage treatment. It has been agreed to carry out a bed search for hidden syringes. Staff must continue to be vigilant. Calorie intake is to be increased to 3000. SOPHIA MUST NOT BE MADE AWARE OF THIS.

Well at least there's only one zombie staring at me now. I am so drugged up that all my strength to fight has gone. I am powerless.

The only time I occasionally feel a bit better is when the night staff don't administer the first feed and the day staff assume they have. Avoiding those 3 syringes of Ensure first thing in the morning gives me that little "high" I desperately crave. I take comfort that despite everything they are doing to fight me, my illness is still lurking there and ready to make me feel better again when I am free from this horrible regime.

Friday

I am so tired. I wake up and don't have a clue what time of day it is or what is happening to me. Each time I wake up, there is a different nurse sitting in the room. They say things to me but I can't understand what they are talking about. Everything is so confusing.

Let your food be your medicine and your medicine be your food.

—*Hippocrates*, Greek physician

Anorexia nervosa is so cruel. Food is a compulsory "medication" in its treatment, and yet the "medication" brings on a reaction in the patient that is as if you are severely allergic to it.

Saturday

Ward round: Sophia has lost half her body weight in fluid since the oedema started to improve. We grossly underestimated the extent of her oedema and her weight continues to drop. Her calories need to be increased further and her electrolytes are now stable enough for us to do so safely.

Sophia gives monosyllabic answers and sometimes does not respond despite being awake. She reports high level of sedation that is "worse every day". The nurses report that she sleeps most of the time. Further sedation is required as the risk of Sophia sabotaging treatment is greater when she is alert. Staff must remain vigilant about observation and searching her bed for hidden items.

Nursing entry: Sophia used the commode and was able to walk the short distance to the sink to wash her hands. She is more stable on her feet and is able to mobilise a little more confidently.

They think I am cheating them but I'm not. I don't understand it because they keep syringing more and more Ensure down the tube, but they say I am still losing weight. I guess the water is still coming out of me. I constantly need to pee.

I am worried they are lying to me about my weight going down. They still won't let me see my weight so how do I know they are not cheating me?

God I feel so fat today. My stomach can't take any more Ensure. Six times a day they bring in those awful syringes full of the stuff. I know fighting them is useless. If I start to kick up, they just call a whole load of staff to come in and restrain me. I am totally trapped and I have no one to talk to about how I am feeling. All I do is sit and think about how I am going to starve myself when I am free again. There is no therapy or anyone to talk to about my feelings so I just obsess more and more about how I am going to reverse what they are doing to me.

Sunday

Nursing entry: Sophia has been more resistant today. We had to hold her hands down whilst her feed was administered. She was shouting throughout the feed and kept moving her head to make it more difficult for the nurse to administer her feed.

I can't stand this. I can't bear being stuck in this room and them stuffing me full of poison. My stomach is getting bigger and bigger and

I can't bear to think how much my weight must be going up. This is my ultimate torture—worse than anything I could have imagined.

The worst part is that there is no end in sight. How long are they going to keep me like this? I've got to find out what the hell they are doing to me. I just need a few moments alone so I can look in the medical folder outside my room. I have to find out—I can't bear all the unknowns.

Monday

Nursing entry: Sophia has somehow discovered that she is now being given 3000 calories per day. She is extremely distressed by this knowledge. Sophia got out of her bed and walked down the corridor to the locked door of the ward. Staff called security and Sophia was returned to her room. Sedation is vital.

I was right—they are pushing me totally out of control. 3000 calories a day is REVOLTING. I can't bear this—I've got to get out somehow. But there is always someone watching me and the bloody ward doors are locked. There is nothing I can do to escape this nightmare.

Tuesday

Nursing entry: No attempts to struggle or resist. Sophia remained very quiet and made no conversation throughout the day.

It's fine. There is nothing I can do for now. I just have to tolerate the misery until I can convince them to discharge me. I will be patient. And whilst all of this hideous "treatment" is going on, I will think about how good it will feel to lose the weight I have gained when I am free. I run through the regime I will follow when I am in control again. God, it will feel so good not to be dirty, gross and fat like this.

Wednesday

Weight gain always makes me feel dirty. I experience fat on my body as repulsive despite the fact I know that rationally the human body needs fat to survive. I am not desperate to be a model or in any kind of lifestyle that requires me to be thin, and yet it is essential to me that I am. I associate fat on my body with being filthy and shameful, and yet I don't judge others with the same standards I insist on myself. I don't look at people of a normal weight and think they are disgusting, but the idea of myself at a normal weight terrifies me. How did my thinking become this way? After all these years, I still have no idea.

Nobody realizes that some people expend tremendous energy merely to be normal.

—*Blanche Balain*, author, with
permission of the Balain family

Thursday

During the initial phase of my illness, I managed to attend school despite restricting my food intake. However, when I reached the age of fourteen, my weight had dropped so low I had to stop going to school and I never returned. The school sent my class notes to the hospital and I schooled myself. I took my GCSEs in hospital during an episode of tube feeding under the Mental Health Act.

Eventually, I made enough progress to be discharged home and I attended a sixth form school in London for my A level years. In this time, I made a small group of friends and anorexia nervosa became an increasingly distant part of my world.

As I stood queuing with my friends for a White Stripes gig outside Alexandra Palace, we scoffed baguettes and drank Pernot. I can remember thinking clearly at this point "Am I normal now?"

I got home at around 2am on a complete high from the night and without thinking ate a bowl of ice cream before crawling into bed. It only occurred to me the next morning that I hadn't even questioned the food I was putting into myself. I just ate because I felt hungry.

I think that was the closest point I have reached to being recovered throughout the duration of my illness. I wish things had stayed like that, but eventually the familiar downward spiral started again.

Friday

Ward round: Sophia has gained more than 1kg. She becomes aroused when talking about treatment and continues to disagree with the treatment approach. She does not believe she can get better and constantly wishes she were dead. She feels damaged by her treatment and that she will never be herself again.

Sophia continues to try and negotiate food. All calories must be given by nasogastric route—no negotiation. Staff must avoid discussion about food. SOPHIA MUST NOT KNOW HER FEEDING PLAN OR HER WEIGHT.

Patience: A minor form of despair disguised as a virtue.

Ambrose Bierce, journalist

Saturday

Day after day is filled with a desperate emptiness. There is nothing to do and no distraction from the misery. A nurse sits in the corner of my hot and stuffy room the whole time. If I kick up, a whole load of staff come in and hold me down. They rush sedatives down my tube and my thoughts slow down so much I feel like my brain won't ever work normally again. I sit in bed, with my stomach groaning with Ensure, and I pray that one day soon this will end.

My dad visits and reads to me but I am too spaced out to take it in properly. We are halfway through "Great Expectations" but I couldn't tell you anything about it. I just listen to the sound of his voice but I can't take in what he is saying. If only I were a little girl again. I wish I could press a rewind button and start my life over again. I have made such a mess of things.

I can't imagine life ever being good. Not after all this. I've had difficult episodes of treatment before that I have managed to come back from, but this time the damage and trauma has gone too far. I don't believe it's possible for me to ever be "Sophia" again.

All I know is that I will do or say anything that will allow me out of this situation. I'll eat deep fried Mars bars—I'd rather that then being pumped full of Ensure through this awful tube. Nothing could be more wretched than this existence.

9. Is the end in sight?

September 2012

Be like the bird who, pausing in her flight awhile on boughs too slight, feels them give way beneath her, and yet sings, knowing she has wings.

—*Victor Hugo*, poet, novelist and dramatist

For many years, I convinced myself that becoming a vet would be my "cure". It was my one passion in life that felt stronger than the anorexia nervosa. Despite all my difficulties, I fought to get the grades I needed. I sat my exams in various hospitals and I worked like crazy to get a place on one of the most competitive university courses.

Sadly, I was wrong. The reality of becoming a vet was not the "cure"—in fact it was the opposite. Failing to cope with the demands of the course only served to make me feel even more reliant on the anorexia nervosa and I felt like I had lost the only weapon I had against it.

Sunday

Ward round: The medical team at the main hospital feel that Sophia will soon be stable enough to be transferred back to the Eating Disorder Unit. She has gained 7kgs in weight.

Before her return, Sophia needs a physiotherapy assessment to ensure safe swallowing after her prolonged period of nasogastric feeding.

We need to continue with the current care plan of feeding via nasogastric tube until she is transferred.

Sophia wants to leave the medical ward and says she will be accepting of a full weight gain diet, dining room attendance, medication, groups and therapy. She expresses despondency about being stuck in the same room for over 4 months. She has asked to be allowed to go to the hospital café in a wheelchair with her parents. This has not been granted. Sophia feels hopeless and is not sure if she can tolerate being confined to one room for much longer.

SOPHIA IS NOT TO BE CONSULTED ABOUT PLANS FOR TRANSFER. Her care plan will not be given to her until she is due to be transferred back to the unit.

I beg you to take out this tube. Please give me a chance to prove myself. I promise I'll eat and I swear you can trust me. I have learnt my lesson. Whatever you put in front of me, I will eat. Chocolate bars, cheesy pasta, chocolate sponge and custard, cheesecake and cream. The rush of cold Ensure as it runs through the tube and down my throat to sit in my bloated stomach feels unbearable. I am desperate to be allowed to feed myself again. I pray that day comes soon.

Who in the world am I? Ah, that's the great puzzle.

—*Lewis Carroll*, Alice in Wonderland

Monday

Nursing entry: I tried to talk to Sophia a little but she appeared very flat in mood and gave single word answers to my questions. She is tearful and states that she feels "awful".

I thought I knew what being bored was, but the past weeks have surprised me just to what extent it is possible to be bored. My days are empty. I am frustrated that throughout all this time I have had no input from occupational therapy to help me find ways of distracting myself. I don't even have my weekly therapy sessions so there is no psychological support—they aren't bothered about how I feel, they just want to see the numbers on the scales going up. They are only treating my body, not my mind.

My world has become so small. I haven't left this miserable room for five months. I think of my life before I was forced into hospital. My life was so much fuller then—I was independent and I still had an identity. There was more to me than just a number on the scales or calories on a meal plan. I loved work and I was proud of the life I had managed to build up despite my illness.

Now I am nothing. I have completely lost sight of who I am and what matters to me. Right now, all I care about is reversing what has been forced upon me—every single kilo.

My body might be healthier, but my head is more fucked up than ever. Being isolated for so long without any kind of help with these horrible thoughts has made them so loud that I can't focus on anything else.

Tuesday

Nursing entry: Sophia spoke about her return to the eating disorder unit. She is anxious about what will happen when she is transferred and what her care plan will be. She worries about how treatment will go and that she cannot trust staff. I have advised her that the team and she will need to build trust and that there will be necessary boundaries to ensure that deterioration in her health will be prevented.

I had desperately hoped that being transferred back to the Eating Disorder Unit would be avoidable but they won't let me go home yet. There are yet more hoops to jump through before I can get the control back. I have been so patient but I don't know how much longer I can bear waiting. I am so wretched and I can't tolerate being this weight. Yet I know I must continue to play ball as it is the only way I will be free to do things my way again.

Wednesday

Nursing entry: Sophia is very down and non communicative. When the nurse came in to administer her nasogastric feed, Sophia noticed that the amount of feed has increased from yesterday. She became very angry, grabbed her purse and ran to the door of the ward. She was prevented from leaving and we struggled to get her back to her room. Her mother arrived to visit and managed to reassure her enough to return to her bed. The feed was then administered.

NO MORE CALORIES PLEASE. Just when I think things can't get any worse, they make things even more miserable for me. I am trying so hard to switch off from it all, but it's so hard when all I want to do is rip myself to pieces.

Every human being has a right to hear what other wise human beings have spoken to him. It is one of the Rights of Men; a very cruel injustice if you deny it to a man!

—*Thomas Carlyle*, philosopher

The night staff are generally more lapse and laid back about things. The nurse that sits in my room at night doesn't have any experience with eating disorders so she never tells me I can't look in my medical folder, which is kept on the wall outside my room.

In the folder there is all the information I have been dying to know and yet dreading knowing for all these past months in the medical ward. I can look at my diet plan and I can read the number of calories they are putting into me. I can see my weight chart. I am disgusted with the numbers. I am being given over 3000 calories a day and my weight has been increasing almost two kilos a week. I feel revolting and yet there is nothing I can do to stop them from doing this to me.

Why do I inflict suffering on myself by looking at the folder? It will do nothing but distress me, but I can't resist. Those numbers being kept a secret from me makes the urge even greater.

Thursday

Review with Dr. Cole: Care plan after transfer to the Eating Disorder Unit

Sophia's medication is to be offered orally or administered via nasogastric route.

Weight to be recorded daily.

Close observations at all times—Sophia must be within eyesight of the nurse with her, even in the toilet and shower.

Staff must monitor for attempts to purge and prevention of calorie intake.

The nasogastric tube must remain in situ even if Sophia is managing her Ensure and medication orally. The nasogastric tube will be replaced at first possible opportunity if removed.

Continue to maintain current level of calorie intake (3300 calories per day). Sophia is to be given an edited copy of this care plan, which omits reference to calorie content. Calorie content needs to be known by nurses only. It has been decided that WE SHOULD NOT TALK TO SOPHIA ABOUT CALORIES.

All meals and snacks must be taken in the dining room at the specified times with the rest of the patients on the unit.

All Ensure is to be completed within specified meal times.

If Sophia requests anything other than prescribed, this is to be denied. She is not allowed to swap Ensure for food. If Sophia does not complete her Ensure—NASOGASTRIC FEED IMMEDIATELY.

Room 12 to be prepared for nasogastric feeding—bed to be moved into centre of room for staff to be able to hold Sophia in restraint. Any potential projectiles need to be removed.

Friday

Nursing entry: Sophia has been informed that she will be transferred back to the eating disorder unit shortly. She asked the nurse in charge when they will be removing her nasogastric tube. The nurse replied that the eating disorder team would be making that decision.

Although I am not happy about having to go to the Eating Disorder Unit, at least I will be allowed to eat and drink there. I am so sick of this uncomfortable tube and my mouth being completely parched. It will be a relief to be able to eat. It feels strange to be looking forward to eating, but anything is better than having the calories syringed into me.

I feel embarrassed at how much weight I have gained. The other patients will see how fat I have become. I feel so ashamed. They are all going to wonder why the new admission is so fat.

Man shall not live by bread alone.

—*Bible*, Matthew 4:4

A re-feeding regime relies not only on three meals a day, but three snacks too. The snacks vary from clinic to clinic, but I think the one I have found the most difficult has to be the sandwiches for snacks served up in the first clinic I was admitted to.

Both morning and afternoon snacks were one or sometimes two sandwiches. Despite having a big breakfast and a main meal followed by a large hot dessert with custard at lunch, we were required to eat these sandwiches. And these sandwiches weren't just any sandwiches. They were an anorexic's worst nightmare sandwiches. The bread was extra thick white slices, there was a generous layer of butter and then to top it all, the filling was swimming in mayonnaise.

I think a lot of "normal" people think that anorexics go into hospital, eat a couple of rice cakes and some lettuce, gain a couple of kilos and then go home. This is so far from the truth. The amount of food you have to consume in order to gain enough weight to be discharged is much more than people realise.

And if it is a shock to a "normal" person, just imagine how much food that seems to someone with anorexia nervosa.

Saturday

Nursing entry: I visited Sophia and gave her the care plan that will be in place when she returns to the eating disorder unit on Monday. She immediately became preoccupied with the amount of Ensure prescribed and was told that she could discuss this with Dr. Cole on Monday.

I later received a phone call from Sophia in a very distressed state with grave concerns regarding her return to the unit. She is very worried about the plans in place. I tried to reassure her but Sophia remained distressed and tearful.

I am in a complete state of terror. I thought transferring back to the Eating Disorder Unit would be better than being stuck here, but it's going to be even worse. I've just read my care plan and it's awful. Nothing has changed—they are going to keep treating me like an animal. I was so stupid to think that I wouldn't have to have this tube down my nose—it's ridiculous that they are insisting on keeping it in. I had just assumed that I would be allowed to eat food again. I don't want Ensure—I want to be allowed to eat but they don't trust me. They have no faith in me and are just assuming I am going to refuse to eat and they will need to use tubes and force-feeding. I've even got my own special room to restrain me in—my own personal torture chamber. I feel sick to my stomach.

Sunday

Discharge summary:

> *Diagnosis:* Anorexia nervosa
>
> *Investigations:* Full bloods, bone scan, CT abdomen pelvis, CXR
>
> *Procedures:* Nasogastric feeding under section 3 of Mental Health Act. CXR revealed bilateral pleural

effusions and shadowing suggestive of noncardiogenic pulmonary oedema. There was poor inspiratory effort and a large volume of ascites throughout the abdomen. The findings of large volume ascites and bilateral pleural effusions are most likely explained by the patient's nutritional status.

Patient was transferred from Avery Lodge hospital for controlled feeding and weight gain under the Mental Health Act. A nasogastric tube was inserted on admission and her calorific intake was gradually titrated upward to achieve weight gain.

The patient was monitored with daily blood tests and electrolyte disturbances were corrected with IV infusions. She developed refeeding syndrome that was corrected through IV phosphate, calcium and magnesium supplementation.

Patient presented with a number of wounds including grade 3 ulcers on her sacrum and right shoulder. These were treated with antibiotics and tissue care.

The patient was observed to have developed bilateral pleural effusions secondary to hypoalbuminaemia that was causing cardiac compromise. These were imaged with X-rays and a CT-abdomen. The pleural effusions were drained under ultrasound guidance in addition to treatment with IV furosemide. 12 litres of fluid were drained from the chest and abdomen.

The patient's haemoglobin dropped to 6, most probably due to depression of bone haematopoiesis. This was rectified with blood transfusions.

The patient was sedated with maximum doses of clonazepam and olanzapine. She was nursed intensively in order to manage her challenging behaviour and ensure her safety.

10. Home sweet home

October 2012

Every human being is the author of his own health or disease.

—Gautama Buddha

It deeply frustrates me when care plans are devised with no input from me. Approaching treatment in this way makes it impossible for any constructive collaboration. Despite my thinking being largely irrational, somewhere underneath all that there is a more rational part of me that wants to get myself a life worth living back. Professionals look at my case history and immediately assume I will be combative. This makes me behave defensively. Having a care plan thrust upon me with no opportunity for discussion is only ever going to be met with complete resistance.

Monday

Nursing entry: Sophia has been transferred back to the eating disorder unit via wheelchair. She is very anxious and says there is too much Ensure in her meal plan. Dr. Cole has told her that her plan will not be changed.

At lunch, Sophia struggled but eventually managed to finish her prescribed two Ensures after an hour and a half.

Sophia has removed her nasogastric tube. After discussion with Dr. Cole, we have decided that the tube will only be replaced if she refuses to take her prescribed calories and medication orally.

Following lunch, Sophia was pacing her room and was asked by staff to sit down. She began to attempt to move her wardrobe and was prevented from doing so. She was escorted to her bed where she was assisted to sit down.

Sophia stated she didn't want to live anymore. She was then assisted to the dining room for afternoon snack.

So it's business as usual in this shit hole I had hoped I would never have to return to. It saddens me that after being through so much, it seems my relationship with staff will be as bad as it was before I was transferred to Avery Lodge. The opportunity for a fresh start has been lost because they are treating me with the assumption that there is no point in trying to work collaboratively. They have automatically deemed me to be unable to take any sort of responsibility for my recovery. But how can that approach keep me well when I am no longer being subjected to the threat of force-feeding?

At least I have learnt one thing—the only way out is to eat my way out. So I'll behave as best I can. At least they have agreed they will gradually allow me to start eating food instead of Ensure over the next two weeks. My meals remain as vile Ensures for now, but the snacks I can have as food. I ripped my tube out and thankfully they haven't insisted on reinserting it unless I give them a reason to.

It is bizarre to taste food in my mouth after so long. Everything tastes so much stronger than I remember. At morning snack, the strawberry Nesquik is unbelievably sweet and putting biscuits in my mouth and chewing feels completely alien. My afternoon snack is a chocolate bar and however scary chocolate is to me, I am grateful I can have the calories in that form rather than a sickly Ensure.

However much I am disgusted with the amount of weight I have gained, I would rather eat food than drink Ensures or have the calories syringed through a tube. I hope that they will allow me to eat food at mealtimes rather than Ensures soon. I am doing everything I can to negotiate. They were planning to keep me on Ensures for two weeks before allowing me to have food instead. If I can convince them I will eat the food and not mess around, surely they will see sense and not insist on giving me Ensures.

I will resign myself to being sat in that dining room and forced to eat. I will take the stupid medication that makes me a zombie. I will keep my head down however desperate I feel. And, one day, I will be allowed to go.

Your purpose in life is to find your purpose and give your whole heart and soul to it.

—*Gautama Buddha*

When I am finally released back into society, what do I want from life? I have come to terms with the fact my dream of being a vet is unrealistic for someone with the level of difficulties I have. So what else is there?

I am not sure if I can find something to do that will make me feel my life is worthwhile. I certainly do not want to be a burden to society living off benefits. I need to do something productive to keep my self-esteem up and I know if I have no other focus, food will occupy my thoughts.

I am the sort of person that needs to be busy. If I don't have distractions I will sink into depression. Through the haze of sedative drugs, I have moments of clarity. I realise I need to think seriously about a goal that is realistic and yet stimulating enough for me.

My hope is that I might be able to go back to working at a pet shop so that I can at least still work with animals even if it's not quite the career I would have had without this illness wrecking my life in the way it has.

Tuesday

Nursing entry: Last night Sophia became tearful as she prepared herself for retiring to bed. Staff intervened and she said she is upset about the Ensures she will be given tomorrow and that she is desperate to be given food instead. She eventually settled and went to sleep.

From the moment I wake up, I am counting down the hours until the evening comes and I can shut my eyes and drift into darkness again.

But I can't, because all I can do is lie in bed and run through what I will have to consume tomorrow. The mountain of calories to endure putting into my body overwhelms me.

How did eating become something that holds so much fear for me? I try to remember a time when a chocolate bar was something to be relished—a treat! Now I just look at my chocolate bar and want the ground to swallow me up so I don't have to eat it.

> The world is so dreadfully managed, one hardly knows to whom to complain.
>
> —*Ronald Firbank*, novelist

I don't think it would have ever dawn on the manufacturers at Kit Kat the amount of emotional trauma that a promotional offer on their product could inflict. I and the other patients I was in treatment with at the time were utterly mortified when our Kit Kat bars at snack time arrived with "an extra finger free"!

Any normal person would think, "Wow—value for money, great!" For us, it resulted in wailing and screaming as the staff insisted we needed to eat the entire bar including the extra finger as it would be abnormal to remove it and we needed to learn to be normal around food. Chaos broke out. The patients took a stand—the chocolate bar in itself was hard enough without adding an extra finger into the equation.

Thankfully the promotion seemed to be a one-off, or the staff decided to make their lives easier by ensuring it never happened again.

Wednesday

Nursing entry: Sophia completed her breakfast but ran half an hour late. She refused to stay for post meal supervision and went to her room. She spent the majority of the time in her room pacing up and down. She refused to stop doing this.

We need to reinsert the nasogastric tube as Sophia is refusing to take her medication. She also refused to be weighed this morning.

I am not a morning person. 6am they drag us out of bed. We queue up outside the nursing room, shuffling in one by one. There is a moment between standing on the scales and the number flashing up. That number will define everything in your world until the next time you are plonked on the scales.

Sometimes that number is the same, sometimes the number goes down and you get a bit of a buzz followed by fear when you realise they will probably increase your calories. In the worst scenario though, that number jumps up and you know that every mouthful you have to consume will be that extra bit harder. Those fears that they are pushing you out of control have become reality.

Really there is no good outcome when you step on the scales, so why bother dragging myself out of bed at some Godforsaken time in the morning to be subjected to it? No thanks. I think I will enjoy being asleep instead—it's much better than being awake. Now that I am allowed to know my weight, the desperate need to know what it is has evaporated. Ignorance is bliss.

Thursday

Nursing entry: After lunch, Sophia returned to her room and requested a glass of water. I agreed and accompanied Sophia to get the water from the water cooler in the dining room.

On returning to her room, Sophia sat on her bed and was taking things out of her pencil case. She then moved her laptop in front of her. I requested Sophia to move it, as I needed to see her face. She did not respond so I told Sophia I was going to have to come over and move the screen myself.

As I approached I noticed a number of oblong pills in her hand. Before I could reach her, Sophia had put these pills in her mouth and drank her water. I tried to open Sophia's mouth but she had already swallowed the pills. Sophia would not tell me where she obtained the pills.

Building my little pill stash has been a long-term project—mostly because it was so hard to get hold of them. In the medical ward, some of the nurses were a bit more lax about checking you had swallowed the tablets. All I had to do was pick the right moment to request some Paracetamol for my "headache".

My stash has been my secret treasure—something to resort to when I can't stand it anymore. I guess that moment came today. Nothing in particular had happened, I just couldn't think of any reason I was keeping myself alive anymore.

I didn't have quite as many pills as I would have liked, but I hoped it would be enough.

Faith is the bird what feels the light when the dawn is still dark.

—*Rabindranath Tagore*, Bengali polymath

I know taking my own life wouldn't come as a shock to those that have known I've been battling mental illness for as long as I have, but I know many people would judge me as being selfish to do so.

I don't want to be remembered or labelled as selfish, but at times where everything has become too much for me to bear, I start to think that I don't care what other people think of me for killing myself. At least I won't be around to hear it.

Doctor's log: Staff were alerted that the patient had taken an unknown quantity of white oblong tablets. The alarm was raised immediately.

The patient stated, "I don't want to live anymore. I don't want to be here and treated like this."

Staff escorted patient to A&E. She attempted to abscond and had to be restrained.

Staff at A&E offered a charcoal drink to protect her liver but patient refused to drink it. Further blood tests

197

show high levels of Paracetamol in her blood. She has been told she will need to stay in overnight. Plan to search patient's room.

Nursing entry: I phoned Sophia's parents to inform them that Sophia had taken an unknown quantity of suspected Paracetamol tablets and has now been transferred to A&E in the main hospital.

Poor mum and dad. It's nothing but bad news when it comes to me.

What you are is what you have been. What you'll be is what you do now.

—*Gautama Buddha*

When I was fourteen, the regulations around placing under-eighteens in adult psychiatric facilities were very different to how they are now. During my first admission to a psychiatric hospital, I ended up in an acute ward with some very unwell adult patients. The woman in the room next door to me seemed to be speaking loudly with someone all night. I couldn't understand who would be sitting in her room talking to her that long until I realised she was talking to herself.

As the ward was not specifically for the treatment of eating disorders, the staff had no concept of how to treat anorexia nervosa. My Rice Krispies were going down the sink and the squirrels would feast on the biscuits I threw out of the window.

My parents were uncomfortable with me being treated in this setting, but the doctors were considering taking them to court if they tried to remove me from my prescribed treatment. I wasn't there long but it is the perfect example of how wrong professionals can get things when making decisions around appropriate treatment.

Although my illness deprived me of a normal adolescence and in many ways has kept me a child, I was plunged into adulthood abruptly and therefore had to grow up fast.

Luckily, now there are regulations in place and a fourteen year old would never be placed in an adult facility. I often wonder if my first admission to hospital had been in a treatment facility appropriate for my age, would I have taken a different path? Could anorexia nervosa have been a "blip" in my teens rather than completely ruining my life?

Friday

Doctor's log: Patient will be medically clear to return to the eating disorder unit today. Her IV infusion will be finishing at some point this morning.

Patient's room has been searched. One tablet was found and disposed of.

Nursing entry: It has been discussed as a team and we feel Sophia may be less resistant to treatment if we allow her to have the standard clinic diet rather than having Ensures. On her return to the unit, all her meals and snacks can be in the form of food, but any failure to consume the food will result in it being replaced with an Ensure drink.

I am annoyed the tablets weren't enough. I should have been more patient and built up my stash a little longer. I was just so desperate for things to be over, I couldn't get through another day of misery. And now I am going back with no stash to fall back on and no escape route.

At least they have relented about the Ensures—I hope that being in the dining room at meal times will feel easier now I am having food like the other patients.

Saturday

Nursing entry: Sophia returned from the main hospital last night. She has complied with her food plan but is taking much longer than the allocated time to complete eating.

When asked about talking with her parents since the overdose, Sophia became upset and stated, "We're not really speaking at the moment." It is reported that she and her parents had argued on the phone regarding the incident.

My parents just don't realise how wretched it is to be in here. If they were in my position, they would understand better why I behave like I do too.

"Normal" people don't comprehend how awful being made to eat a weight gaining diet is for an anorexic. When that delightful bowl of chocolate sponge and ice cream is dished up for me, it feels just as bad as being forced to eat my own excrement. That is the best way I can think to describe what it's like.

During my first admission to an eating disorder unit, the patient group was incredibly supportive of each other. We faced our difficult meals together and we tried to console ourselves after eating through empathy and daft coping mechanisms. After a particularly large meal of a cheese quiche with jacket potatoes the size of our heads, followed by a brick of treacle sponge with custard, our stomachs were fit to explode. In order to minimise our discomfort, we created our special post meal posture. This was known to us as "the starfish" and involved lying on the floor with limbs as spread out as possible in order to spread the weight of our laden stomachs against the force of gravity. Obviously, it didn't help much, but it made us laugh which helped us distract ourselves from the feelings of fullness while we counted down the minutes to the next dreaded trip to the dining room. Good company and the ability to find humour in a situation can get you through the most difficult aspects of treatment.

Childhood is a short season.

—*Helen Hayes*, used with actress's permission

Visiting my grandparents in Sussex was probably not the way I would have chosen to spend Sundays if I had been given the choice. The drive there was boring and although my grandparents had a swimming pool, my grandfather would usually put the chlorine treatment in just before our arrival so that we couldn't swim in it. I don't think he liked children very much, or maybe it was just other people in general he objected to. His precious Jack Russells were certainly much more worthy than pesky grandchildren. We used to joke that they ought to have their own seats at the dining table.

The part of the visit I did like though was helping granny with her crumble. Sunday lunch would always be a roast. The chicken was usually dry but not too bad, but the potatoes often had worms in them and the gravy was always cold.

But the main meal was irrelevant; dessert was much more important. I would always help granny peel the apples and chop them into pieces while she made the crumble. It would smell so delicious while it was cooking and I would linger near the Aga so that I could enjoy the aromas.

When it was time, granny would take it out and serve it with vanilla ice cream. The ice cream would melt almost immediately when it was placed on the steaming hot crumble so you had to eat it quick.

Remembering just how much pleasure this dessert gave me makes me realise how much things have changed. Crumble is a dessert that has featured in almost all of the eating disorder clinics I have been treated at, and in all of them I sobbed with fear and disgust at having to eat it.

Sunday

Nursing entry: Sophia has expressed feelings that she cannot tolerate the weight she has been forced to gain. She states "I will have to just eat my way out of here so I can lose the weight again."

I wish I could keep my thoughts to myself more—expressing them does me no favours in terms of getting out of here any time soon.

If you kick a stone in anger, you'll hurt your own foot.

—*Korean proverb*

I am seventeen and I am in yet another treatment centre. There is a particular nurse who I am certain hates me. At lunch, she portions out the dessert for all the patients. It's a nasty strawberry sponge cake that's loaded with synthetic foamy cream that makes the whole thing a bit of an unpleasant mush. As she cuts the gateaux into messy slices, there is one slice that is clearly much larger than the others. I know exactly what direction that slice is headed, and of course, yes, she plonks it in front of me. I sit and stare at it for a minute. I try to fight the anger bubbling inside me but it's hopeless. I explode. I pick the bowl up and throw it against the wall. Strawberry cake splatters across the wall and the bowl smashes. My fork bounces off the floor and lands on the nurse's foot. She starts to scream and shout, saying she is calling the police because I have assaulted her. Despite claiming to be distressed, she has a slight smile on her face and I realise that I have reacted in exactly the way she wanted me too. My anger always gets the better of me.

Monday

Ward round: Sophia wishes to know her target weight so that she can get there and be discharged. Her only goal is to leave hospital.

Sophia must continue to gain 1kg a week until the next ward round.

She is to attend all meals and has not been granted any leave.

She remains on close observations (within eyesight of her nurse at all times).

Nursing entry: Sophia complied with eating her breakfast but refused to attend post meal supervision. She returned to her room and would not stop pacing.

Sophia attended ward round and became very distressed when told that she will need to put on more weight. She threw coffee cups at the team and struck Dr. Cole on the arm. She was escorted back to her room where she sobbed on the bed.

Two members of staff were needed to assist her to the dining room for lunch. She completed her meal and returned to her bed. Her mood remains very low.

The police have been informed that Sophia was physically abusive towards Dr. Cole. They will arrange a time to visit Sophia.

Stupid bastards. Sitting around that table tucking into their coffee and lovely biscuits whilst they decide your fate.

If I were a decent person I would feel bad about my behaviour, but I stopped being a decent person when I was dragged in here against my wishes. I hope the police do come—at least in prison they won't make me eat.

Tuesday

Nursing entry: Sophia was observed trying to hide part of her peanut butter sandwich at snack time today. She initially denied she had hidden anything but eventually placed it back on her plate.

At 6pm, she refused to come to the dining room for supper, saying she felt "too full". With persuasion she eventually attended but ran over an hour late.

Sophia returned to her bedroom and paced her room. She could not be persuaded to sit down. She is reluctant to interact, even when pressed.

I guess I'm bored and fed up of just trying to go along with things. As I am sure has become clear to you, it is not in my nature to be compliant. The effort of not acting out has become too much for me. I can't hold the feelings of destruction in anymore.

Wednesday

Nursing entry: Sophia struggled to complete her meal at lunchtime and was initially reluctant to attend the dining room. She remains low and withdrawn.

Sophia has been told by Dr. Cole that the police will be coming tomorrow to discuss the assault she perpetrated in her recent ward round. Dr. Cole has reminded her that assault of staff is unacceptable and we have zero tolerance of violence. Sophia was dismissive and simply asked if the police would move her to prison. Dr. Cole told her that her behaviour would not affect the treatment she receives and that there is no option of transfer to another service or prison. Sophia rolled over in bed, covered her face and asked Dr. Cole to leave.

Sophia's evening dose of sedative has been brought forward as night staff have struggled to make her comply with her medication.

My violence towards you is nothing compared to what you have subjected me to. I still have scars on my body from the rips and tears I sustained when you brutally held me down. And I can't go running to the police because I am "crazy" and those injuries are a result of "treatment".

So, please tell me, do you think that my "treatment" has helped me, or are you fully aware of how violated and damaged I feel?

Damaged people are dangerous. They know they can survive.

—*Josephine Hart*, writer, used with permission of Ed Victor

When I have had periods of release in society, there are good days and bad. Sometimes, I can get out and about, I see friends and I interact in "normal" ways. I feel well because pretending is working out for me. I don't think about how ill I have been and all those years locked up in hospitals. I can walk down the street and no one has to know I am a nutcase. And then on bad days, I don't go out because I am scared of the world and I don't know how to find my place in it. I've missed out on so many years and in many aspects I still feel thirteen—the girl I was before the onset of anorexia nervosa. I don't have the strength to hide from the world that I am damaged goods. What hope do I have? Who would want to know someone as messed up as I am? I can't stop these insecurities from taking over my thoughts and knocking the little self-esteem I have.

Thursday

Ward round: The nursing staff report Sophia is not fully compliant with her medication. Sophia is being treated under the Mental Health Act and must have her medication. If refusing to take it orally, Lorazepam must be given by injection.

Sophia is clearly exercising by pacing in order to burn calories. Staff need to intervene and restrain her to sit on her bed. If her arousal escalates and she does not sit or lie down, administer Lorazepam by injection.

Sophia must comply with all prescribed food. If she refuses she is to be fed via nasogastric route.

Close observations to continue. Sophia must be observed at all times—including in the bathroom.

Glorious pills—they make me so much easier to manage. The more they pump me with, the drowsier I am and the more alone I feel. I can't talk or interact at all. My brain is being slowly fried. I used to be intelligent but I certainly couldn't hold an intellectual conversation in this state.

Perfect as the wing of a bird may be, it will never enable
the bird to fly if unsupported by the air. Facts are the air
of science. Without them a man of science can never rise.

—*Ivan Pavlov*, Russian physiologist

Anorexia nervosa turned me from a C to an A grade student.
Not only had I committed to restricting my food intake, but I
had also committed to improving my grades. I was aiming for
"perfection". I was sick of feeling fat and lazy. After months of
misery, I had to get my act together.

When I wasn't at school, I was studying in my room. If I
managed to get the studying I wanted to do done, my reward
would be allowing myself something to eat.

As time went on, my standards became higher and higher.
It was more difficult to achieve what I wanted so my reward
of food became increasingly scarce. With anorexia nervosa, the
goal posts always move. Nothing is ever good enough.

Friday

Therapy session: Sophia feels "tormented and brutal-
ised" by treatment. She is unable to experience being fed

211

as care and feels powerless and out of control. She is also not engaging well with staff and sees everyone as oppressors. She is not willing to explore activities to minimise her exercise or manage her agitation.

Pacing my room takes the edge off my anxiety. It also pisses off the nurse sat staring at me, which gives me a small ounce of satisfaction. Simple pleasures are all I have these days.

Saturday

Nursing entry: Sophia was reluctant to attend lunch and had to be assisted to the dining room. Her face is impassive with little spontaneity evident. Says that she feels miserable.

I hate it when they say, "Do we need to assist you?" It implies that you will be gently supported and helped. In reality, it is just a way of making being dragged along the corridor by your arms and legs sound a more acceptable part of treatment.

The nightmares come in batches. I'll have a week where I don't have any at all, and then I'll have a week where every night I wake trembling and nauseous. In the nightmares, I am always in a hospital bed and my hands are always bound. I don't feel the pain that I felt when I was actually being treated, but I do feel the desperate frustration. Often, something happens that I don't like but I can't do anything to stop it because my body is paralysed and my hands won't work. The dream I hate the most is where I can see an animal is suffering but I am unable to get my hands free to help it. I see a dog drowning or rabbits trapped in a hutch as they are engulfed by flames. I am screaming for help but no one around me hears me. Sometimes the hospital room is full of strangers, sometimes it's empty, and sometimes there are people I recognise. They never speak.

They don't make eye contact. They just stand there and I don't understand why they won't help me free myself so I can rescue the animals. As I am forced to watch them suffer, I feel part of me dying too.

The only voice that is 100 per cent safe to have, in your own head, is your own. Something true and joyous and reliable, with its never-ending golden ticks.

—*Caitlin Moran*, columnist, copyright of Caitlin Moran, with permission of Rogers, Coleridge & White Ltd.

Sunday

Nursing entry: Sophia remains low in mood with no interaction with staff. She used the toilet, came to the dining room for lunch, refused to attend post meal supervision and returned to bed. I asked her why she is so tired the whole time and she said that she couldn't bear "being awake and aware of it all".

Bed, medication, eat. Medication, eat, bed. Eat, bed, medication. That's about as varied as my life gets right now. Not exactly stimulating is it?

There is so much of the day that is empty and all I have to fill the time is thoughts about food. I obsess over the hospital menus—what to choose, what do I allow myself to have? Do I allow myself to have what I want deep down—what I would have chosen before I became

214

anorexic? Or do I stick to the safer option that is more bearable for my anorexia nervosa and is what the majority of the other patients will choose?

I spend hours devising meal plans for when I leave here—what I will do to cut down my calories and lose the weight they have piled on me. I am so desperate to get rid of the "fat" thoughts screaming at me and to feel like my body is mine again.

Monday

Nursing entry: Sophia is still on close observations. She does not respond to prompts to communicate with her and spends most of the time lying on her bed. She is reluctant to attend the dining room but eventually completes her meals.

Small talk is so lame. You have nothing to say of interest to me and I certainly have nothing decent to say to you. So let's just be silent. You will stare at me because you are being paid to do so. And I will stare at my bedroom wall because it has become a familiar view.

I used to be creative. Art was my favourite subject at school and I took A levels in art and textiles. After being discharged from one of my more lengthy episodes of treatment, I did a photography course for a year. Even in hospital, I used to fill my days with making quilts or doing cross stitch and tapestries. My home is full of colour and the walls are adorned with various bits of artwork. It is such a contrast to my environment now. In early admissions, I would decorate my room in whatever way I could to make it feel more homely. But now I can't be bothered. I don't have the drive to try and hang on to my identity like I used to. My existence is sparse and dreary and I can't pretend otherwise.

A bird does not sing because it has an answer. It sings because it has a song.

—Chinese proverb

The only times I have smoked have been during periods of treatment in psychiatric units. The main reasons I started smoking was boredom and the fact that most of the other patients smoked. When the smoking ban was introduced, being a smoker also meant that you were permitted to go out into the grounds of the hospital to smoke. Although staff would accompany you, at least you got out of the ward for brief moments in the day. Taking up smoking was the only way I would get to go outside. Unfortunately, it wasn't exactly a breath of fresh air.

Tuesday

Group therapy: Sophia attended the session of her own accord. She was able to listen to others as they spoke. With some encouragement she was able to share that she was feeling particularly low in mood. She spoke briefly about not wanting to be on the unit and wanting to go

home. Her interactions were minimal but she stayed until
the end of the group.

*My day consists of regular visits to the dining room for the next dose
of trauma. That dreaded, greasy macaroni cheese that will be plonked
on my plate. The vegetables that have had all the goodness blasted
out of them after being overheated from frozen. The sticky lumps of
sponge pudding drowning in custard. It's vile, but I'd rather eat it
than being force fed Ensures. At the end of the day, however hard eating is, it's better than being violated by shoving a tube down my nose.*

*The boredom has broken me down. I can't take another day of being
curled up on my bed. The groups might be a waste of time, but it has
become apparent that I certainly have plenty of time to waste.*

Wednesday

Nursing entry: Sophia didn't want to attend snack so
she was assisted to the dining room. She sat down and
I asked another patient to swap places so that I could sit
next to Sophia. Sophia then left the dining room. She said
she felt very embarrassed and angry with me for asking
another patient to move.

With assistance from staff, she was returned to the dining room to complete her snack and take her medication.

*The other patients don't speak to me. I guess having a nurse constantly with me is pretty off-putting. And my at times violent behaviour probably freaks them out. At various points in time, little groups
form within the patient group. But I am always an outsider, just like
at school.*

217

You can't have your cake and eat it.

—French proverb

Most teenagers are probably relieved when the lunch bell goes at school, but for me it was the worst time of the day. The lunch hall was huge and scared the hell out of me. Everyone sat in their groups, chatting, laughing, saving seats for each other. I would often sit down at a table only to be told that I couldn't sit there because the seat was saved for someone else—no doubt someone deemed more interesting and confident than I was.

It got me so down that before long I just stopped going into lunch at all. Before anorexia came into play, I would buy three or four chocolate bars at break time. When the lunch bell rang, I would go to the toilets and sneak into a cubicle. I would lock the door and breathe a sigh of relief. Despite the unpleasant toilet smells suppressing my appetite, I would wolf down the chocolate and then sit and wait until lunch was over and it was safe to venture out of my cubicle. It felt so disgusting to eat whilst in the smelly toilets and eating became associated with feeling dirty and revolting.

Thursday

Ward round: No changes to current plan. No leave granted. If Sophia continues to complete meals, take her medication and attend post meal supervision we can consider some limited leave in the near future.

Therapy session: Sophia continues to feel tortured by the team for forcing her to eat and gain weight. Today we spent the last 5 minutes of our session in the ward garden. Sophia became more animated in speech when she talked about her garden at home, her memories of playing in the garden as a child and her pet rabbits.

I miss animals so much. They are such an integral part of my identity. I trust that they will not reject me or hurt me in the way that people have.

Until one has loved an animal, a part of one's soul remains unawakened.

—*Anatole France*, poet, journalist, and novelist

I was never allowed pets as a young child, and I was the happiest eleven year old in the world when my mother conceded to getting a cocker spaniel. I remember going to collect her from the breeders so clearly.

My dad and I drove to the breeder on a Saturday morning to take our beautiful new puppy home. From the moment I saw her I was in love. She was a stunning dog—black and white with symmetrical markings. She curled up on my lap, wrapped up in a tartan blanket, and peacefully slept the whole two hour journey back home. Unfortunately, she did not sleep so easily at night and whimpered and whined until someone came to cuddle up with her.

Everyone in the household adored her, and it wasn't long before we got a second dog—also a cocker spaniel but an orange roan colour.

Dogs can definitely sense when you are upset. There were many occasions when I have been crying my eyes out on the sofa and they would come and curl up with me. Their eyes were full of concern and love. I hated that my illness took me away from them during times when I was hospitalised. I missed precious moments of their lives and I wasn't able to be with them when they passed away. My struggles with food took yet another thing away from me.

Friday

Nursing entry: Sophia had a bit of a wobble at morning snack today. She demonstrated some distress, which she attributed to a staff member saying that she needed to sit next to her in front of the other patients. Sophia said she "didn't want the others to know that" and appeared very embarrassed.

Why do they insist on humiliating me at every given opportunity? I am alienated enough from the other patients as it is, I don't need them adding to it.

It's probably just as well I am alienated from them. They are mostly younger and although very unwell, they are not chronic and I don't want them picking up bad habits or "tricks" from me. I remember I certainly picked up on these from others during the first few admissions I had.

Warren life doesn't make for secrecy.

—*Richard Adams*, Watership Down, used with
permission of Oneworld publications

If you haven't already picked up on a compensatory behaviour
before you are admitted to an eating disorder unit for treatment, it is likely you will learn a lot of treatment sabotaging
behaviours before you are discharged. There is a strong temp-
tation to copy others when you are struggling to accept the
realities of treatment.

I can clearly remember in my first admission that it dawned
on me that I could discreetly hide food when I saw another
patient pocketing half her turkey escalope. As much as the
rational side of my head knew that what she was doing was
not going to help her situation, the desperation to avoid some
of the calories the dietician had prescribed was too difficult to
ignore. My turkey escalope went swiftly up my sleeve a few
minutes later.

Saturday

Nursing entry: When asked to come to the dining room to attend snack, Sophia said she was feeling too drowsy.

Staff nurse Debbie came and encouraged Sophia to attend the dining room. Sophia said she felt she was putting on too much weight. Debbie explained to her that she was putting on weight at the rate that the doctors require.

Sophia was reminded that, as per her care plan, she would need to be fed via nasogastric route if she refuses to have her snack. Sophia came to the dining room and completed her snack.

I eat not because I am hungry. I don't even remember being hungry. I am constantly full. But I have to eat because I will NOT give them the excuse to shove a tube down me and stuff me with absurd quantities of Ensure. I have endured enough of that for one lifetime.

Sunday

Nursing entry: Sophia became distressed this morning when weighed as she has gained 0.8 kgs. She lay on her bed and refused to come to breakfast. She was assisted to the dining room and completed her meal. She then returned to bed. Her mood remains low.

I am so sick of my world being ruled by numbers. Calories or kilos, the numbers are always higher than I want them to be.

At times where I have felt the need to weigh myself every single day at home, even an increase of 0.1 kg is enough to make me feel I need to restrict my food intake. Rationally, I know that 0.1 kg is nothing and that your weight has to fluctuate. And yet I can't get it out of my mind. I have a gram less of cereal, I will choose a lower calorie yoghurt, a smaller banana—it's stupid, but I can't ignore that 0.1 kg. Of course, if I have lost 0.1 kg, it doesn't have the opposite effect. But I can't tolerate a slight increase without cutting back.

Monday

> **Nursing entry:** Sophia finished her lunch 10 minutes after the given time and was encouraged to attend post meal supervision but went to her bedroom instead.
>
> She brushed her teeth, sat on her bed and read the newspaper. She appears stable in mood but very quiet and passive. She responds to questions but does not engage in further conversation.
>
> Sophia was encouraged to join the rest of the patients for film group but said she didn't feel like it and prefers to be alone, as she "does not belong here".

I don't like being in the communal areas of the unit. I prefer to be safe in the confines of my room and my solitary routines.

There are generally two categories of patients in eating disorder treatment. There are those that have suffered for a relatively short period of time and the aim of treatment is full recovery. And then there are those that are "chronic", who have suffered over many years and needed several inpatient admissions. Their goal of treatment is often just to learn how to manage their illness better.

I always struggle in the group dynamic in hospital as it reminds me so much of school and how afraid I felt of others. My illness has denied me the life experiences that "normal" people of a similar age to me have had.

Better to be seen alone than in bad company.

—French proverb

Growing up, Saturday lunchtime was my favourite meal of the week. It was a rare occasion where my father wouldn't be working and the whole family would pile into the car and head for our favourite Chinese restaurant.

In the window, the crispy ducks would be turning on their spits, the fat dripping from them as they turn and the cooking aromas would fill your nostrils before you even stepped through the door. We would order a huge meal. Duck pancakes, char sui buns, steamed dumplings, sweet and sour pork, sticky rice wrapped in lotus leaves were all among our family favourites.

We would all fill ourselves to the brim but somehow still find room for dessert—deep fried, sticky toffee bananas with coconut ice cream. My dad was a particular fan of those and I have definitely inherited his sweet tooth.

It makes me so sad to think how much this weekly treat made us a family. Anorexia nervosa takes that away—you can't eat like your family and friends do, so it's best to avoid situations where you will be expected to. You become increasingly

225

isolated. Anorexia replaces your family and friends as you push them further and further away. The more they try to help, the more you retreat from their company.

Tuesday

Nursing entry: Sophia completed her supper but needed extra time. She left the dining room at one point saying that she could not do it. Staff nurse Debbie discovered some pastry in her cardigan pocket. She told Sophia that she would not replace it this time but she would have to in future. Sophia has been told not to take a cardigan with pockets into the dining room.

I do feel embarrassed when I am caught hiding food in the dining room. I hate the other patients being made aware of it and I know they gossip and bitch about me when I've retreated back to the safety of my room. I also feel pathetic when the staff tell me off like a naughty child. I wish I could resist the urges I get to hide food, but I just can't bear putting all these calories into me.

Wednesday

Nursing entry: Sophia was agitated and distressed at dinner tonight. She was observed by staff to be removing food from her plate. Sophia was confronted and she became tearful, saying she could not manage the meal. Her pockets were checked and both had food in them. She denies being told not to take a cardigan with pockets into the dining room. She has agreed to have her pockets searched at the end of each meal but asked that this would be done discreetly and not in front of the other patients.

I'm not stupid. I'm not vain. I can see the damage anorexia nervosa causes to not only me but also those around me. I don't think I look good this thin and I have so much to get better for. So why is it so hard for me to eat? Why does being a healthy weight fill me with horror? Why do I constantly try to sabotage treatment? I have so much determination and willpower, why can't I channel that into getting well? Over so many years, I have spent hours in therapy trying to get to the bottom of these questions and yet I still don't understand it.

I do not give up on things easily, but I know that I will never be fully recovered. Anorexia nervosa has conditioned my brain in a way that I can no longer reverse. The self-destruction has gone on too long and caused too much damage for full recovery to be a possibility. Sometimes you just have to accept that all you can do is get the best quality of life you can whilst managing your illness. I wish the doctors would accept this. They are wasting time and money on me when it could be spent on someone with a much better prognosis than mine.

It's in these rare moments of clarity, which break through the sedative effects of the drugs they pump me with, that I feel most frustrated.

Thursday

Nursing entry: Sophia completed her meals but was struggling a little more today. She was late coming in to community meeting. When asked how she felt about the community, Sophia said she didn't feel good about it. The therapist asked if she felt people didn't like her and she nodded her head.

There was a time when I felt recovery was possible for me, but I have accepted that it is not a realistic goal anymore and I think the other patients snub me for it.

Animals are such agreeable friends—they ask no questions, they pass no criticisms.

—*George Eliot*, writer

Friday

Group therapy: Sophia has had a difficult week and is struggling with gaining weight. Although she has spent much of her life in hospital, she said she had previously enjoyed working in a pet shop and that this was something she would like to go back to when she is discharged.

I love animals. I love being around them. I love looking after them. I love working with them. I love that I don't feel scared of meeting new animals like I do with new people. Their behaviour is more predictable than humans. People can be mean and malicious. Animals aren't like that. Yes, they can snap and growl, but they can't hurt you with words. They're not prejudiced and they don't judge you.

But animals also make me feel sad. They are a reminder that I will never fulfil my life passion. I will never be what I wanted and worked so hard for. Anorexia nervosa is not compatible with being a vet—I've learnt that the hard way.

Ward round: Sophia has gained 1.2 kg over the week. She is completing her meals but not attending post meal supervisions. Her close observations must continue and will only be stopped if she starts attending post meal supervisions. No leave off the unit granted—only up for discussion if she is taken off close observations.

Nursing entry: At the beginning of the shift, Sophia met with matron Simon to discuss her management round feedback. She expressed her frustration at not seeing any benefits for her compliance with meals and weight gain. It was explained to her why it is not appropriate for someone who is on close observations to have leave off the unit due to risk. Sophia was congratulated on all she was doing and was told that the close observations will be reviewed if she starts attending post meal supervision.

I know the score by now—another hoop to jump through. Yet another little bribe in the battle to make me behave. Fine, I'll go and sit in that depressing lounge after meals and join the other patients all dwelling in their own misery at having just eaten. I am that desperate to get out of this place, even if it is just for 15 minutes in the grey streets and I've got some pain in the arse nurse escorting me.

Saturday

Nursing entry: Sophia completes her meals but is quiet and anxious while eating. She does not engage with others in the dining room. The occupational therapist Karen met with Sophia to plan a home visit.

Sophia attended post meal supervision after dinner.

Even the thought of a brief visit home makes me well up with emotion.
I can't imagine how it will feel to be in my home after so much misery
and suffering. I just worry that coming back to this place will feel so
dreadful that it will spoil the day completely.

Sunday

Nursing entry: The occupational therapist and staff nurse
Tracy accompanied Sophia home this afternoon for an
assessment. Sophia was quiet for the majority of the trip
but did engage at times and responded to questions being
asked. She was notably brighter when interacting with
her rabbits. She was able to groom them and her mood
notably lifted when she spent time with them.

Sophia ate her prescribed chocolate bar for snack with
her parents. Her parents expressed their happiness at the
progress Sophia has made and were able to identify much
improvement in her physical state.

Sophia returned to the unit without issue but was
upset that the time had gone so quickly. The home visit
felt bittersweet because she is desperate to be at home
instead of hospital. She believes she can keep herself
safe now and is complying with treatment. I suggested
to her that "compliance" was all she was doing and that
my worry was she still felt very angry and perhaps not
very well underneath all the façade. The risk of her losing
weight as soon as she leaves hospital remains high.

This is the happiest day I've had in the past year. A glimmer of hope
has reappeared. Maybe they will let me go home eventually. Maybe
I can put my life back together again, piece by piece. Being back in
my own environment has reminded me of the person I am beyond
my anorexia nervosa. I still have my identity. Anorexia nervosa and
treatment hasn't completely swallowed me up.

I don't think of all the misery but of the beauty that still remains.

—*Anne Frank*, The Diary of a Young Girl

On good days, I start to contemplate what I would like from life once I am well. I want to travel—both returning to places I have been to already and loved and also venturing to places new to me.

I would love to travel around India and witness the riot of colour and bustling streets. I want to go back to Japan during cherry blossom season and sit in the cascades of pink petals floating through the air. I want to go to Italy and enjoy delicious pizza washed down with wine in the hills of Tuscany. I could go to Brazil and watch the toucans and macaws flying in the trees. Perhaps a trip to Hawaii to swim with turtles in the ocean? I want to walk in the mountains in Switzerland among the alpine flowers. And most of all, I want to make it to my sanctuary in Bali.

There is so much to see and do. If only I could tolerate putting food in my body. Why aren't these ambitions enough to overcome my terror?

Monday

Nursing entry: Sophia was pacing up and down the room when I took over close observations. When I asked her what was wrong she said she was "fed up with this place". She says she feels like a prisoner and is sick of having no privacy. I acknowledged her feelings and said that she has been doing really well and just needs to keep going.

Sophia feels the team are using the prospect of leave from the unit like a carrot. When she does what we ask, we only ask more of her and keep moving the goal posts. She became even more frustrated talking about this and started banging her head really hard against the wardrobe. I got up and put my hand between her head and the wardrobe to prevent Sophia from hurting herself. Sophia's parents arrived to visit her and Sophia's mum told her to stop. Sophia started to cry and her mum calmed her down. I left the room to give them some privacy but stood outside the door so I was still in eyesight of Sophia.

Yesterday was full of hope and positivity, but today I only feel frustrated. I am sick of being locked up and watched every second of the day. I can't remember the last time I was allowed to go to the loo or shower in private. Yesterday, freedom felt so reachable. But today, it just feels further away than ever.

Tuesday

Nursing entry: Sophia completed her supper and attended post meal supervision with the other patients. At the end of the supervision period, Sophia remained in the lounge after the other patients had left. Sophia talked about how hard it is at the moment and how "fat and gross" she feels. She worries that she will never be able to rebuild her life and will be friendless and alone. I encouraged her to think of things she could do to build up her confidence again.

Sometimes I question whether it's even worth fighting for life anymore. Is it really that great? Is it really worth all of this hard work to be allowed to return to the real world again? I am not sure I really like the real world that much anyway. Just because it is better than this doesn't count for a lot.

Oh, my friend, it's not what they take away from you that counts. It's what you do with what you have left.

—*Hubert Humphrey*, politician and 38th vice president of the United States, used with the permission of John Simkin

As happy as I was to get a place to study veterinary medicine, my first year of university was miserable. I was terrified of the other students and didn't speak a word to anyone. I hated having to work in groups and I felt like an idiot every time I opened my mouth. I forced myself to go into the cafeteria at lunchtime on the first day, but found the experience so difficult that I never ventured there again.

As other students got to know each other and established friends, I felt more and more lonely. Maybe if I had been fully recovered I would have felt more accepted and happier, but I was far from recovered and therefore had no chance of thriving in that kind of pressured environment.

I still have all my veterinary textbooks and notes from my first year. Whenever I see them on my bookshelf I am reminded of what a failure I am, and yet I can't bear to throw them away. I don't want to accept what anorexia nervosa has robbed me of.

Wednesday

If I have to eat even one more peanut butter sandwich I think I will have to kill someone. The bread is always stale and the peanut butter cakes the roof of my mouth. Why eat something you don't like? It's such a waste of calories. And the next person to put another bloody Kit Kat in front of me should be prepared for a tirade of abuse.

I am so bored of eating the same thing over and over again. Nothing changes in this bloody place. Other patients come and go, but I seem to have become a permanent fixture.

11. The wings start to flutter

December 2012

There are two freedoms—the false, where a man is free to do what he likes; the true, where he is free to do what he ought.

—*Charles Kingsley*, historian, priest, and novelist

My anorexia nervosa convinces me that I need to get away from those trying to control me in order to be free. I used to be convinced by this, but over the years I am beginning to have my doubts. What is true freedom? Deep down I know, it doesn't matter whether I am in hospital or not, I will always be a slave to anorexia and I will never truly be free unless I can break away from its clutches.

Thursday

Ward round: Sophia continues with the full weight gain diet and has gained a further 0.8kgs this week. She complains of being tired and lacking in energy because of the medication she is being made to comply with. Nurses confirm that Sophia spends most of the day in bed and often nods off in post meal supervision.

Sophia says her mood is constantly low and worst in the mornings. She states that she does not find being on close observations useful and feels that leave off the unit would help her.

Sophia doesn't agree with the need for further weight gain and thinks the chances of maintaining her weight in the community are very low if she is made to gain further weight.

Sophia reports ongoing depression and says the therapeutic groups aren't helpful—she only attends them to kill time. Sophia has been advised to keep attending the groups.

The team feel it is now reasonable to consider removing Sophia from close observations and start allowing her some leave, although staff must escort her. This needs frequent review in terms of managing the risk of her absconding. Sophia denies the will to abscond and says she knows the possible consequences of absconding.

Sophia can have 15 minutes escorted leave daily from the unit, starting tomorrow. If Sophia overstays her leave or refuses to return to the unit, all leave will be stopped.

Her sedative medications can start to be reduced next week but no change in medication for the moment.

Therapy session: Sophia worries that her feelings of despair will never leave her and she will always feel this way, especially if her weight increases further. She has identified that when she is at a lower weight, her emotions are duller and the anorexia nervosa feels easier to control. I advised Sophia that being a low weight is what led to the physical ill health she experienced recently and that she found being physically unwell unbearable. She acknowledged that her thoughts were contradictory and it is hard to know what she actually wants.

I never want to get that physically unwell again. I know my quality of life is so poor in that state that it doesn't justify being alive at all. However, I also know the amount of weight they have forced me to gain is not something I can tolerate.

There is a halfway ground and my goal is nothing more than to have some quality of life outside hospital. For some people, this will seem sad. But after so many years of hospital and various treatment approaches, it's a lot more realistic.

In the end, only three things matter: how much you loved, how gently you lived, and how gracefully you let go of things not meant for you.

—*Gautama Buddha*

When I got into vet school, I was determined that I would cope with the demands of the course despite being unwell. My family and the doctors tried to convince me to defer my studies and focus on making a full recovery but I wouldn't listen.

I struggled with the academic side of the course because my concentration was poor and I struggled even more with the physical aspect. As a student, I was expected to complete a three week work placement on a sheep farm during lambing season. After two days of the placement I had to admit defeat and go home. I didn't have the strength to lift up a bale of hay and the farmer was becoming increasingly frustrated with me.

I stuck it out on the course until the day of the end of year exams, when I was sectioned and taken to the nearest eating disorder unit. It has taken many years for my dream to be battered out of me, but I have now made peace with the fact I won't ever fulfil my desire to be a vet.

Friday

Nursing entry: I woke Sophia up for breakfast but she ignored me. I prompted her by suggesting it will be a good day because she is coming off close observations and can have some privacy. She attended breakfast and post meal supervision.

After so many months of being watched like a hawk, at last I get the privilege of being able to go to the toilet without an audience. I almost feel like I've got my dignity back. And then I am reminded that I'll be dragged to the dining room (or "assisted") if I don't attend breakfast.

Although I am very happy to be off close observations, suddenly being without company feels strange. For the first time in months, I am able to shut the door of my room and have some privacy. But the silence isn't as welcome as I expected. In fact, it only makes me even more aware of how lonely I feel.

Saturday

Nursing entry: Sophia has coped well with being taken off close observations. She responds when prompted and is completing meals without issue. She used her 15 minutes escorted leave to go and buy some magazines from the newsagent.

I live for those 15 minutes I have out of this place. Each second is precious. Just for those 15 minutes, I am back in the world, albeit with some staff member being with me and telling me not to walk so fast.

Sunday

Nursing entry: Sophia left snack today without explanation. When I spoke to her she said that it was because there was no white bread and she couldn't eat a peanut butter sandwich made with brown bread. I retrieved some white bread from the kitchen upstairs and Sophia returned to the dining room to complete her snack. Despite her weight gain and improvement in mental health, sudden changes in plan still throw Sophia.

The brown bread has five more calories per slice than the white bread. Obviously, this is unacceptable and I will not eat that stupid sandwich if it is not made with white bread. There are enough calories in it as it is without an extra ten calories than usual.

Better bread with water than cake with trouble.

—*Russian proverb*

To most people, an evening meal out or a takeaway is an appealing option—no cooking, no washing up, and no effort. Generally, for someone with an eating disorder, restaurant dining or a takeaway is terrifying. What's in it? How have they cooked it? What will the portion size be? The anxiety of selecting something off the menu and then waiting for it to arrive is unbearable. You can't enjoy the experience because the feelings of impending doom dominate your thoughts.

In one of the eating disorder clinics I was treated in, a weekly takeaway night was part of the programme as the staff felt we should learn to cope with normal eating. Some weeks it was pizza, others it was an Indian curry or a Chinese. Whatever the type of cuisine, we all struggled. Sometimes the meal would take over two hours as patients sobbed and forced small mouthfuls of the food down. Often we covered our eyes so we couldn't see what was in front of us. The only comfort was that we were all in it together—we weren't alone in battling the anorexia nervosa screaming in our heads.

Monday

Nursing entry: Whilst eating her toast at breakfast, Sophia did not open her second portion of margarine and refused to eat it. She returned to her bedroom. Three staff members assisted her back to the dining room. Sophia's margarine was applied to an additional slice of bread and it was explained to Sophia that she needs to comply to take this orally or an Ensure would be prescribed via the nasogastric route. Sophia showed extreme distress but completed the margarine and bread. She returned to her room and curled up on her bed sobbing.

Every time I push the boundaries, I am brutally reminded of who is in control. I still have no say about what is put in my body—I just get a choice of whether I swallow it or it's forced with a tube stuffed up my nose.

I'm such an idiot—now I've ended up having an extra slice of bread and it's my entire fault. I am disgusted with myself.

My head is constantly swimming with numbers. How much have I had so far today? How much do I have ahead? Guessing, estimating every single calorie in every single mouthful. Any calories I have managed to avoid, the calories I've had the day before, what member of staff is doing the portioning at lunch today, what do I have to eat later, etc. I am drowning in these constant thoughts. It's exhausting.

Tuesday

Nursing entry: Sophia was woken up at 6am to be weighed but she refused. She complied with her medication but was observed hiding small bits of biscuit at snack time and she was challenged on this.

Okay, caught red-handed. I just can't resist when I see an opportunity. Whatever anyone says to me, I am certain I am eating too much food and I am gaining too much weight.

Where do you go to get anorexia?

—*Shelley Winters*, used with
permission of Gloria Sullivan

I am mortified by "thinspiration" and "proana" websites on
the Internet. I do not understand how anyone could want to
be anorexic. Maybe they just don't realise how crippling the
illness can become, the extent of the damage it can cause, and
the pain and suffering it inflicts on the sufferers and everyone
around them. How anyone who could think that would be a
positive thing completely baffles me.

It bothers me that "normal" people might look at or be
aware of those sites and draw the conclusion that all anorexics want to be the way they are and have purposefully made
themselves ill. Certainly for me, that is so far from the case.
I have never looked at those websites and they really anger
me. I wish I didn't have the anorexic thoughts that plague me.
If I could undergo brain surgery to cure it or take some miracle
pill, I wouldn't hesitate to do it.

Wednesday

Nursing entry: Sophia expressed that she feels over-weight, uncomfortable and that she will lose weight upon discharge. She is frustrated with not knowing more about the future of her care plan. I advised her to discuss with the team at her next ward round.

I look in the mirror and I can see that I am not as underweight as I used to be. This makes me unhappy and I don't understand why because I don't think skeletal is a good look. As a child, I was much taller than most my age and I saw myself as big. I disliked being big because I felt it brought more attention to me and I didn't want to stand out. Those feelings have stuck with me and I don't know how to get rid of them. Even when I have gained the tiniest bit of weight, I feel and see myself as fat.

Thursday

Nursing entry: Sophia tried to hide one of her marga-rine packets at breakfast. When questioned on this she removed it from her lap and completed her breakfast. She was also observed hiding a biscuit in her sock at snack. She remains quiet and isolates herself in her bedroom.

I've been hiding the second margarine pack every day recently and now they've noticed I've got to eat it again and that will make me FAT. I need to dispose of food somewhere else in the day to compensate for having that stupid margarine pack this morning. Oh God, this is a nightmare. All I can think about is that awful margarine and how panicky I feel. I wish they had noticed the first day I did it. It's much harder to start having it again now. Why did I do it in the first place? I am so stupid.

Friday

Therapy session: Sophia's mood is still very low and she feels despairing most of the time. She sometimes feels a little brighter when on leave from the unit but this does not last long.

We discussed what anorexia nervosa gives Sophia and she stated that it provides her safety from the world, which may hurt her and cause her pain.

In my late teens, I became close friends with a couple of girls who were a similar age to me. I met them in treatment, but we lived together for a while after being discharged. I felt so happy that I finally had friends who accepted me for who I am, especially as much of my adolescence was very lonely and disrupted by periods of hospitalisation.

One Christmas, I planned to spend the morning with my family and then drive up to Cambridge to be with my friends in the afternoon. It was a four hour drive but, being Christmas Day, the roads were empty. As I whizzed along the motorway, I can remember how excited I felt about seeing them and giving them their presents.

When I finally arrived, I could sense something was wrong. One of my friends was upstairs and I was told she wasn't feeling well. I thought it was a bit rubbish that she didn't even feel well enough to say hello but I tried to just enjoy spending some time with my other friend. But things felt really odd and my friend didn't seem to want me to stay and suggested it might be best if I go home. I felt so rejected and distraught, but I got in my car and drove away. When I arrived home, my flat was cold and dark. I had managed to hold myself together throughout the journey home, but once I got through my front door I fell to pieces. Christmas Day ended with me sobbing my eyes out on my sofa.

I left their presents, but I never got a thank you. I don't know what changed and to this day I don't really understand why they behaved the way they did. But I felt so crap about myself that I just accepted it as what I deserved. I didn't deserve friends. I didn't deserve people being nice to me—I deserved to be treated like shit.

It is necessary to distinguish between the virtue and the vice of obedience.

—Lemuel K. Washburn, Is The Bible Worth
Reading and Other Essays

The lunch hall at my preparatory school was not an easy place to be. There were a lot of rules and humiliating punishments for breaking them. The head master sat at the top of the lunch hall and would ring a bell to instruct the pupils when they were allowed to speak, when they were allowed to eat and when to say the Lord's Prayer. Desperate to avoid humiliation, I did my best not to violate any regulations. During my seven years in that lunch hall, there was only one occasion where I was caught whispering to the girl next to me. My punishment was that I had to stand up on my chair for the duration of the meal. This might sound like not much of a punishment, but for me it meant that I had every pupil in the entire school looking at me, which was my worst nightmare. You were only allowed to sit back down again when it was time to say the thank you prayer.

Saturday

It would be so nice to be able to walk the streets and pretend to be just like everyone else I pass by. That nurse walking with me makes it impossible to forget that I still don't fit in the normal world. Also I am desperate for a Diet Coke.

I think it is fairly universal in eating disorder treatment centres to have a complete ban on diet drinks. Many anorexics are addicted to these and I admit that I certainly have drunk way too much Diet Coke for way too long.

Being in hospital would initially prevent me from getting my Diet Coke "fix", but as soon as I was granted time out into the big, wide world I would buy as many Diet Cokes as possible and sneak them back into the clinic.

This was not necessarily an easy task as the standard procedure is a bag search by staff on return to the ward. I therefore wore high leg socks to enable me to stuff Diet Cokes down the sides of my legs. It was hard to walk normally with cans strapped to your legs but I was never caught doing it. I think staff are so focused on looking through your bag they don't notice that you are waddling down the corridor. Getting rid of the empty cans was easy—they don't search your bag on the way out.

Sunday

self-harm. One reason for this is that she thinks that were she to do so, it would merely prolong her admission.

There is no way I am getting to the weight they want me to be, so my only option is to falsify my weight. I am already drinking large amounts of water before being weighed but I hate doing this when I then have to stuff breakfast down me. I've got to get my hands on some weights to strap onto myself for weigh-ins, and my only hope is being given some unescorted leave.

Monday

Ward round: Weight has increased by 1.4 kg this week. Sophia remains on the full weight gaining diet.

Sophia is constantly drowsy and low in mood. It is objectively hard to assess her due to the level of given sedation but she has prominent anorexic cognitions.

The team has agreed to reduce her sedatives. We acknowledge she is doing well (although there are occasions where she has been observed hiding food).

Sophia remains distressed about her weight gain and the rate she is gaining weight. The team feels she still needs to gain weight.

Although Sophia's weight has improved relatively, she still remains in the weight range for severe anorexia nervosa and her illness itself remains severe. She continues to lack capacity in respect of treatment (including food, therapeutic activities and medications) owing to prominent anorexic overvalued ideas interfering with her ability to weigh decisions relating to these areas of her care in the balance. For this reason, it is appropriate and in her best interests to continue the boundaries in her treatment, including requiring her to complete all meals and attend supervision, as well as taking medication (restricting her liberty using restraint if necessary).

Tuesday

Nursing entry: At suppertime, Sophia was observed hiding butter. She walked out when challenged and refused to return to the dining room. She remains in bed and says, "I am rotting in here".

The team have discussed her progress and feel it is appropriate for her to have unescorted leave from the unit, but this will be dependent on her complying with her meal plan.

45 minutes unescorted leave and task accomplished. To the shops and back, weights strapped around my ankles and undiscovered by staff when searched upon my return. What a relief.

Wednesday

Nursing entry: Staff are reminded that Sophia's leave from the unit is conditional on her completing all of her prescribed meals. She was allowed out unescorted yesterday but is still hiding food. She had to be brought back to the dining room at snack time to complete her food. Her unescorted leave from the unit today has been denied. She remains subdued and isolative.

Bastards. Of course they have the perfect punishment now. If I don't eat the ridiculous amount they want me to, I lose my right to those precious moments of the day when I am not stuck in this miserable unit. I wish I didn't care about my leave so they weren't able to use it to blackmail me. I hate them. Every mouthful I swallow makes me feel more and more hateful of them all.

At least I managed to get my weights before they took my leave away. They are surprisingly lax about the weighing procedures in this unit—other places I have experienced have been a lot stricter. Most units insist on patients being weighed in their underwear, but not here. In some places, the nurses will even listen outside the toilet door to check you have emptied your bladder before being weighed.

Beware of little expenses; a small leak will sink a great ship.

—Benjamin Franklin, one of the
founding fathers of the United States

If you ever have the opportunity to look underneath the tables in eating disorder dining rooms, be prepared for a nasty surprise. The underside of the table is likely to be smeared with food. Usually it's butter or margarine from breakfast and occasionally a nice bit of yoghurt or jam. Peanut butter is a common favourite too.

Most seats in a dining room will have a cushion, which is necessary when your rear is so bony that it hurts to sit down. Unfortunately, the cushion introduces the option of hiding elements of your meal or snack underneath it. Chips, nuts, bits of pastry—whatever fearsome delight that featured on today's menu can be leaked from your plate. Of course, if possible you will dispose of the evidence quickly after the meal is over and the dining room is empty, as long as a member of staff or another patient hasn't got there first.

Disposing little bits of food in this way demonstrates how fearful patients can be of weight gain and the acts of desperation they will resort to. However small, the scraps of calories you are avoiding mean a lot to your eating disorder. As long as you are engaging in such behaviour, the illness can take comfort that it still has some control.

Thursday

Nursing entry: Sophia spent much of the morning in her room. She completed her meals in the dining room but had to be prompted to finish the crumbs on her plate.

Some of the staff are so obsessive about making you scrape your bowl and pick up every little crumb. It's not enough you've just eaten four biscuits—if you have left a crumb you haven't finished. Sometimes it's as if they want you to actually lick your plate clean. Every calorie counts as much to them as it does for me.

Friday

Nursing entry: Sophia attended the dining room for evening snack but left with some of the snack still in her mouth. Staff approached her and asked her to swallow the food but she refused and spat it out into her bin. She has refused to be weighed this morning.

Take my leave away—I don't care. I'm not going to give in to blackmail and bribes.

Out of this nettle, danger, we pluck this flower, safety.

—*William Shakespeare*

Saturday

Nursing entry: Sophia completed her meals today without issue although there was a little bit of smearing of food at breakfast. She has been quiet and isolated in her room throughout the day.

So what if I smear my Weetabix around the bowl? I've got two slices of toast to get through as well. If it makes me feel safe to eat my breakfast then that's what I have to do.

At times when I am learning to feed myself again after a period of starvation, I develop many rules and strategies to help me cope. These involve behaviours that purposefully try to reduce the intake of calories. Smearing food around the bowl or plate is a classic example. Somehow "getting rid of" the tiniest bit of food can make eating the rest of it more bearable.

Sometimes the behaviours don't really serve a purpose and are more just quirky rituals. I tell myself it is okay to eat the food because I have performed a particular ritual. These rituals take many forms—breaking the biscuit into a set number of pieces, counting the number of peas and then eating them two by two, cutting toast into particular shapes, wiping cutlery, drinking the milk before eating the cereal, turning the plate at certain angles, etc.

When you are being made to do something you feel very scared about doing, you will do anything to try to lessen that fear. My weird rituals help me curb my irrational thoughts enough to allow me to feed myself. Somehow it makes doing the most terrifying thing feel bearable.

Sunday

Nursing entry: I accompanied Sophia on a home visit today. Sophia spent time with her rabbits and appeared much brighter in mood and more talkative during this time. We spoke about numerous aspects of her care. I raised the fact that she has been found to hide food on numerous occasions. Sophia feels embarrassed when challenged on this and says she has an overwhelming compulsion to hide food as she worries about her weight increasing and feeling out of control. I advised Sophia that to achieve her goals for the future, she must learn to feed herself and demonstrate to us that she is able to do this. Sophia acknowledges this but states that she finds it very hard to eat the volume of food she is currently prescribed.

Before returning to the unit, Sophia had her snack in a café. She coped well with having her snack and was able to engage in conversation throughout.

It was so nice to be at home today. When I was with my rabbits I could escape the constant thoughts around food and weight that plague me all day. I wish I could be out in the world so my life could actually have some quality to it.

I have survivor skills. Some of that is superficial—what I present to people outwardly—but what makes people resilient is the ability to find humour and irony in situations that would otherwise overpower you.

—Amy Tan, author, used with
author's permission

Those caring for someone with an eating disorder can make unfortunate blunders without even realising it. I was being looked after by one particular carer who was very kind but had no concept of what anorexia nervosa was.

At my dreaded snack time, the carer consulted my meal plan and removed two biscuits from the pack for me to eat. I told her that if she would like she could have some biscuits with me. Her response was "No, no. Biscuits make you fat!" I don't think she noticed how mortified I looked.

Luckily, I was at a stage in my illness that I was able to just laugh at the whole situation and not let my anorexia nervosa latch on to her words. Maintaining a sense of humour has helped me cope with such comments rather than let them trigger off a whole load of irrational thoughts that have the potential to sabotage my eating. Dark humour has helped me through some very bleak times.

Monday

Ward round: Sophia will soon be at her agreed target weight. Her sedatives can be reduced further and two hours leave home next weekend has been granted.

I thought this day would never come. Finally I feel like I am closer to getting out of this dump. What they don't know is my weight is a fair bit less than what they think. Falsifying my weight is clearly the only way out of this mess and it's working.

Tuesday

Nursing entry: Sophia was weighed this morning and has reached her target weight band. Her meal plan has been reduced—she can now have yoghurt instead of the full weight gain hot pudding with custard. Should her weight fall, puddings will have to be introduced again.

THANK THE LORD! At last there is less food to have to stuff myself with. No more bowls of sickly coconut sponge or bread and butter pudding swimming in custard.

Of course, it is now even more crucial they do not find out I am deceiving the scales. I know I am playing with fire, but it's the only way of getting out of this place that I can tolerate.

Wednesday

Nursing entry: Sophia continues to stay in her room all day and only comes out when she has to attend the dining room or post meal supervision. She does not interact

with other patients or staff. She has completed her meals
and complied with medication.

I've just got to keep my head down and be a "good girl".
THEY MUSTN'T FIND OUT.

It is no measure of health to be well adjusted to a profoundly sick society.

—*Krishnamurti*, philosopher and writer, with
thanks to the Krishnamurti Foundation

The atmosphere on eating disorder units varies. Some units are stricter than others and some are posh private facilities while others are run-down NHS clinics. Whatever the environment, the grim reality is that the patients will all struggle to manage their biggest enemy—food.

Sometimes the atmosphere is supportive, with patients genuinely looking out for each other. I have made some very close friends with people I have been in treatment with and I and they have remained close many years after discharge.

Unfortunately, the atmosphere can also sometimes be deeply competitive. Who's managing to not gain weight? Who's getting "special" treatment? Who's got out of having a chocolate bar? Why has so and so got a different meal plan? How come they can go home? It's not fair. They're getting away with something. How come I'm not allowed? You get the idea.

Eating disorder units can be a breeding ground for bitchiness and gossiping. I have been hurt many times by patients who

I thought of as friends only to find they have been discussing things I told them in confidence and bitching about me to the rest of the patient group. It is better to stay isolated and alone than risk being hurt or humiliated.

Thursday

Group therapy: Sophia says she is feeling brighter in mood but is bored. She engaged well and offered suggestions to others. She acknowledged how much has changed since her admission. She set a goal of wearing a new jumper to practise being more flexible.

Oh please. These groups can be so pathetic. Has my life really deteriorated to the point that my goal for the week is "to wear a new jumper"? It's all so patronising and yet the boredom of not going to the groups is unbearable. I have been here way too long. I can't hold in all my hatred for this place—I feel like I am going to explode and it's not going to be pleasant.

Friday

Ward round: Sophia appears to be doing much better. She has started to attend groups and is generally more positive. However, her Section 3 detention under the Mental Health Act is up for review and the team agree that it should be renewed. On discharge, the team feel Sophia should be placed under a Community Treatment Order.

Sophia's parents are keen for Sophia to continue to gain weight above her current target weight. They want a "safety margin" should she begin to lose weight when she is discharged. Sophia feels this is too ambitious at the moment—she refuses to gain more weight.

Sophia's parents have agreed for Sophia to have overnight leave from the unit this weekend.

As if. I can't even tolerate the ridiculous target weight I am supposed to be, let alone a higher weight than that. Why is everyone around me so unrealistic? And why do I need my parents' "permission" for overnight leave? I'm 26 years old for fuck's sake. Well at least I am getting what I want. And all it took was acquiring some weights. Yes, I toss and turn at night, fretting over being "discovered", but so far there has been no suspicion about things. They must just see how fat I am and therefore it doesn't enter their heads that I might be falsifying my weight.

Saturday

Nursing entry: Sophia was weighed this morning and she has gained weight over her target weight band. She is extremely distressed. I have agreed that she does not have to have her toast at breakfast anymore and her diet has been amended. Sophia is much calmer now and is generally much brighter in manner. She received her medication and went on leave this afternoon. She is due back on Sunday for lunch. I have advised her to call us if there are any problems.

Yes—no more toast loaded with margarine and jam. This is great. The more my meal diet plan is decreased, the more weights I add around my ankles when I am weighed and the happier I feel.

Okay, so there is the constant fear that I will be found out, but it's worth the risk. I am desperate to satisfy that anorexic voice and I can't accept being the weight I am and having to consume the meal plan they have me on. I won't go back to my extreme regime I had before, but I have to find a compromise between that and what they are expecting of me.

Best of all, I can't believe I have a night of freedom from this miserable place! I am euphoric. I might as well see what I can get away with and extend it slightly. I don't see what the big deal is if I return to the unit a few hours late. I really don't want the dreaded roast dinner on Sunday lunch time and being stuck in that place on a Sunday afternoon is so depressing when I should be out in the world and doing something other than rotting in my miserable room here.

A human history begins with the man's act of disobedience which is at the very same time the beginning of his freedom and before the development of his reason.

—*Erich Fromm*, Psychoanalysis and Religion, p. 82, used with the permission of Rainer Funk

There are times in hospital where a patient rebellion breaks out. The most memorable one for me was a revolt against the evening supper menu. The patient group was small and only three of us were actually being subjected to the dreaded creamy cheese and broccoli soup that smelt of feet and very smelly feet at that. We decided to take a stand. It wasn't a locked unit, so when suppertime came, we walked out and jumped in a taxi. We went into town and got drunk passing from pub to pub, downing cider and cocktails. I wasn't much of a drinker, and I got drunk quickly. We didn't return to the unit until gone midnight, and the night staff were not happy with us.

The next day we were separately called into the nursing office to be read the riot act by our consultant. Although I can see that they needed to tell us off, I think our behaviour should have been somewhat celebrated. Yes, refusing to have the meal was going against treatment. But our little rebellion gave me a taste of the adolescence I missed out on and although I didn't relish being told off, I felt proud that I had done something so "normal".

Sunday

Nursing entry: Sophia was due back at lunchtime but remained on leave. It seems there has been a miscommunication regarding her return time. She arrived back at the unit this evening and says her leave went well.

Yes my leave went wonderful thanks. Yes I ate everything I was supposed to. No I didn't over exercise. Yes I took all my medication.

Lies, lies, lies. I don't even feel bad for lying because I lost all respect I had for you people when you hurt and violated me in the name of "treatment". But I know I have to nod and smile and be pleasant to you because it's the only way out of this dump.

Every vice has its excuse ready.

—*Publilius Syrus*, Roman writer

I don't think I was a great liar before I got ill. I certainly remember feeling very guilty about lying when I was a child. It shocks me how easy I find it now. Some of the time it isn't lying, I am just stuck in denial about the reality of my health and behaviours. But sometimes it is most definitely blatant lies that are so convincing I begin to believe them myself. Years and years of lying about food and my behaviours around food have made me an expert.

Monday

Nursing entry: Sophia was weighed this morning and her weight has dropped. She needs to regain this weight and show that she can feed herself adequately when she is at home. She will start self-catering some of her meals on the unit to help her manage food better when she is on leave.

I messed up. I underestimated the number of weights to put on me before being weighed this morning. I'm so annoyed with myself. Will they let me have overnight leave again?

At least I can start self-catering some meals—I most definitely won't be making that vile cheese and tomato flan that is a regular feature on the unit menu.

Tuesday

Ward round: Sophia is reported to be working collaboratively with staff. The initial goal is to be discharged to day patient treatment that will be 7 days a week and all meals at the unit.

While Sophia asserts her intentions to do things differently and to build a life outside of hospital, discharge from hospital with minimal or no after care has in the past resulted in relapse and near death.

Sophia currently has huge ambivalence about her weight and has no desire to gain more weight. Ongoing boundaries provided by the Mental Health Act are crucial to manage the risks from her illness and to prevent another relapse.

Sophia is at risk of disengaging from treatment prematurely and rapidly declining to a life threatening medical state. The current plan is for continued care under the safeguards of a Community Treatment Order upon discharge to support her to remain stable out of hospital and provide the contingency of rapid recall to hospital much earlier should she relapse.

Under the Community Treatment Order, Sophia will need to attend for treatment as per her care plan. Physical and psychological monitoring including spot weighs will be non-negotiable. Sophia must continue to take her medication as prescribed. Her weight must remain within her target band. We have acknowledged the risk of weight falsification and the importance of spot weighs. Sophia will be recalled to hospital immediately if she does not meet any of these requirements.

I really resent this Community Treatment Order. I don't think it will help me manage my illness, I think it will only make me resistant to treatment because I am constantly under the threat of re-admission. Dr. Cole is so adamant that it will be the best way to stay "in control" of me, but in reality I think it will mean that I just continue to hide my struggles from those trying to treat me. I guess it just goes to show that, even after all this time, they still don't understand how my head works.

Wednesday

Nursing entry: I met with Sophia today to discuss meal planning and self-catering. She acknowledged her recent weight loss and says she had difficulty planning her meals last week when she went home. We have made a meal plan for her to follow when she goes on her one night's leave this weekend.

Well obviously I will try to eat more than last weekend, but this meal plan is excessive. If they weren't so unrealistic about things, I would be able to follow their advice more. Do they seriously think I am going to be tucking in to a cheese loaded jacket potato at home?

When was the last time I actually cooked myself a meal and sat down and ate it at home? I can't remember it was so long ago. When I am not in treatment and condemned to my regular trips to the dining room, I don't sit down to eat a meal under my own will. I haven't even used the oven in my current flat. I allow myself to snack late at night, but other than that I don't eat. I would like that to change. I would like to be able to cook and sit down and enjoy a meal. Except I know I wouldn't enjoy it. I would be wretched with guilt and panic about what I was doing. I really hate my brain.

Thursday

Nursing entry: Sophia self-catered her meal at lunchtime today but staff are concerned she did not eat adequately. There is worry she will not manage whilst on leave this weekend. She needs to put more structure into her meal plan. Her self-catering needs to be discussed and has to be more strictly monitored.

The only time the staff come and speak to me is when they want to talk about food. That's all they've got time for. I am so sick of being constantly nagged and hassled about what I am eating. They have no idea how tedious it is to be hounded with meal plans and watchful eyes detecting every morsel you consume. I hate being stared at while I eat and barked at when I do something wrong. They don't see me as a person—I have spent months here and yet very few staff know anything about me. Of course, they are familiar with my anorexia nervosa, but they have no idea about the person underneath it. I am not sure I am anymore either. My illness has become so fused with my identity.

Friday

Nursing entry: The occupational therapy team have met with Sophia to discuss the issues around her nutrition. Sophia is doing more self-catering than has been authorized and is choosing only safe, low calorie foods. We discussed how we could best help her manage her nutrition with set boundaries.

Sophia found it difficult to hear this. Her self-catering has been suspended for now and she will rejoin the main dining room again at meal times.

Great—so it's back to being stuffed full of that evil crap they serve up in the dining room. I don't want to put that shit in my body. I am never going to eat macaroni cheese or corned beef hash when I leave here so why do I have to force myself to eat it here? What's the point? As far as they're concerned, I've reached my target weight so why can't I eat what I want now?

God, I am dreading supper. Typical that it would have to be possibly my most despised meal—the delightful cheese and onion quiche. The pastry is always a soggy mess and it is impossible to serve it up in an attractive manner. It's just lumped on the plate as an enormous dollop of egg and cheese mush. The onion is slimy and pungent. Even the limp salad served up with it is ladled with oily dressing. I dread how I shall feel after I am made to eat it. This is so unfair. I shouldn't have to do this still, after I've gained so much weight.

Today I signed up at a gym near the unit and I will go and exercise there during my unescorted leave. I am only supposed to have 45 minutes per day, but most of the staff are really lax about it and don't even say anything if you are gone longer or go out more than once. It is rarely handed over between shifts whether I have taken my leave that day yet so I can go in the morning during the early shift and in the afternoon during the late shift. All they care about is that you are there for the meals. Stuff your face and then you're free to do whatever you want.

Pretty much all the patients exercise during their daily leave if it's unescorted. We walk the streets regardless of the cold winter, the dark evenings and the typical British wetness.

We must accept finite disappointment, but never lose infinite hope.

—*Martin Luther King Jr.*

Saturday

Nursing entry: At lunch, Sophia refused to eat her chicken skin and walked out of the dining room. I spoke to Sophia and she stated she was sick of being here and that she wasn't going to eat the chicken skin because it was disgusting. I explained to Sophia that it would be unfair of me to allow her to leave the chicken skin when the other patients have to eat it. I advised Sophia to finish her meal and not to throw away the hard work she has done over the past months.

Sophia returned to the dining room and had her yoghurt but refused to eat the chicken skin.

No one would eat flabby chicken skin that's all congealed and rubbery. Punish me whatever way you like, but I am not eating that. They better not use that as an excuse to deny me my unescorted leave—I need to get to the gym.

Whole baked trout was a weekly feature on the menu in one of the treatment centres I have attended. It was one of the nicer meals in terms of quality, but unfortunately it resulted in major conflict between patients and staff.

Some nurses felt that patients needed to eat everything—the skin, the head (including the eyes) and the tail. Other nurses were too lapse and would be oblivious to all the perfectly edible pieces of fish that were being hidden underneath the skin they were allowing us to discard.

It was a Russian roulette as to who would be on duty. However much a nurse insisted, I would never consume the eyes of a fish and I don't think any of the other patients did either. Luckily, when patients are all in agreement about something, there is some security in numbers.

Sunday

Nursing entry: Sophia's weight has dropped and she is now under her target weight band. We need to discuss increasing her food intake. If Sophia refuses to eat more, we may have to suspend her leave from the ward.

Oh God. I messed up with the weights again. It's just so hard to judge how many weights to strap on me when I feel so fat the whole time. My disgust at what I have to eat and how big my body feels makes me underestimate how many weights I need when I am weighed. I can't bear the thought of being stuck in here. I have to have access to the gym. I will pile on weight if I can't exercise.

Monday

Ward round: There is concern that Sophia is losing weight and withdrawing from treatment. She says that she does not want to attend the day patient programme and wishes to be discharged to outpatients. The team feel she needs to remain in treatment longer.

It is unclear whether she is taking her medication when on leave—probably not.

She still isolates herself from staff and other patients. Sophia says she doesn't feel being here is helping her.

Sophia's last blood tests show elevated CK, indicating her activity is much higher than her nutritional intake. There are concerns that Sophia has lost weight and that she is possibly falsifying her weight. The team suspects she may be struggling more than she is outwardly displaying.

Dr. Cole is concerned that her current weight is insufficient to enable Sophia to live and recover and we need to support further recovery. Sophia's anorexia nervosa continues to impair her capacity for decision-making. It may be too soon to consider transfer from inpatient to day patient treatment.

The team have decided we need to start routine spot weighing to rule out weight falsification.

Nursing entry: At dinner, Sophia said she is prescribed 2 scoops of ice cream. Staff informed her that she should be having 3 scoops. Sophia then walked out of the dining room and refused to come back to complete her meal.

Shit. I really don't like the way things are shaping up at the moment. I have a feeling of impending doom. They have got their suspicions and it's going to be hard to convince them they are wrong.

I am using more and more weights and the risk of being caught out is increasing every day. I feel sick. I am in a constant state of anxiety. They can't find out. My life really will be over if they discover my real weight.

> Praise and blame, gain and loss, pleasure and sorrow
> come and go like the wind. To be happy, rest like a giant
> tree in the midst of them all.

> —*Gautama Buddha*

One of the eating disorder clinics I was in was part of a very large psychiatric hospital with various wards. Most of the wards were locked and held patients being treated under the Mental Health Act. Every Friday night, someone in one of these wards would set off the fire alarm. This meant that all patients in the entire hospital had to evacuate and stand in the hospital grounds until the fire brigade arrived and checked it was a false alarm. This gave patients their best chance of a break for freedom, which was a particularly appealing option on the night before the start of the weekend.

Although I kind of admired their determination to escape, it got pretty tedious to be chucked out into the dark and cold of winter in just our slippers and pyjamas every week.

Tuesday

Nursing entry: Sophia was reluctant to come to breakfast this morning. When I prompted her she shouted at me saying, "Why don't you just piss off?" I told her that speaking to me in that way made me feel uncomfortable, but she replied that she didn't care.

They are going to find out and there is nothing I can do. Can I run? Where won't they find me? How can I get past the locked doors? I can't sleep, I feel sick the whole time and I just want this nightmare to end. The only thing that helps reduce my anxiety is going to the gym. I feel a lot better about putting all this food in me if I've been able to exercise—it's the only thing that takes an edge off my anxiety about being made to eat so much.

I wouldn't say I am addicted to exercise in the way some eating disorder sufferers are. I don't get a "high" out of doing it—I am simply trying to do everything I can to prevent further weight gain. I would love to stop as I don't enjoy my trips to the gym, but because I am being made to eat so much food I have to go in order to bring my anxiety levels down to a level I can tolerate. When I am not being made to eat, I do not feel the urge or need to exercise.

Wednesday

Nursing entry: Sophia continues to be withdrawn and hostile. She is reluctant about attending meals and always arrives at the dining room late.

The more anxious I get the worse my obsessions and rituals are. If everything is tidy, if everything is straight, if everything is clean, then maybe, just maybe my world won't fall apart. The more rituals I have to do before I can eat, the later I am in getting myself to the dining room and the more panicked I feel.

I must shut and open my cupboard. Then I wash my hands. I must straighten my bedcovers and smooth my pillow. Then I wash my hands. I must wash my mouth out with mouthwash. Then I wash my hands. I must brush my teeth. Then I wash my hands. I must check my phone battery. I must go to the toilet. Then I wash my hands twice. I must touch my radiator. I must check my cupboard again. Then I wash my hands. Only then can I go to the dining room, sit down, and eat. If my rituals are interrupted, I must start them again and then I am late and people get cross. They don't understand.

I will not let anyone walk through my mind with their dirty feet.

—*Mahatma Gandhi*

If I have learnt anything in life, it is that you should be very careful about who you let into your head. It takes me a long time to trust someone enough that I feel able to speak my mind, and even then I feel scared that they will react in a way that hurts me. When your self-esteem is rock bottom, you feel even more vulnerable. I think this adds to the secrecy that is commonly associated with anorexia nervosa. I feel the need to keep things to myself so that my illness is not challenged or threatened. I don't want my coping strategies to be taken away.

Thursday

Therapy session: Sophia remains unhappy about being on the unit and does not want to attend the day patient programme. She wants to leave the service completely and continue her recovery at home.

I told Sophia that these feelings are understandable but having support upon discharge from hospital after

such a long admission would be advisable and give her
the opportunity to practise feeding herself and building
a life.

Sophia stated that she did not agree with this.

*Why the hell would dragging myself into this place every day after I
am discharged be remotely helpful? I don't have any respect for the
programme, I hate everyone here and I'm pretty sure everyone hates
me. I want to get as far away from this place as soon possible.*

Friday

Nursing entry: Sophia was spot weighed this morning. She has gained enough weight to be back in her
target weight band. She complied with her meals and
medication.

*Phew—that should get them off my back for a bit. I had a feeling they
would spot weigh me today so I strapped myself with weights before I
left my room this morning. Maybe they won't find out. Maybe I can
convince them I am well enough for them to discharge me and leave
me the hell alone. I am so relieved they won't have a reason to take
away my leave from the unit—I couldn't cope without being able to
go to the gym.*

A lot of gyms seem to turn a blind eye to the physical
appearance of those applying for membership. I suppose
they are focused on the financial gain of securing payment
for a membership contract, but they don't consider that
they could be held liable if someone collapses whilst using
their facilities. I have been able to secure a gym membership
despite being noticeably very underweight and physically
frail. The only time I have had questions asked of me was
when another member of the gym had alerted management
of the gym that I was clearly very unwell. Only at that point

did the gym put my membership on hold until I had medical clearance.

I managed to secure medical clearance rather easily because the GP didn't even ask to see me. I just spoke to him on the phone and picked up a signed doctor's note declaring me well enough to use the gym facilities.

Despite this, I felt uncomfortable knowing that other members had noticed my appearance and my embarrassment stopped me from going to the gym anymore. I guess I should thank the person who alerted the staff, although at the time I was furious with whoever it was.

We cannot live only for ourselves. A thousand fibers connect us with our fellow men.

—*Henry Melvill*, priest of the
Church of England

Despite telling myself I don't care, it always hurts to feel left out. I can't count the number of times at school where I was wretched because one of the girls in my class had invited everyone to their party but me. To be fair, I was an incredibly shy child and I found it hard to interact with others. But knowing they would all be playing party games, eating sweets, and having a nice time without me made me miserable. Hearing about how much fun it had been at school the next day got me down. I was desperate to be included, and yet too scared to interact with anyone.

Saturday

Nursing entry: Sophia prepared her own breakfast today. Another patient reported that she only had a half portion of porridge and made it with water not milk.

I met with Sophia to discuss the fact that I was concerned she is significantly undercutting calories when self-catering. Sophia became tearful and said her weight had gone up "so why did it matter"? She feels controlled by us and says "everyone is on my back trying to get me to a higher weight". Her self-catering sessions have been suspended for now.

I am so annoyed that another patient has snitched on me to the staff. It's none of their business what I eat and they should just focus on themselves. Why do they think they have the right to interfere with my treatment? I am not meddling in their affairs.

Sometimes this illness is just so desperately competitive—it's horrible. Everyone looks at what everyone else is doing. That's why I am wise to keep my distance from the other patients as much as possible. Others have betrayed me too many times in treatment—I must remain wary.

Anorexia nervosa can make you pretty oblivious to the impact your behaviours have on others, and even if you are made aware that your behaviour is inconsiderate you don't feel able to change your behaviour.

In one of the clinics I was in, every breakfast would be the same argument. Patients were expected to take two slices of bread out of the loaf and toast them to their liking. A normal person would obviously just take the first two slices in the loaf. Anorexics don't think like that. Your impulse is to go for the two thinnest slices. This led to patients squabbling over slices that are suitably thin enough, and a lot of complaints that it was unhygienic to rummage through the entire loaf in your quest for the end crust, which was sometimes barely a slice at all.

I'm amazed it wasn't stopped sooner, but eventually the staff decided that they would issue the slices to each patient from the loaf to end the escalating shouting matches that were becoming a frequent event at the start of each day.

When angry, count to four; when very angry, swear.

—*Mark Twain*, author

Before I became unwell, I hadn't had much contact with very elderly members of the population. During my time spent in medical wards, it has never failed to make me chuckle at how abusive the elderly can be. It seems however much you lose your faculties, you rarely forget how to be insulting. The language I have heard coming out of the mouths of frail old ladies is the worst I have ever heard, and some of them are still able to punch doctors so hard that they yelp. To be fair, if I make it to old age, I am sure I will be equally vile to those interfering with me. I'm pretty vile now so I can't imagine how insufferable I'll be if I make it to old age.

Sunday

Nursing entry: Sophia refused to have milk in her coffee at snack time and claims it is in her care plan that she doesn't have to have it. We need to check this with the rest of the team. She is getting slower in eating and completes her meals later and later.

The only things that make the days bearable are keeping to my routines and obsessions. So what if they mean I eat slower? At least I'm bloody eating. Isn't that enough for them?

Monday

Ward round: Sophia refused her spot weigh today. There has been concern that she has made large reductions in her diet when preparing her own meals.

Sophia feels she has been to hell and back in this admission. She says the worst point was at Avery Lodge as it was unable to manage her and they would have let her die.

We discussed the plan for a Community Treatment Order when she is discharged. Sophia doesn't want to be on a Community Treatment Order. Dr. Cole sees a need for it, as Sophia is likely to leave treatment too soon without it.

Fuck them and their stupid Community Treatment Order. So basically, I won't ever be free? I will always be wearing invisible handcuffs. I will always have to go to sleep at night fearing that any day they could drag me back to this miserable hellhole. I won't agree to this. There has to be a way I can find my freedom again. I don't deserve a life sentence.

Don't cry over spilt milk.

When you have an eating disorder, you often have strong feelings about the presentation of food or the way it "should" or "must" be in order to make it acceptable to eat. It's often little things—food being the right temperature, toast being toasted to a certain degree, tea or coffee not being the right strength, how the food is served on the plate, etc. The list is endless. Everyone has personal preferences and when you have an eating disorder it is very hard to accept being given something that "isn't right".

Almost at every meal on every day there will be some sort of upset in an eating disorder unit dining room because staff are refusing to reheat food to a higher temperature, toast bread to the preference of particular patients, etc. This usually involves shouting, rowing with staff, storming out, throwing food and all sorts of distress.

Dining room regulations and rules are usually posted on the dining room wall, but those rules go out the window when someone is completely freaking out. Little preferences with food are massively important when you have an eating disorder.

Being given food that is barely warm is just unacceptable for me. I get very angry if staff won't heat up the food when I feel it is not hot enough. I have stormed out of the dining room on many occasions because of this, only to be "assisted" back to the dining room when the food will be even colder than it was before. I also hate my toast being cut into squares—it has to be cut in triangles. There is no rationale behind this; it's just the way it has to be in order for me to feel able to eat it.

Tuesday

Nursing entry: Sophia agreed to be spot weighed this morning and her weight is within her target weight band. She can have her leave from the unit this weekend.

Another stroke of luck—I am getting pretty good at predicting when they are going to surprise me with a spot weigh. At least I can get out of this place at the weekend.

Wednesday

Nursing entry: Sophia was due back from leave for supper this evening. She did not come back until 9pm and says she was told that was when she was due back. She reports that her time at home went well.

Oh dear, really? I was expected back for supper? I must have misunderstood. Of course I followed my meal plan and took my medication. I am a good girl and there is no need for me to be here anymore.

Oh, bird of my soul, fly away now, for I possess a hundred fortified towers.

—Rumi, Islamic scholar

Thursday

Care Plan Approach meeting: We acknowledged the progress, distress and difficulty Sophia has experienced in treatment. She has a severe illness and has been unable to benefit from treatment for many years. She has been in near death from starvation and this has been a long and traumatic admission.

Sophia remains frightened and sticks to safe foods whenever she can. She is unwilling to take the risk of doing anything different. She remains very lonely and distant from others and feels she has failed at life.

The nursing team feel she has been less engaged recently and has pushed the boundaries of her care plan. She still has blood abnormalities and is attending groups less and less.

The staff are suspicious about Sophia's weight and there has been little change in her thinking. Her sole motivation is to get away from the eating disorder unit.

In this meeting, Sophia expressed clear sadness and then became very increasingly hostile and dismissive. Sophia feels humiliated, exposed and ashamed. She says that groups and treatment are useless and she doesn't want to change. She has agreed to work towards discharge to the day patient programme and this will initially be intensive—all day and seven days a week. She will be placed on a Community Treatment Order and will be readmitted as an inpatient if she violates any of the conditions in her care plan.

I am so sick of these stupid meetings. Fine, make me do the day patient programme, put me on a Community Treatment Order, but you won't control me forever. I will be patient and one day freedom will be mine again. I've come this far; I can't give up now however angry I am about being made to do the day programme.

Friday

Nursing entry: Sophia took her 30 minutes leave from the unit this morning but did not return. I phoned her and she stated she had gone home and wasn't coming back. I explained to her that because she is under a section 3 of the Mental Health Act, I would need to inform the team of her absconding and circulate her to the police for them to return her to the unit.

Sophia's mother then phoned to say she has found Sophia and they will return to the unit together. Sophia arrived back just before lunch. She stated that she was not going to eat in the main dining room because she was meant to be self-catering her meal today. There is no record of this. We discussed what to do as a team and entered

Sophia's room. Sophia was restrained and escorted to the dining room. She was told she had to drink two bottles of Ensure or she would not be allowed to go home on leave. Staff exerted boundaries and did not react to Sophia's distress and pleas—"Please, don't do this to me".

Sophia drank the Ensures and was returned to her room. She completed the rest of her meals today but appeared vacant and sad.

There are no words. My desperation is overwhelming and I feel numb. Being dragged down the corridor by my arms and legs hurt, but that's nothing compared to the emotional trauma.

I thought all that was behind me now—I wouldn't be subjected to it ever again. How wrong I was. I won't ever be able to forget the events of today. All I can do is crawl into bed and hope I wake up to a different world.

I want to feel happy that I can at least go home and they haven't got an excuse to take my leave away, but I know I will feel traumatised and miserable about what happened today whether I am stuck in this shit hole or at home. There is no way of escaping the wretchedness.

Saturday

Nursing entry: Sophia has been low in mood, self-isolating and withdrawn. Attempts made to engage with her have not been successful and she avoids eye contact.

I can't look at them. I begged them to stop yesterday and they acted like I didn't exist. Why should I respond to them now when they have treated me that way? I can't act like yesterday and all the other occasions when they have abused me didn't happen. I can't smile and make small talk. I know that I am nothing to them. They don't see me as a person—if they did they would not continue to damage and traumatise me.

Sunday

Nursing entry: Sophia had her snack and then asked to go to the post office before it closes. She reassured staff that she would be coming back for supper. Sophia did not come back. Staff nurse Patrick spoke to her on the phone. Sophia said she is fine and at home. She stated that she would return to the unit tomorrow. This incident will be fed back to the team.

I feel safe for now—no one can hurt me here. I was worried they would threaten to call the police to drag me back, but luckily the ward matron had gone home already and I guess the nurse in charge just decided to leave it. I am so relieved, but how am I going to face going back to the unit?

Three things can not hide for long: the Moon, the Sun and the Truth.

—*Gautama Buddha*

No matter how many times I pull the wool over people's eyes, I never learn that I am only cheating myself. I am so fixed on convincing everyone around me that I am not deteriorating that I start believing it too.

Anorexia nervosa does everything in its power to convince you that you can be well and happy but still cut corners and avoid your fears. Even after years of battling this illness, I am still fooled.

Monday

Nursing entry: Staff noticed that Sophia had weights underneath her clothes when she was weighed this morning. She will be spot weighed tomorrow morning.

They've noticed. They know. So I guess the shit really hits the fan now.

Tuesday

Nursing entry: Sophia was spot weighed today. She refused and we explained that it was important for the team to have a real weight from her and we had a feeling she was not in her target weight band.

Sophia became very distressed and said she would rather kill herself then to stay in treatment any longer. She was informed that until she agreed to be weighed, the team would just assume that her weight has declined and act accordingly. Sophia agreed to get on the scales. Her real weight is 6kgs lower than her target band.

Sophia attended meals and did not discuss this morning's events. Her room has been searched and the weights she has been wearing to get weighed have been confiscated.

Six kilos is probably a lot more than they expected. Gradually I have been adding more and more weights around my ankles. So now I have to wait to hear what they are going to do with me. I just pray they realise they aren't helping me by keeping me here like this. They can't force me to be something I don't want to be. Will they see sense now?

Whenever they catch you, they will kill you. But first they must catch you.

—*Richard Adams*, Watership Down, used with permission of Oneworld publications

During one of my admissions where I was being treated involuntarily under the Mental Health Act, I managed a short-lived escape. The unit was part of a larger hospital, which also treated voluntary patients so the doors weren't locked. I got past the nurses and the receptionist and made it a few metres down the country lane that led to the train station. Unfortunately, the receptionist had sounded the alarm and a team of six nurses quickly caught up with me. I was swiftly returned to the unit, carried by my arms and legs. The stupidest part was that I was running away over something ridiculously pathetic—the nurses had said I had to have crumble and custard for my dessert that day instead of my yoghurt. At the time it felt like the end of my world, but looking back I can see how much of an overreaction my behaviour was.

Wednesday

Ward round: Sophia's leave from the unit has been suspended. Sophia is very upset and adamant that she does not want to stay on the unit any longer. We discussed informing Sophia's parents that she has been discovered falsifying her weight. A joint meeting with her parents and staff has been agreed.

So I am stuck here now. No leave. They only thing that keeps me going is that small period of the week where I can be at home and now that's gone. My parents are going to be furious with me. All I do is mess things up. And how the hell am I going to eat all this food knowing I can't go and burn it off at the gym?

Thursday

Nursing entry: Sophia has phoned her mother to tell her she has lost weight. Sophia is very upset. Her mother is angry with her and says that Sophia was stupid.

My parents don't realise how hard it is to have the thoughts I have. They are frustrated I can't just change the way I think. I can't turn off the anorexia nervosa. It's not a choice.

Yes, my mother is right I have been very stupid. I am not a stupid person but anorexia nervosa taints my mind and I can't resist doing stupid things even though I know they aren't going to help me.

Friday

Nursing entry: Sophia has remained very upset. She has been kicking against the front door to the unit and says we are punishing her and that she would rather die than be here any longer. She then started to slam her head against the door. Staff restrained her and administered Lorazepam.

I have officially lost the plot. I have nothing to lose—they have taken away everything I care about. I am in such despair. I just want them to dose me up so the drugs block all the misery out. I am falling down that deep black hole.

We swallow greedily any lie that flatters us, but we sip only little by little at a truth we find bitter.

—*Denis Diderot*, philosopher and art critic

Isn't life just so much easier when you can stick your head in the sand? At the back of your mind, you know you are not coping, but as long as you can pretend to everyone else that it's fine then it's easy to convince yourself you're fine too. Reality is a pain.

Monday

Care Plan Approach meeting: Sophia, Sophia's parents, nurse matron, occupational therapist Karen and staff nurse Debbie all present.

Sophia has been found to be falsifying her weight. We need to restore her weight loss. Her leave has been stopped—Sophia is not to leave the ward. Sophia must now be put back on the full weight gaining diet plan.

Sophia's mother was angry and upset by Sophia's lack of motivation for recovery and she left the meeting. Sophia continued conversation, but then became upset and left the room when told she will not be allowed any home leave.

The unit staff interrupted the meeting to inform us that Sophia had left the unit when a cleaner opened the door. We agreed we needed to involve the police to return her safely. I noted the high risk of serious suicide attempt— Sophia has an impulsive and dangerous history of over-doses when she feels exposed and trapped in treatment.

I wasn't even thinking. I just left the meeting, went directly to my room, grabbed my bag and coat and headed for the unit doors. I knew they would be locked as they always are, but miraculously, my tim-ing was perfect. The doors were wide open as the cleaner brought his hoover through. He shouted as I slipped past and tried to stop me, but I pushed through and ran as fast as I could (which unfortunately isn't very fast because my leg muscles are pathetic). Thank god I got out. A nurse came after me but I managed to jump on a bus and get away. I've escaped, so now what do I do with myself?

Nursing entry: The cleaner alerted staff that Sophia had sneaked past him and managed to leave the unit. I ran after Sophia and tried to speak to her. I told her that is would be much better if she stayed on the unit. Sophia looked very angry and shouted "Fuck off Sally, I don't want to have to hurt you." She crossed the road and jumped on a bus. I have phoned the police to inform them.

Doctor's log: The police returned the patient this after-noon after her mother found her hidden in a cupboard in her flat.

On return to the unit, patient has refused to speak and crawled underneath her bed. A number of empty Paracet-amol packets were found in her coat pockets. She appears to have taken at least 40 tablets. Her mother eventually persuaded her to come out from under the bed and she was taken to A&E in an ambulance. Nurse Steve and myself accompanied her. The patient vomited three times and was sobbing, apologising to her mother.

Patient remains in A&E. The levels of Paracetamol in her blood are extremely high and she has a saline drip.

Forty tablets. I didn't realise how hard it would be to take that many. I had to swallow handful after handful. I went to multiple chemists in a daze to buy packet after packet. I got on the Tube and kept taking tablets bit by bit. I sat in a coffee shop and forced myself to swallow the last lot. I knew I had to take enough to do the job properly—there is no way of rectifying my life. Today has to be the last day. Today is the day all the misery stops.

I have been in the back of a police car many times, but I have never been arrested or committed a crime. The police have always been so nice and reassuring, but they are naïve. They tell me that they are sure the doctors will understand and that we can come to an agreement with them when I am returned to whatever hospital I have broken out of. They have no idea that I have absolutely no say on my treatment. I am not even allowed to make the most basic decisions for myself—everything is decided for me. Part of me is lifted when I have their reassurance—I want to believe them that everything will be okay after a nice chat with the doctors. But as soon as I am escorted back into the hospital, I know the police officers don't have a clue. I am mad and therefore I must not be listened to.

The truth will set you free, but first it will make you miserable.

—*Attributed to James A. Garfield*, 20th
president of the United States

The cycle of readmission is exhausting. It takes so much courage and perseverance to go through the process of re-feeding and weight gain, and then you are released back into the world. But freedom has always been short lived for me. Each time I am admitted, the painful process of treatment seems so pointless when the likelihood is you are just going to relapse again on discharge, and the next relapse is usually worse than the one preceding it.

Tuesday

Doctor's log: Patient has required 3 saline drips. She remains distraught and says she can't bear the thought of returning to the unit. She continues to have a nurse with her at all times.

I do not want these drips in me and I do not want to be kept alive—not if life is spent day after day in the unit with nothing improving

298

for me. I took a lot of pills, but unfortunately I couldn't stop myself from vomiting some of them up. I am so frustrated. I slip into sleep and hope that I will not wake up.

Wednesday

Nursing entry: Staff have been informed that Sophia may need to be transferred to another hospital due to the damage the overdose has had on her liver. She continues to be on a drip.

I don't want to be fixed. My head can't be fixed and they won't accept that. But if my body can't be fixed, may be they will finally listen to me and give up.

Adam and Eve ate the first vitamins, including the
package.

—*E. R. Squibb*, inventor and chemist

Thursday

Nursing entry: Sophia's bloods have improved so the
medical team have decided transfer is not necessary but
Sophia still requires a drip and needs to stay in the medical ward. She remains on close observations.

Sophia has refused to eat her lunch. She became
angry and stated the meal looked and smelt disgusting.
She threw it in the bin so I asked the kitchen staff for a
replacement. Sophia said she would throw the food at me
if I attempted to replace it. She eventually agreed to eat a
sandwich.

*In the grand scheme of things, is there really much point in getting
into more rows about food? I can't escape the constant nagging. As
usual, all they are bothered about is food.*

I find it ironic that the food in medical wards is so bad. Surely those needing to be in hospital due to ill health, for whatever reason, need to have decent nutrition? Yet hospital food is generally atrocious. Even the smell of the food as it is rolled into the ward on a trolley is unpleasant. The vegetables are usually cooked from frozen and have had any nutritional benefit blasted out of them. They appear as an unidentifiable mush on the plate. Most dishes contain some sort of gloopy, white or grey sauce and any meat or fish is pretty indistinguishable. The pasta is always stodgy, the rice hard, the potatoes like bullets and any pastry is a soggy mess.

From what I have witnessed, very little is actually consumed by the patients. To compensate for the lack of nutrition in the food, patients are prescribed multivitamins and expensive supplement drinks. I know I have an eating disorder and it isn't really my place to pass judgement on what healthy eating is, but being anorexic has meant I have acquired a vast knowledge about food and I've spent too many endless days frustrated in a hospital bed.

Friday

Nursing entry: Sophia's father visited Sophia this afternoon. He tried to reassure her and her mood lifted a little. She agreed to eat a snack but remains anxious about returning to the unit. The doctor has informed her that she will be discharged back to the unit soon.

Please don't send me back. It isn't working and I can't take another day in that place. How much longer will they be able to justify keeping me there?

Saturday

Nursing entry: Sophia continues to talk about not wanting to return to the unit. She had a sandwich for lunch.

I pointed out to Sophia that this didn't seem to be enough food to me but she refused to have anything else.

Nothing is ever enough for them. I think I've done well to manage a sandwich given the circumstances, but they constantly have to push for more. I don't know why I bother at all. I might as well have refused to eat anything.

Sunday

Nursing entry: Sophia is returning to the unit shortly. Dr. Cole has said she will start back on phase 1 of the feeding regime. Sedative medication has been increased. Sophia must have a nurse with her at all times.

I am not giving up. I will find a way out. I can keep storing pills. Somehow, I will get what I want.

12. A prisoner again

February 2013

Patience and perseverance have a magical effect before which difficulties disappear and obstacles vanish.

—*John Quincy Adams*, 6th president of the United States

Monday

Nursing entry: Sophia has been transferred back to the unit by wheelchair. Her room and belongings have been searched and no items of concern were located. She expressed a wish to have her supper after all the other patients had left the dining room. She remains on close observations—a nurse must have her in eyesight at all times.

Therapy session: Sophia states that she does not feel she needs to be in hospital. She justifies this by saying that her physical health has improved significantly. She does not wish to take sedative medication. She denies suicidal ideation but does not regret her actions. She is still at a high risk of self-harm in the context of frustrations at her current situation.

And so it starts all over again. No freedom, no respect, no say about my treatment and someone staring at me at all times. Why would anyone want to be alive like this?

I am sure recent events have been a popular topic of gossip for the other patients. I don't want to be around them.

Tuesday

Nursing entry: Sophia refused to drink her juice at breakfast this morning and walked out of the dining room. Staff restrained and escorted her back but she refused to complete her meal. Sophia is furious with staff and acknowledged that when she is told to do something she immediately does not want to do it.

No, I am not going to do what you want me to. Do whatever you want. Drag me, grab me, hold me, and inject me with your stupid drugs if you can but I am not going to make it easy for you. I am going to be so vile you will dread coming to work.

That is my new strategy—before long you will be desperate to get rid of me.

A chattering bird builds no nest.

—*African proverb*

With each year that passes, I become more distraught that life is running away without me. My fellow schoolmates are getting married, earning a salary, and having babies. I am rotting away my days in hospital. My birthday is just a reminder of the fact I am wasting my life and the older I get the more ashamed of myself I become. Yet another year I have failed to conquer my demons.

Wednesday

Ward round: Sophia has requested to be allowed home on her birthday. Leave has not been granted.

Her diet will be increased over the next week to the full weight gain diet.

Sophia states she is not going to comply with her increased diet. She remains on close observations and is generally in fighting mode. She is projecting her anger onto the staff.

Medication must be complied with.

I guess I am doomed to yet another miserable birthday in hospital with a head full of anorexic thoughts.

My fourteenth birthday was a marker for the onset of extreme restriction. Although it had already been established that I was suffering from anorexia nervosa, I am not sure my mum had realised the severity of it. When I got home from school, a birthday cake was presented. If my memory is correct, it was a lovely looking coffee cake all decorated with pretty candles. I was horrified. As if I could allow myself to eat something so loaded with fat and sugar! You don't get the day off from anorexia nervosa on your birthday. Even my mother's disappointed and hurt face could not persuade me to have a slice. After that year, we didn't bother with birthday cakes for me.

Thursday

Nursing entry: Sophia is very disappointed and angry that she will not be allowed any time off the unit for her birthday. Sophia walked out of the dining room this morning and refused to complete her meal. She went into the bathroom and pushed a metal shelving unit into the hand of nurse Simon. An incident form has been submitted.

I've got a feeling you might need quite a few of those incident forms in the near future. Not being allowed to go to the gym is torture. All I want is to burn all these calories off, but the only thing I can do is pace my tiny room. It's not enough to counteract all the calories I am having.

Friday

Nursing entry: Today is Sophia's birthday. She remained in her bedroom for most of the day. Her mother brought in her rabbits and she appeared visibly brighter during

306

the visit. Her mother has brought in a cake. It has been agreed that Sophia is allowed to have a slice of her cake instead of her normal snack this evening.

Yet another year lost to anorexia nervosa. I thought last year was the worst I would have. I was wrong.

At least my long-suffering parents haven't given up on me. I have caused them so much pain and there have been so many birthdays ruined by my eating disorder. If there is one thing I have achieved this year, I have eaten a slice of birthday cake. After having it agreed by the staff, I asked my mum to bring in a cake. I thought I would feel a lot guiltier about eating it than I did. Somehow, I felt proud. I just wish I could have enjoyed it with my mum rather than all the other patients gawping at me with horror. Today has been one small flickering of light but how long will this feeling last before everything is a battle again?

Diplomacy is to do and say
The nastiest thing in the nicest way.

—*Isaac Goldberg*, author

During one of my many episodes of treatment, I managed to make more progress than I ever had done. My weight was almost at a normal level and I had a job in a high street shop. Although I didn't exactly feel proud, as I had worked hard to get the high grades I needed to get into vet school, but after so much time in hospital being in any kind of employment felt like an achievement. I didn't have many friends but I had begun to socialise a little.

At that time, I was seeing a therapist who, despite her rather brash manner, I had confided in a fair bit. Just when I was feeling a bit better about myself, I was swiftly crushed. Out of the blue, during my weekly therapy session the therapist asked me if I cared about my appearance. I guess I do care about the way I look and I had started to wear make-up occasionally. I liked clothes despite feeling self-conscious about myself. My therapist then declared that perhaps I should think about my appearance more because "I looked like shit". I felt like she had just kicked me in the stomach. It came out of nowhere and was an extremely harsh way of telling me I could perhaps put a bit more effort into how I look. I was so hurt I couldn't even speak. With hindsight, I am angry with myself for having let my defences down and giving my therapist the power to hurt me so much. Her words played in my mind over and over. I don't know what she was trying to achieve and maybe she made an error of judgement. I'll never know—I felt too humiliated to attend another session with her. I never saw her again.

Saturday

Nursing entry: Sophia is depressed and only responds minimally to staff. She has been sitting on her bed and says she doesn't feel there is any point in living.

Sophia refused to finish her afternoon snack and stormed out of the dining room. She was blocked from entering her bedroom by staff but managed to get past. She has been lying on her bed and crying.

I let the sobbing overwhelm me. I am drowning in sorrow. I feel pathetic. I am selfish. All I can think about is my own misery and suffering. I have to get more meaning in my life. I know I won't feel any better about myself until I do.

Sunday

Nursing entry: Sophia has been extremely distressed today. She has been banging her head against her door. Staff managed to get her to stop but she continues to say she has had enough and remains withdrawn.

I can bang my head all day but it still doesn't get rid of the thoughts. As soon as I stop banging and it stops hurting, the thoughts come flooding back. I am horrible, I am disgusting, and I am revolting. Over, over and over.

Monday

Nursing entry: Staff have attempted to communicate with Sophia with no success. She has been violent towards herself with residual red marks on her knuckles from punching the wall.

I would do anything for a blade right now. I want to slice myself into pieces. I want the outside to reflect the inside. I am overwhelmed with horrible feelings and thoughts and I have no outlet for them.

Tuesday

Nursing entry: Sophia completed her lunch and attended community meeting. In the meeting, the patient group talked about there being a divide between patients that want to get well and those that don't. Sophia sat quietly but looked tearful.

After community meeting, Sophia returned to her room and curled up on her bed. She refused to attend afternoon snack voluntarily so had to be assisted to the dining room by staff.

The other patients dislike me because I am honest about what I feel is realistic for me. It's none of their business and I wish I could just tell them to stop bitching about me. But I can't because I am forced to be around them and speaking up will only make the bitching worse. All I can do is pretend to be invisible—just like I did at school.

The trouble with always trying to preserve the health of the body is that it is so difficult to do without destroying the health of the mind.

—*G. K. Chesterton*, writer and philosopher

At preparatory school, I was the captain of the swimming team and often took part in swimming galas where we would race against other schools. Even at the age of eight, I felt self-conscious about my body. I was much taller than my classmates and I felt huge compared to the other girls around me. At swimming competitions, I would wait for my race with a towel wrapped around me. When it was time, I would drop my towel and scurry over to my lane. Waiting for the whistle to be blown was torture. I could feel everyone's eyes on me, I could sense everyone looking and seeing how big my body was. When the whistle blew and I hit the water, I would channel my feelings of self-repulsion into putting everything into my strokes. My big shoulders and strong arms would be going like the clappers as my legs propelled me through the water. The worse I felt about myself, the faster I would go. Often I wouldn't even look at if I reached the end of the pool first—all

311

I could think about is getting back to the security of my towel and covering up my body again.

Wednesday

Ward round: Sophia is to remain on close observations. The nurse is to remain with her at all times, including use of the bathroom. Her medication needs to be increased.

Group therapy: Sophia discussed her struggles and describes feeling there is no point in continuing. She feels angry towards staff, particularly Dr. Cole, and was barely responsive when asked questions about her day.

I feel completely numb. The meds must be kicking in. I don't like being pumped with drugs, but I have no choice. They are so watchful now when I take my medication and they have changed most of them to liquid form so I can't store up pills. I have a little stash left that they have not discovered, but it's not enough to do the job.

Thursday

Nursing entry: Sophia's weight this morning is up by 0.8 kgs. Sophia was an hour late to breakfast and reluctant to attend because she feels her weight is out of control and we have been giving her too much food. She refused to complete her meal and returned to bed. Sophia was told that she needed to go to the dining room and complete her breakfast or she would be made to drink two meal replacement drinks. Sophia told staff to "Fuck off". The nurse that was observing her reported she thought Sophia had taken some tablets. She approached Sophia and asked her to open her mouth. Sophia crawled under her bed and she hit the nurse who was trying to stop her. The alarm was sounded but staff were unable to move

Sophia out from under her bed. Eventually, she became drowsy and we were able to move her out from under the bed. Both her arms were shaking and she was transferred to A&E via ambulance.

The night staff are generally a lot less observant than the day staff. I have been storing my evening medication. I should have waited longer to build up more pills, but I couldn't bear to be dragged back to the dining room and force-fed this morning. The violence and brutality has to stop.

Friday

Doctor's log: Patient has been transferred to the High Dependency Unit in the main hospital. She has been stabilising from an episode of arrhythmias and receiving IV fluids.

It is unclear what the overdose consisted of, but it is suspected that the patient had been hoarding her medication.

When I drift in and out of consciousness, I am not sure where I am or what time of day it is. I don't care about anything—all that matters is that I am not in that unit anymore. I am safe. No one is going to manhandle me here. I don't feel happy but I feel peaceful. I don't want that feeling to go.

Do not look for sanctuary in anyone except yourself.

—*Gautama Buddha*

Over the years, I really have put my family through hell. I am surprised any of them are even on speaking terms with me, and some of them aren't and probably will remain hostile towards me for the rest of my existence. There have been times when I have not been welcome in the family home. I think my parents thought that they were perhaps enabling me to stay ill by allowing me to live with them, and they had to protect my siblings from further disruption. I wasn't really around much during their lives because I was mostly in hospital, but I caused a lot of distress which I am sure had a very detrimental impact on their lives. As a result, relationships are strained. Whatever the situation, anorexia nervosa takes its toll on everyone involved, not just the sufferer. And sometimes, saying sorry just isn't enough to release the anger and hatred towards me.

Saturday

Nursing entry: Sophia is very drowsy. Her mother visited her but left when Sophia was not communicative with her.

Sorry mum. You did everything you could to give me a good life, and I threw it all away.

Sunday

Nursing entry: Sophia woke up today and says she doesn't remember anything. She seems very confused. She is now stable and will be transferred back to the eating disorder unit shortly. Sophia states she does not want to return to the unit and her mood remains low.

I wish my body were less resilient. It keeps going no matter how much I abuse it. It is as determined to keep me suffering as they are.

Monday

Doctor's log: Patient has returned to the unit and remains on close observations. She continues to have suicide idea-tion, lacks capacity to make decisions regarding treatment and remains hopeless about her care here. Risk of harm to self remains high. Continue with sedative medication and prescribed meal plan.

I really wish they would start hearing my opinion on my treatment. It is my treatment after all. It's my treatment and my life. Why is that so hard for them to accept?

Tuesday

Nursing entry: Sophia attended the dining room for snack. She crushed up her biscuits and had to be prompted to finish the crumbs. She completed her snack.

Sophia had her evening meal and then sat patiently in post meal supervision. She took her medication but did not engage with others in any way.

Just go through the motions. Don't think just do.

Wednesday

Nursing entry: After breakfast, Sophia was informed she would not be allowed to attend the group this morning because she was not allowed to go to the therapy room upstairs. The team have decided it is safer to keep her downstairs.

Sophia became very angry with this and feels we are punishing her. She became tearful and then curled up in a ball on her bed, saying she did not want to speak to anyone.

I know the group wouldn't have made me feel any better about my situation, but at least it would have got me out of bed and passed some time. The days are endless when all you do is lie on your bed between trips to the dining room. My head is full of thoughts and fears. Even having an extra two baked beans (and yes, I do count my baked beans as I eat them) will make me feel anxious throughout the rest of the day. My mood lifts a little in the evenings, just because I know the day is nearly over with.

You will not be punished for your anger, you will be
punished by your anger.

—*Gautama Buddha*

Thursday

Therapy session: Sophia spoke in detail about how she
does not feel able to get better here as she has too much
"hate" for the staff. She is struggling to put any faith in
her treatment.

We need to discuss her treatment as a team—clearly
the current treatment plan is only pushing Sophia to dig
her heels in further.

I admit that I enjoy releasing my anger. I am not proud of this
quality, but sometimes I can't find any other way to express my
frustrations. I will smash and throw things. I will hit myself,
scrape my skin with my nails, and bang my head against the
wall. I will lash out at people who get in the way of this. I will
hit and scratch them. If they hold down my arms, I will resort
to biting them. I turn into a raging animal and in that moment
I feel good. I know I will feel ashamed about my behaviour

afterwards, but in that moment the relief of letting all my anger out is immense. In no way am I justifying being abusive towards staff, but I don't have a less destructive way of releasing my anger. I feel like a pent-up animal.

> **Nursing entry:** At evening snack, Sophia refused to take her medication and stormed out of the dining room. I followed her and she told me to leave her alone. I explained I could not leave because she is on close observations and needs to have a nurse with her at all times.
>
> Sophia went into the laundry room, dragged the drying rack and tried to throw it at me. She then started throwing anything she could get hold of and I set off my alarm. Staff were able to calm her down and she retired to bed. I didn't speak to Sophia but sat silently in her room.

My anger builds up until I can't keep it in me anymore. I explode and lose control. I just want to destroy everything around me, I want to hit myself, I want to hit others and I will do anything to release the anger. When I am completely exhausted, I fall into blissful numbness.

13. Stalemate

April 2013

Honest disagreement is often a good sign of progress.

—*Mahatma Gandhi*

Friday

Nursing entry: Sophia was in a very depressive state this morning and did not wish to get out of bed. After much encouragement from staff, she attended the dining room but refused to eat half of her breakfast. When asked why she responded with "I have given up".

Sophia was given an Ensure at morning snack to make up for the breakfast she had refused to eat earlier. I asked her to drink it and she said "just piss off and stop being a bitch". She is not following her prescribed meal plan and refuses to attend post meal supervision.

Sophia attempted to leave the unit this morning. When returned to her bedroom, she started banging her head against her wall and says she "can't take it anymore". I advised her to discuss how she is feeling in her Care Plan Approach meeting this afternoon.

I am sure this afternoon will be yet another meeting that is pointless for me to attend. Even if I am asked my opinion, it falls on deaf ears. As always, I am the lunatic and they know best.

Care Plan Approach meeting: Sophia feels that relationships with staff have deteriorated due to her struggles around food and she does not feel that treatment here is helping her. She attributes her low mood to being kept here against her wishes.

Sophia identifies that conflicting with staff over food and medication is a trigger for her thoughts of self-harm. She does not find being on close observations helpful and is sick of having no privacy.

It appears that Sophia continues to experience the team as punitive and uncaring. Although Sophia's physical condition has improved, she does not feel her quality of life has improved.

As a team, we agree to have a trial period of removing Sophia from close observations. Staff will check her every 15 minutes. Close observations will be reinstated if staff have concerns.

Sophia does not feel there is anything to gain by staying in hospital. The team acknowledge she has made progress and she is physically much better than she has been in many years. We had wanted her to have an opportunity for greater recovery, but Sophia has become more and more resistant to treatment.

We have agreed to transfer Sophia from the inpatient to the day patient programme next week (7 days a week and full day attendance). She will not be given her medication to take off the unit—she must take it before she leaves in the evenings.

Sophia can stay at her current weight and will no longer have to eat the full weight gain diet. A maintenance meal plan will be prescribed. If her weight falls, she will be given a week to regain it. If she fails to gain the weight back within this time frame, she will be readmitted as an inpatient.

Sophia will be removed from section 3 of the Mental Health Act and placed on a Community Treatment Order. She must comply with the conditions of her Community Treatment Order or she will be recalled to hospital.

Today has really surprised me. After so long of not being heard, maybe they are starting to realise what I have been saying to them for months. I am not happy about the Community Treatment Order or having to attend the day programme, but at least I won't be stuck like this and they won't force me to gain more weight. And best of all, I've got my unescorted leave back so I can start going to the gym again.

Peace cannot be achieved through violence, it can only be attained through understanding.

—*Ralph Waldo Emerson*, essayist and poet

In whatever setting I am being treated, being locked in combat with those treating me usually results in complete lack of progress. I tread water for months while everyone around me is determined to make me eat and gain weight, and I put every ounce of my existence into doing the exact opposite. Any weight gain is immediately reversed as soon I am discharged. The more I fight, the more they fight back and the more pointless treatment becomes.

It is only when some kind of understanding and mutual agreement occurs that things can move forwards. When I feel like I have a voice, I stop seeing those trying to treat me as the enemy and I start taking some responsibility for my treatment and my future. When I am treated with respect, I want to collaborate and I can engage with doctors and nurses on a more rational level. This is when things can turn a corner.

Saturday

Nursing entry: Sophia is now in a more collaborative stance after the meeting yesterday and is pleased she will no longer be an inpatient. She thinks her mood will improve now because she will feel less trapped in treatment.

How I feel today is such a contrast to recent days. There is a little glimmer of hope now—maybe life can get better.

Sunday

Nursing entry: Sophia has completed all meals today with no problems or concerns reported to staff. She is quiet in manner but made conversation when engaged by staff. She accepted her prescribed medication.

They are treating me with a lot more respect now, so I should do the same. It's only fair and I am not a spiteful person really. It doesn't make me happy to be horrible to people but I can't help it when I am being bullied and forced into things.

It isn't what they say about you, it's what they whisper.

—*Errol Flynn*, actor, used with permission
of Robb Callahan

I hate it when I walk into the lounge and all the other patients stop talking and look sheepish. They hate me for fighting treatment and I suspect they slag me off when I am not around.

I guess it is only human to be annoyed by someone who is refusing to comply when you are forcing yourself to do it, but it pisses me off that they act like they are all committed to treatment when I know many of them are engaging in self-sabotaging behaviours. After supervision, the bathrooms are usually occupied with patients desperately trying to purge the scraps of calories that haven't been digested yet. And pretty much everyone engages in exercise to burn off the calories we are forced to consume. And yet they sit in the groups and insist they are working hard towards recovery. Some of the patients genuinely believe they can comply with treatment, but the anorexic voice is too strong. After so many years of fighting it myself, I know how much of a dilemma this can be. I just wish I could be honest and express my feelings without being judged or snubbed for it.

Monday

Group therapy: Sophia spoke briefly about the recent changes to her treatment. She feels good about these changes but also acknowledges feeling rather unsettled. She identified that it will be hard to attend the unit every day as planned.

The other patients think it's unfair I don't have to gain any more weight. I've overheard comments about "how ridiculous" it is that I've got a maintenance meal plan now. I don't care—I am not close with any of them. I wish I had more friendships with people not suffering with anorexia, as I know that would be a good influence on me.

14. A step to freedom

May 2013

Those who expect to reap the blessings of freedom, must, like men, undergo the fatigue of supporting it.

—*Thomas Paine*, political activist and philosopher

I have started looking at the website for that hotel in Bali. It is more of a retreat than hotel—the perfect sanctuary for me. When I feel like giving up, it reminds me of what I am fighting for. When I get those little glimmers of hope, I allow myself to think that actually going there could be achievable. Maybe it's not just a dream, maybe it isn't as unrealistic as it felt all that time in the medical ward. Just maybe.

Tuesday

Ward round: Sophia has requested to have breakfast at home before attending the unit. The team feel the current boundaries should be maintained. If Sophia does not attend the unit for breakfast, she will not be allowed to go home in the evening and will need to stay at the unit overnight.

They are NEVER readmitting me. The staff constantly remind me they are still in charge, but I will find a way past their boundaries.

It is nice to be in the comfort of my own home again, but it does feel strange and I admit I find being alone in the evening quite frightening after being surrounded by staff and patients for so long. I put the TV on to block out the silence so being back home feels less lonely. No longer being an inpatient has made me even more aware of how few friends I have. My anorexia nervosa has led to greater and greater isolation and I can't remember the last time I had fun.

Gosh, when was the last time I had fun? Hospital life is not always full of gloom. In one of the nicer treatment clinics I spent many months in, I had got to know the nurses well and became close friends with a couple of the patients.

On New Year's Eve, we stayed up watching horror films and running around the hospital garden waving sparklers in the darkness. At midnight, we cracked open some champagne which we shared with the nurses and got very tipsy. We laughed and laughed, totally forgetting our troubles and just enjoying each other's company. It was the best New Year I have ever had. Staying up and drinking champagne made me feel I could almost call myself "normal". I was actually celebrating the New Year in good company, instead of being alone and depressed that yet another year of wasting my life away had passed.

Wednesday

Nursing entry: Sophia says that it was hard to get up this morning and being alone in the evening was difficult. She was weighed this morning and says she is unhappy about her weight. She feels she is being prescribed more food than she needs.

I don't like being split between the unit and home. I hate having to eat at the unit during the day and then returning home to sit with the guilty feelings. I want to be completely discharged so I can move on with my life. The groups don't help me and I don't find the dining room supportive, so it all feels a bit pointless to drag myself in. I guess I will have to go along with this for a while to keep them happy, but there is no way I am doing this for much longer. I want to get a job and do something productive with myself and having to come here is just getting in the way of that.

Thursday

Nursing entry: Sophia phoned this morning to say she was not well and would be in late. She will not be attending the unit until this afternoon.

Sorry but if I am feeling ill I really shouldn't come in to the unit. I wouldn't want to pass any germs to the vulnerable and underweight patients.

Excuses, excuses, and excuses ... I am good at those.

I think it would be impossible for me to count the number of times I have made excuses to avoid eating. It just rolls off my tongue now—"Oh, no I've just eaten thanks", "Actually I don't really like chocolate", "I've got a stomach pain", "I'm not really hungry". My family don't even bother now. My parents saw through my excuses years ago but that doesn't stop me from making them.

The weak can never forgive. Forgiveness is the attribute of the strong.

—*Mahatma Gandhi*

I wish I were better at forgiveness. It's hard not to dislike people that are making you do something you don't want to. Even when it's all smiles and fun chit-chat, I can't forget all the times they have pinned me down and violated me. Sticking tubes down my nose, shoving tablets down my throat, sticking sedative injections in my backside. Do they really think I can just forget about that? Am I supposed to somehow block out the bad memories? How can that be possible when you know the threat of that happening again is still looming?

When someone lets me down, I shut that door. I don't want to know them anymore. I can't tolerate being hurt by some-one. I feel I would be an idiot to trust them again and I may pretend to accept an apology, while inside I am thinking, "Just piss off". Sometimes I am very childish and try to ignore them. I stop speaking to people and I find I can't even look at them anymore.

I don't fully understand why I am like this, I just know I have to put my defences up and perhaps that is a reflection of how vulnerable I feel. I know my inability to forgive is a huge flaw in me and it has resulted in a lot of hurt not only to friends but even members of my own family. Although I am lucky that most of my family can forgive me for my behaviour, there are some things that they are unable to forgive and I have to come to terms with that sadness.

Friday

Group therapy: Sophia spoke about finding being on the unit all day extremely hard as it is all about food and so boring.

Now I am spending more time at home, I am painfully reminded what a failure I am by the sight of all my textbooks on my bookshelves. Animal anatomy, biochemistry, dissection manuals, and animal husbandry—everything I was passionate about now evokes nothing in me but feelings of regret.

Am I dead inside? My ambition, my hopes, my desires have deserted me. I have lost it all and now too much damage has been done for me to get it back again.

Even if I can get my head around that, what does my future hold? How am I going to make the best of things and establish some kind of existence that doesn't make me miserable?

Saturday

Nursing entry: Sophia did not turn up this morning. She was phoned but did not answer. I left a message encouraging her to call us and attend the unit.

I can't resist—I have to push the boundaries. Let's just see what they do about it. It's time to find out if their threats are empty ones. I've got a lot more important things to think about than being stuck in the bubble of eating disorder treatment.

Sunday

Nursing entry: Sophia attended late today. She says she has a cough and is unwell. She has been advised to stick with the plan of attending the unit as otherwise she is violating the conditions of her Community Treatment Order.

I hate this Community Treatment Order. I will get out of it somehow. I am not going to live with a constant threat over my head. Even though so much is uncertain in my future and I am not entirely sure what I want from life, I know that there is no way that I can feel happy when I am trapped under their control.

Monday

Nursing entry: Sophia attended the unit as planned today but was observed to be very withdrawn. She appears to be maintaining her weight but staff have noticed she is struggling more with food.

So the weights are back. I know it puts me at risk of being caught out, but I can't tolerate being the weight I am. I need to drop a few kilos—they pushed me way too far and it should be up to me what I weigh. I know the lower my weight is, the more restricted my life will be, but I have come to terms with that, and those around me need to accept that at some point.

It's no good trying to keep up old friendships. It's painful for both sides. The fact is, one grows out of people, and the only thing is to face it.

—*Somerset Maugham*, playwright
and novelist, used with the permission
of the Royal Literary Fund

When it comes to gaining weight, I am full of good intentions, but I am useless at fulfilling them. I buy clothes in bigger sizes in the hope that they will motivate me to gain some weight so I can look nice in them. When a close friend of mine said she was getting married in six months' time, I thought that was the perfect goal for me to work towards. I devised a meal plan and vowed to myself that I would stick to it and gain some weight so I would look nice for the wedding.

Six months later, my weight was even lower and I felt too ashamed to even attend the wedding because I didn't want anyone to see how frail and ugly I was. Not only had I failed myself, I had also let my friend down. I don't blame my friends for "growing out" of me—anorexia nervosa makes a tedious companion.

Tuesday

Group therapy: Sophia attended the group today and spoke about how hard it is to be here. She is finding going home and being alone in the evenings a struggle. She has some friends that she sees, but has fallen out of touch with a lot of friends due to being in hospital for most of her life.

Being a day patient has made me even more aware of how alone I feel. I know it is the quality of the friendships you have rather than the quantity that matters and I value the few friends that I have, but my social life is pathetic. I need relationships with "normal" people—I know that will be much more healthy than forming friendships with patients on the unit. But, you have to be particularly cautious about making friendships with fellow sufferers. I have learnt to recognise true friends from those that just want to nose into your business for warped reasons.

Wednesday

Nursing entry: Sophia did not attend the unit for breakfast but arrived just before lunch. She completed her meal and said she had overslept this morning. In post meal supervision, the other patients expressed their concern about Sophia and that they felt she was deteriorating. Sophia stated that there was nothing to worry about.

Sophia is not adhering to her treatment plan. She misses breakfast most days. If she continues to do this, she will be recalled to inpatient treatment.

Why won't they just leave me alone! Everyone is on my back the WHOLE TIME. It's bad enough that the staff nag me, but now I've got other patients having a go at me too. I can't even get away from it because I have to attend the stupid programme every day to avoid "violating" my Community Treatment Order. I am being forced to spend every single day with people that hate me.

Faith is the bird that feels the light when the dawn is still dark.

—*Rabindranath Tagore*, Bengali polymath

I once had a housemate. It was nice to be living with someone and we became good friends. When our lease ran out, I suggested we move into another flat together. My housemate seemed keen and we went to the estate agent to view a number of properties. We fell in love with a small cottage in a pretty mews and put an offer in. Everything seemed to be working out great and the estate agent rang me to say we just needed to pop in and sign the contract.

When I relayed this to my housemate I didn't get the response I expected. She told me she was really sorry but she didn't think she could live with me anymore. She was finding it hard living with someone who was ill and she didn't want to commit to taking out another lease with me.

I was devastated. I didn't understand why she didn't say this in the first place and I felt like such a fool when I had to ring the estate agent and tell them we were withdrawing our offer. More than anything, I felt angry with myself. I was stupid to trust someone and allow myself to be hurt. I could understand why she didn't want to live with me anymore, but stupidly I had hoped that for once my illness wouldn't stand in the way of companionship. I had forgotten that you mustn't rely on anyone, no matter how well you think you know them.

Thursday

Therapy session: Sophia discussed her feelings of being controlled and unheard with regards to treatment. She doesn't want to attend the day patient programme and resents being on a Community Treatment Order.

Sophia described the atmosphere on the unit as difficult. She thinks the other patients avoid her and she dislikes being in the dining room with them.

The patient group is quite cliquey at the moment and Sophia feels very much excluded. Sophia admits this is partly her fault because she is shy and doesn't put herself out there much.

I informed Sophia that my role is changing and I will no longer be able to see her for therapy. Her therapeutic care will be transferred to Nancy and I have told Sophia that I think they will work well together.

Great—yet another person dumping me. I don't want to see someone new. I would rather stop therapy altogether. The sessions are a waste of time anyway. I used to find them helpful, but now I think I am being held back by everything associated with this shit hole—including therapy.

You know what? You are not dumping me—I am dumping you.

Friday

Nursing entry: Sophia remains ambivalent about attending the day programme and feels alienated from her peers.

Sophia identifies that she has been ill for so long now that she doesn't fully understand the purpose of the illness in her life, she is just aware of how petrified she is of weight gain and change.

Why does every gram I weigh feel so important? Why is my self-worth based on a number? It's a big, wide world and yet I've reduced mine more and more. My life seems so stunted and insignificant compared to how it used to be. I feel desperately sad when I think back to earlier years where I had so much potential. If only I had dealt with this illness before it completely destroyed my life. Is there anything left to live for? Can I really summon the energy to try and piece things back together yet again?

I don't know the answers to these questions so I fill my head with obsessive thoughts about food and rituals instead, even though I know that will only make me feel even more lost in the world.

Nothing is more difficult, and therefore more precious, than to be able to decide.

—*Napoleon Bonaparte*, military and political leader

Supermarkets are a place of great trepidation for me. I have wasted hours wandering along the aisles doing "market research". I look at every packet to scour the ingredients and nutritional information. I put products in my basket only to take them out again five minutes later when I have changed my mind. I try to convince myself to buy foods that would help me get well, but usually I'll end up buying the usual diet foods and the few items that feel "safe" for me to eat.

When it comes to paying, I feel self-conscious at the checkout. I get so embarrassed about what I am buying and I feel guilty for spending money on food. Somehow it feels greedy, despite the fact I know food is a basic human need.

I can't walk past food shops without going in, just to see what they have and if I can discover a label I haven't read. I can spend a whole day just going from supermarket to supermarket. My head is swimming with numbers but I can't stop.

I know my brain is desperate for food, but when I am not allowing myself to eat, looking at food will have to suffice. The more I look at food, the hungrier I am and the more I have to keep looking.

Saturday

Nursing entry: Sophia attended as planned today. She appears to be managing food but does not engage with others on the unit.

It's all so utterly pointless. They know my illness is stronger than they are. Their attempts to manage me are futile now I am free to make my own decisions for most of my time. It's my battle with anorexia nervosa now—I either eat or die and that is the ultimate decision I have to make.

Sunday

Nursing entry: Sophia did not attend today—we need to discuss her non-attendance urgently. I have phoned Sophia and left a message reminding her that her Community Treatment Order requires her attendance.

I don't answer the calls. I immediately delete the voicemails. I don't need to listen to them because I already know what they will say and I don't want to hear it.

I feel so hostile and resentful towards the staff and it is impossible for me to communicate with them. I am completely alone and unable to reach out to anyone—hardly the supposed purpose of this Community Treatment Order.

Monday

Nursing entry: Sophia did not attend today. Staff have left a voicemail asking her what her plans are. She has

again been reminded that her attendance is a condition
of her Community Treatment Order.

*I can't face going in but I also don't want to suffer the consequences
of not going in. If only I wasn't on this painful Community Treatment Order. I'll probably get away with it for a few days before they
actually decide to do anything about it so I am giving myself a well-
earned break from the misery of the unit.*

Tuesday

Nursing entry: Sophia phoned during the night to say she
has a migraine and will not be attending the programme
today. She says she will attend tomorrow.

*I will give myself another day off but tomorrow I have to put on my
happy face—all smiles, no need to be concerned about me, I am doing
great.*

"The tongue like a sharp knife ... kills without drawing blood".

—*Gautama Buddha*

I loved working at the pet shop. After so many years of being stuck in psychiatric institutions, I couldn't believe that I was doing something "normal" people do. I was part of a world I feared I would never find a place in.

I liked working the extra hours, and I was more than happy to work Christmas Eve. After my shift ended, I waited ages for a bus home, eventually giving up and deciding I would have to walk it instead.

It was already dark and the streets were icy so I was concentrating hard on treading carefully. I was too focused on the pavement to notice a figure step out from an alcove and before I knew it something hard hit my face. After a few seconds of shock, I registered what had hit me was a football. I stopped and looked at the man in disbelief. I couldn't understand it so I said, "What was that for?" He responded with words that cut right through me and hit upon the years of self-hatred I was trying to leave behind, "Because you're an ugly girl." I walked away as fast as I could.

341

I wish there was something I could have done to retaliate, but I knew nothing I could say or do would hurt him to the same extent those words hurt me.

As I trudged home in silence, all I could think was it doesn't matter how hard you try to pretend Sophia—you will always be ugly.

Wednesday

Nursing entry: Sophia attended today and seemed very bright in mood. She was laughing more and very animated in speech. She has been offered a job at her old place of work and feels very positive about this. She looks visibly thinner but her spot weigh did not show any weight loss.

I can't believe I could go back to work. After so long, my life would actually have some value to it. It makes me sick that the doctors could stop me from going back.

Thank goodness I decided to strap my weights on this morning—I had another sixth sense that a spot weigh was going to happen.

They HAVE to discharge me from day patients. Surely they can see that going back to work would be better than attending a programme that isn't helping me? This is my big opportunity to find a way of being happy in the outside world again. If they deprive me of this I will be furious.

There is just one life for each of us: our own.

—*Euripides*, classical Greek tragedian

All my life I have felt crushed by pressure to conform. I have always felt forced into the way I live my life. As a child, I followed the regulations of my parents and school, and as an adult, I have conformed to the rules of my anorexia nervosa or the rules of treatment for my anorexia nervosa. I would like to be a free spirit, and yet I do not know how to function that way. With rules, I am safe. Without rules, there are too many unknowns.

Thursday

Ward round: Sophia has requested that she be allowed back to work 3 days per week. She doesn't feel that coming to the day programme is helping her and she states she has "done her time here".

She would like to reduce her medication, as she is unsure that it helps. The team feel that it is important she continues to take her medication. We also need to continue to spot weigh her regularly as she looks like she has lost weight despite her spot weighs not giving us evidence she is falsifying her weight.

I'm not taking that Olanzapine anymore regardless of whether I have their blessing or not. They have stopped making me have my meds before I leave and I just bin the tablets when I get home. I never wanted to take it in the first place and since stopping I have felt much less drowsy and I haven't been falling over like I often did whilst taking it. It's pointless trying to justify this to them—they don't listen to anything I say anyway because as far as they are concerned I am not capable of rational discussion.

Friday

Nursing entry: Sophia phoned the unit today to say she will not be attending. She says that she is fine and able to feed herself. She feels it is time for her to get on with her life.

I've made as much progress as I can with my illness and now I need to find a way to survive and support myself in the world. For the first time in ages, I am thinking clearly. Who knows, maybe when I go back to work it will inspire me to look after myself better. I know eating will be easier if I am feeling happier about my life. The only problem is, deep down I know that I can't be happy if I'm not eating. At least I can see that, even if I don't feel able to change it.

15. Flying the cuckoo's nest

June 2013

The reason birds can fly and we can't is simply because they have faith, for to have faith is to have wings.

—*J. M. Barrie*, The Little White Bird

There is no denying that when you are in an eating disorder treatment programme, you feel like your life is food. When you're not eating it, you are talking about it and when you're not talking about it, you are thinking about it. It is hard to think about anything else.

I feel so greedy and pathetic for not having anything more worthwhile to focus on. All my creativity is gone and my self-esteem just gets lower and lower. I might be struggling to eat it, but my mind feasts on food all day every day. And the more I am stuck with my obsessions over food, the shittier I feel about myself. I've got to get out of this trap.

Monday

Nursing entry: The weekend staff have reported to the day care team that Sophia did not attend at the unit over the weekend.

Sophia has not arrived today and is not answering her phone. I have left her a message asking her to call the unit immediately as I was very concerned that she is flouting the conditions of her Community Treatment Order. This will be discussed in the team meeting and Dr Cole has been informed.

This time I am not giving in to your threats—I know what I am doing is the right thing to do. I will make you see that it is the right thing to do.

Tuesday

Nursing entry: Sophia attended the unit today and her weight is stable. She says she wants to be an outpatient. She has returned to work and says she feels supported by her employer and colleagues.

I won't be labelled as crazy. I am not a lunatic. I am a rational person. I can be part of the normal world and it isn't right to keep me trapped in psychiatric care. Please accept that this is as far as I can be pushed. End this miserable chapter of treatment and let me go back to life and freedom.

I saw the angel in the marble and carved until I set him free.

—Michelangelo, Italian artist and architect

When I am at work, I can pretend to be normal. I know I don't look normal because rationally I know I am still underweight, but I am still accepted as part of the team and the customers seem to treat me like I am no different from the rest of the world. I enjoy the company of my colleagues and when I am at work I can fully appreciate how lonely I have been in treatment.

Most importantly, I am being treated as "Sophia" again.

Wednesday

Ward round: Sophia is not keeping to the conditions of the Community Treatment Order. She has requested to be discharged into the community. We have discussed the situation as a team and feel it is best if we reach a compromise with Sophia and end her time on the day patient programme.

Sophia needs to attend the unit two days a week for the next two weeks and then she can be transferred to outpatient care.

Sophia must be aware that she will have become more active on return to work and she needs to increase her nutrition to manage this.

Her spot weighs show no evidence of weight falsifying.

It's a lot easier to falsify your weight when you're not an inpatient. It's harder for them to catch you off your guard. It will be even easier when I am an outpatient, as long as I don't slip too far and my bloods start becoming deranged. There's no getting around that one.

Thursday

Therapy session: Sophia did not attend her last session with me today. She has her first appointment with Nancy next week.

I probably should have attended the last session but I feel angry that they are making me change therapists and I guess I wanted to demonstrate my feelings to them in some way.

Deep down though I am not angry, I am hurt. I was stupid to form a relationship with my therapist. If I hadn't then I wouldn't be feeling rejected and sad. I hadn't realised how much I had invested in the therapeutic relationship, but it is almost impossible not to become attached when you have been seeing the same therapist every week for years.

Why do the end of relationships always feel so bitter? It's not so bad when you are the one who wants to move away from someone else, but when someone else cuts you out, the rejection feels unbearable.

In order to cope with this, I will quickly reject someone if they give me even the smallest indication that they might hurt me. This has alienated me not only from friends but even members of my immediate family. It is an extremely selfish and confusing response for people and I know it has caused a lot of hurt, and yet I can't help but react in that way. My levels of insecurity heighten with every knock I get in life.

16. Keeping them happy

July 2013

Holding on to anger is like grasping a hot coal with the intent of throwing it at someone else; you are the one who gets burned.

—*Gautama Buddha*

I have been angry in every episode of treatment I have had, but particularly when I have been sectioned and I am not a voluntary patient. In one such admission, I was called into ward round to be told I wasn't allowed to have home leave that weekend and my diet plan was going to be increased because I had lost weight. I was furious. What they were saying was just unacceptable to me. I swore at them and refused to leave the room until they agreed to change their decision.

After about ten minutes of silence, my consultant announced they would commence ward round for the other patients in a different room. Everyone got up and left and I sat in an empty room with just my fury for company.

Outpatient session: Today Sophia attended her first appointment. She feels very sad about the end of her sessions with her last therapist and doesn't wish to attend appointments with me. She says she has attended today

349

because she doesn't wish for those involved in her care to think she is not okay as they might recall her to hospital. She is enjoying work and does not feel that the Community Treatment Order is necessary.

Sophia's weight has dropped a little and she became angry when I said I wanted to discuss this with her. We spoke about how to have these conversations without her feeling attacked, as I need to make her aware of the realities of her situation.

We will meet with the outpatient consultant, Dr. Fresher, next week to make a clear plan regarding what to do if Sophia deteriorates.

Despite having 8 kilos of weights strapped around my middle, I am still below my stupid target band. I can't hide more weights on me without it being blatantly obvious. I am surprised Nancy hasn't noticed I seem to be a bit bulky around my middle. I would never have got away with it with my old therapist—she was too on the ball. I suppose that's one benefit of being lumped with someone new.

It's great not having to drag myself into day care and I love being back at work. I still have low moments when I feel crap and I can't think about anything other than what a failure I am, but on the whole this is the best I have felt since that fateful day when I was dragged into that awful unit.

My eating is a lot more disordered than I would like, but I had come to terms with the fact that was probably going to be the case. Certainly, this most recent episode of treatment did nothing to help me address my fear of food—if anything it made me even more scared and fearful of it. Unfortunately, I have started to struggle with food in new ways that make me feel deeply ashamed.

Out of all the horrific behaviours associated with eating disorders, binging is the worst for me. I never binged throughout the first years I had anorexia nervosa, but I think I reached a point where my body was so starved it stopped listening to my head.

I would be shovelling food into me and unable to stop despite how terrified I felt. I can't deny how wonderful it felt to eat foods I had been denying myself for years, but I knew the torture that lay ahead. Once I had managed to stop myself and vomited, I would feel absolutely terrible. The floodgates open and all I can think about is how disgusted I am with myself. However much I am determined to never do it again, it is only a matter of time before I break down and my ravenous body takes over again.

The worst aspect is the shame. I feel so revolted by my behaviour that I cannot confide in anyone about what I am doing to myself. The eating disorder has exactly what it wants—it completely engulfs you.

17. Denial is not a river in Egypt

August 2013

A man who is "of sound mind" is one who keeps the inner madman under lock and key.

—*Paul Valéry*, Mauvaises pensées et autres

Despite my frail appearance, I can pretend to myself that I am just a "normal" person when I am at work. I take on another identity. Deep down I know that my colleagues and customers can see how emaciated I am, but it is rarely mentioned. However trapped in my illness I am feeling, after a shift at work I always feel so much better about myself. As long as I am working, I haven't lost my identity completely to anorexia nervosa and there is still a place for me in a world that I have struggled to fit into all my life.

Outpatient session: Today, Dr. Fresher joined Sophia and I for the duration of our session. Dr. Fresher explained some aspects of the Community Treatment Order and we discussed at length what Sophia wants from treatment. Sophia explained that she is trying to get her life back and is working hard to stay well. Dr. Fresher raised the fact that Sophia's bloods were becoming more abnormal. Sophia appeared to take this on board but did not share our concern. Sophia would like to stop attending outpatient appointments but we feel this is not currently appropriate.

We agreed that we would continue to monitor Sophia's weight and bloods regularly and try to support her as an outpatient. However, if she loses further weight or her bloods deteriorate further, we will have no choice but to arrange an inpatient admission. Sophia feels she would rather die than have another admission to our unit. We will review things in a month's time.

The bloods are a real pain. You can falsify your weight, but you can't fudge your blood results. My liver is starting to play up. I am sure it's fine though—I mean I feel okay so things can't be that bad. At least I've got a month to improve things so I will definitely have sorted out my liver function by then. I'll make a meal plan to stick to and I'll try to reduce my activity. I am most definitely not going to give them a reason to shove me back into inpatient treatment.

I have so many genuine good intentions. I spend hours devising new meal plans that make small steps to improving my eating. I swear to myself I will start the meal plan the following day, but then breakfast would come and go and my good intentions would go out the window. Sometimes I do manage to make a step forwards but after a few days I usually slip back again.

It's so hard to stay on track. However determined I am, when it comes to actually putting plans into action, it's too easy to find excuses not to do it.

18. My life, my rules

September 2013

The trouble with always leaving yourself a way out is that you always take it.

—*Robert Brault*, used with author's permission

At times where I have managed to gain weight, I have needed to buy new clothes in bigger sizes. However determined I am that I don't want to relapse and that I have had enough of this illness, I still keep my "skinny" clothes. In the back of my mind, I know I am not throwing them out in case one day I can fit them again—and secretly I desperately hope I will.

> **Outpatient session:** Sophia did not arrive for her appointment. When I phoned her, she said she didn't want to attend appointments at our unit anymore. She says she dreads attending now, especially as she cannot see her old therapist.
>
> I have told her it is very important that she attends her Care Plan Approach meeting tomorrow, but Sophia stated she didn't want to.

Okay, so making improvements didn't work out so easy. I make meal plans but they never stick and I am soon back to my bad habits. I just keep thinking I'll eat later—I can't give myself any food yet. Now I don't even drink during the day, which makes getting through a shift at work very hard. It's such a relief when the clock strikes 11pm and I can allow myself some food and something to drink. But usually I am so starving by then that I eat and eat and eat until I'm sick.

When I wake up in the morning I feel disgusting, but I put on my "happy" face and pretend as best I can that everything is fine. I know my bloods will be bad because even I can tell my body isn't in good shape. I can't let them find out. I have to fix things before they get the chance to lock me up again.

I love being back at work and I don't want to have to stop and go back into hospital. Despite this, I still don't feel able to improve my eating. I so hoped that getting some positive things back in my life would be enough to keep me stable, but nothing is enough to stand up to my anorexia nervosa.

What the hell am I going to do?

To keep the body in good health is a duty ... otherwise we shall not be able to keep our mind strong and clear.

—*Gautama Buddha*

I am ravenous. My mind says no but my body won't listen. I need food. I need all of it, everything, the entire tub, the entire packet and every last spoonful. I can't stop myself. I am mortified about what I am doing but I can't resist any longer. And now I've started, I might as well keep going. At least then everything in the freezer, the cupboards and the fridge will be gone and I will never be able to binge again.

That is, before I next go and buy it all again.

I eat and vomit, eat and vomit, eat and vomit until I collapse into exhaustion. When I wake up it hits me what I have done and I starve for days until I break down and binge again.

It's a vicious cycle of misery and I am so ashamed I can't breathe a word of it to anyone.

Care Plan Approach meeting: Sophia did not attend the meeting today and has expressed that she no longer plans to attend her outpatient appointments.

Sophia's weight continues to be below the specified weight in her Community Treatment Order. Her bloods have become increasingly abnormal. Sophia feels that she is managing to support herself and feels that "things could be a lot worse". Sophia attends outpatient appointments under duress and only due to being on a Community Treatment Order.

Although physically compromised, Sophia is trying to create a fuller life for herself outside of her eating disorder, which is very important for her to move on from anorexia nervosa. She also struggles with inpatient admissions and makes little gains during these, sometimes actually deteriorating. Given this, I think we should give Sophia the chance to continue being managed in the outpatient setting whilst taking some risk.

Sophia has discussed in her outpatient sessions that she would like to go on holiday. I explained that there would be great risk involved in travelling at her low weight.

Thank goodness they can also see that an inpatient admission would not be in my best interests. I can stop being so scared now I know that is not an immediate threat. I just wish I could be honest with someone about how much I am struggling without the fear of them recalling me to hospital.

I wasn't expecting them to agree to me going on holiday, but I thought I would ask anyway as it might give them a sense they are more in control of my actions.

My daily struggles are becoming more and more difficult for me to hide. I can't walk normally—my body is eating the muscles in my legs. I keep falling over because my reflexes aren't what they should be. It scares me when that happens because sometimes it takes me a long time to gather the strength to stand up again. I panic that I won't be able to get up and I will be stuck. I can barely lift up a tin of dog food at the pet shop and I feel so embarrassed. I can't climb stairs and quickly become breathless and dizzy at any kind of physical exertion. Worst of all, deep down I know things have gone too far—beyond the point where I can even pretend it is possible I can fix them.

How much longer can I keep up the façade? I'm an expert at disguising my deterioration, but even I can't perform miracles.

19. Running out of options

October 2013

Even a hare will bite when it is cornered.

—*Chinese proverb*

Outpatient session: Although reluctant, Sophia did attend today's appointment.

Sophia's blood tests show further deterioration. Sophia acknowledges this and has committed to being more mindful of the amount of exercise she is doing and trying to eat more.

We spoke about her Community Treatment Order. I explained to her that I think this needs to be continued. She feels she is being punished for being ill. She remains angry that her relationship with her previous therapist was ended.

It's not Nancy's fault. I just feel rejected and I don't want another new therapist to get used to. I don't feel able to talk to her and even if I did I don't think she could say anything that would help. I think she would just go running to Dr. Fresher and before I know it I'll be dragged back into hospital. Being on a Community Treatment Order has made me feel even more defensive and unable to ask for help because they have the power of immediate recall to hospital.

361

But for once, I can actually admit to myself how much I am deteriorating. I know I am slipping closer and closer towards medical crisis and I would not survive another traumatic episode of treatment. I've got to come up with some kind of plan to escape. Maybe if I can get some distance from my situation it would help me to change. I have to try it—it is the only hope I have left.

20. Treading on thin ice

November 2013

Freedom is never voluntarily given by the oppressor; it must be demanded by the oppressed.

—Martin Luther King, Jr.

Care Plan Approach meeting: Sophia has not attended this meeting.

There is continued high risk of death through starvation and suicide. Powers of recall to hospital need to remain in place to ensure any level of safety in the community. The Community Treatment Order has been extended for a further 6 months. Sophia is very angry about this decision.

Sophia's most recent blood tests have become alarming—her liver function has deteriorated further.

Sophia has been contacted to set up an appointment but she refused to attend. The implications of saying no to appointments whilst on a Community Treatment Order were explained, at which point Sophia put the phone down.

We need to start organising a bed for her and she needs to be recalled to hospital.

It is also possible she is falsifying her weight and her blood tests certainly suggest she is losing weight.

Last night, I woke up at about 3am and found that my freezer was surrounded by water. I opened the freezer door to find all my precious ice creams were defrosting. The freezer wasn't working and I couldn't work out what was wrong. I went into a complete panic and I couldn't bear the thought of throwing out all my special ice creams.

I feel very possessive about food when I buy it and wasting it is unbearable, especially when there are so few things I feel able to eat and I have to go to so much effort to source specific products.

In my panic, I decided I would eat the lot rather than allowing them to defrost and end up in the bin. I ignored the terror at spiralling more and more out of control, spending the remainder of the night stuffing myself with ice cream and then vomiting until I collapsed.

When I came round, there was still water all over the floor and there were ice cream tubs filled with vomit at various sites around my kitchen. I shook with a wave of disgust that crushed me and I knew I could no longer exist like this. I can't bear feeling this way about my behaviour and being so miserable.

This time I am not waiting for someone else to intervene—I am going to take a leap of faith and this time it will be on my terms.

I believe in getting into hot water; it keeps you clean.

—*G. K. Chesterton*, writer and philosopher

I am exhausted. It takes every ounce of motivation in me to get me out of the house and into work. When I get home, I collapse on the sofa and I am unable to move. I don't even have the energy to get up the stairs and sleep in my bed, so I sleep on my sofa instead. I keep falling and hurting myself. I feel scared of going out because sometimes it happens when I walk down the street and I can't get myself up without help. It happened on my way to work the other day and a police officer happened to be walking by and helped me up. I was bleeding where I had hit my head but I assured him I was absolutely fine and I had to go or I'd be late for work. I have periods where my eyesight goes and all I can see is black. I can't tell anyone what is happening because I know they will intervene and I don't want to be forced into treatment again. I can't survive another round of battling with doctors. At the same time, I can't ignore that my body is packing up and I know if I attend my outpatient appointments they will immediately see how bad things have got. My last set of blood tests was bad enough; they would be even worse now. And hiding the weights is getting more and more risky because I am requiring more of them with each week in order to appear to be maintaining when the reality is that I am losing weight rapidly. I am well and truly in hot water.

> **Review by Dr. Cole:** I have been informed from the outpatient team that Sophia is not complying with her treatment plan and the conditions of her Community Treatment Order. Her bloods are deteriorating, she has appeared weaker and she is not attending her outpatient appointments.
>
> There is a bed available next week. The process of getting Sophia to come in to hospital is likely to be traumatic, based on previous history. The recall papers will therefore not be posted and police will go and get her from her flat or place of work.
>
> IT IS CRUCIAL THAT SOPHIA IS NOT INFORMED OF PLANS TO READMIT HER TO HOSPITAL.

I keep looking at the website. I keep pondering, wondering if I have the strength to do what I am plotting. I am nervous about it, but it looks like I am getting closer to the point where I need to start putting things into action. I am scared because I will be throwing myself out of my comfort zone and into a complete unknown, but maybe this is the drastic action required for me to make the changes I need to make.

I know there is a high chance I won't survive, but I would rather take that chance. At the end of the day, I would rather die than be put through further traumatic treatment. I think of those dreaded hand bandages and the pain and misery I went through. I know what I must do.

I ring the travel agent.

21. The final break for freedom

One week later

No bird soars too high if he soars with his own wings.

—*William Blake*, painter, poet,
and printmaker

All week I have known something bad is coming. I've made all the arrangements and everything is in order—my bags are packed, I've booked the time off work and my animals are all being taken care of.

Now all I can do is pray that I manage to pull this off.

Report by Dr. Fresher: Sophia has just phoned my secretary to cancel her appointment with me today. I managed to speak to her, she told me she is at Gatwick airport and that she is about to leave the country. She feels things aren't going well for her and she needs some time to recuperate. She says she is going to Tenerife and she will be back in a week's time.

I explained the risk to her life at present given her recent blood tests. She said that her treatment under our care has not helped her and put the phone down.

I will investigate whether Interpol can track her down in Tenerife. We need to inform the police to help us recall her to hospital when she returns to the UK.

I didn't expect the secretary to put me through to Dr. Fresher. It was stupid of me to ring before I had actually taken off and safely out of the UK.

I gave them a red herring—wrong airport and the wrong destination. But, it won't take them long to work out that there are probably no flights from Gatwick to Tenerife this morning.

When I arrived at Heathrow, the taxi driver helped me with my bag, as I am too weak to carry it. I managed to check in without any problems—I was worried they might take one look at me and question whether I was well enough to fly. I had considered forging some kind of medical clearance that I was safe to fly, but it would only take one phone call from the airline to confirm it was a fake. Thank goodness the airline I was flying with didn't seem remotely concerned at my appearance on check-in.

The plane was held up on the runway for about 30 minutes and I was convinced any minute the cabin crew were going to approach me and kick me off the plane into the hands of the police. I had no idea how easily they would be able to track me down and discover my true location and destination.

The moment we started to speed into take-off, the moment the wheels lifted off the ground, I felt a rush of relief and euphoria. I had done it. I had broken free. I couldn't hold back the tears rolling down my starved face. Even if I didn't survive the plane journey, I would be happy to die right now if it meant avoiding forced treatment.

I hadn't even told my parents I was going. I couldn't trust them not to tell the doctors.

Phone call: Sophia's mother has just phoned the unit. She has gathered information from the travel agent from Sophia's computer. It turns out that Sophia has gone to Bali and will not be back for two weeks. It is very unlikely

Sophia will survive travelling that far in her current state and her parents are aware of this.

Unfortunately, there are no direct flights to Bali. I stop over in Shanghai and have to wait four hours before my next flight. I have no local currency or US dollars so I can't even buy a drink. I am shaky and nauseous. I am having serious doubts I will survive the next leg of the journey. Despite that, I have no regrets. Making a run for it has been the best decision I have made in a very long time.

No one else can take risks for us, or face our losses on our behalf, or give us self-esteem. No one can spare us from life's slings and arrows, and when death comes, we meet it alone.

—*Martha Beck*, with author's permission

I am fully aware that my BMI is at a life-threatening level and has been for a long time. My immune system is weak and I am at immediate risk of organ failure. Despite knowing this, the thought of increasing my weight fills me with terror. Each time I relapse my weight reaches lower and lower levels. My body has begun to adapt to being such a low weight but I know I can't afford to be complacent about that. I have accepted the reality that any moment I could drop dead and no one would be surprised. It's pretty extraordinary that I have survived as long as I have. I guess I am unfairly resilient. It saddens me to hear of teenagers with this illness that have lost their lives to it. Sometimes people die after suffering just six months of anorexia nervosa, and I've battled with it for fifteen years. I feel guilty for still being alive when people that have a much better chance of recovery have lost their lives to this horrible disease. I wish the resources for treatment were more focused on those with the most potential to make a full recovery. I feel angry that so much time and money was spent treating someone who didn't want such interventions. I feel selfish for it, especially when I hear of young patients that have died waiting for appropriate treatment.

When finally I reach Bali, I drag my suitcase through the airport. I can barely walk but I keep going. I have to. The immigration officer checks my passport, looks concerned and asks if I'm okay. I smile and assure him I'm fine—just tired.

I feel dizzy and terrified I will collapse, but somehow I keep going. When I see a friendly man holding a sign with my name on it, it takes every ounce of self-restraint I have not to burst into tears of relief. He takes my case and leads me to a car.

It's late—about 2am. Everyone is sleeping, yet there is a buzz of electricity in the air. I open the windows as we whiz through the city of Denpasar and then out through winding hills and rice paddies. The warm air instantly lifts my spirits and despite how tired I am there is too much adrenalin pumping through my body for me to sleep.

It's a four hour drive but the time flies by despite having been travelling for almost 24 hours now. I am not disappointed by what I see—Bali's more beautiful than I had even imagined.

I can't believe I am here—I finally made it.

22. In full flight 7,769 miles away

20 hours later

No one saves us but ourselves. No one can and no one may. We ourselves must walk the path.

—*Gautama Buddha*

Crisis review: Dr. Cole, Dr. Fresher, Sophia's parents all present.

In the past month, Sophia's physical state has deteriorated. Recall back into hospital had been considered over a few weeks but there had been reservations about putting this into place as previous admissions have been so difficult and have escalated risks. A decision was however eventually made to recall her due to concerns about further deterioration to her physical state.

Whilst arrangements were being put into place, Sophia phoned to say she going on holiday and her flight was just about to take off. Although Sophia said she was going to Tenerife, it eventually transpired that she was on her way to Bali. Sophia has emailed her parents to say she has arrived safely and she is hoping to return in a better physical state. She has revealed to her mother that she has been using weights and is 10kg lower than the weight specified in her Community Treatment Order.

She therefore felt she had no other option than to flee the country.

It is clear Sophia lacks capacity to make decisions regarding her treatment. However, Sophia has previously exhibited a high risk of suicide when she feels trapped by treatment and therefore it is not in her best interests to initiate a search for her.

I'm sure it is a lovely place, but I have no long-held desires to go to Tenerife. I have no idea why I even came up with that decoy destination—it just sprung to mind in a moment of panic.

Those many grim days of lusting after the beauty of Bali were nothing I made a secret of, but perhaps they were wishfully thinking that it wouldn't be somewhere so far away.

They should know me by now though—my actions are usually quite extreme.

Somehow our devils are never quite what we expect when we meet them face to face."

—*Nelson De Mille*, with author's permission

The journey here really took its toll on me. I am weak all over and the breathlessness I experienced during medical crisis in hospital is back. I fall and hit my head on the marble floor in my room. I have a huge gash in my forehead that a local doctor is called to stitch up for me. The hotel staff aren't sure what to make of me—they have never seen a Western woman so underweight before and their eyes widen with shock at the sight of me. The doctor has never heard of anorexia nervosa and is completely puzzled when I try to explain what an eating disorder is to her.

Now I have made my epic journey, relief seeps through my emaciated body. I sink into sleep, unsure if I will wake up.

Review by Dr. Cole: I have made contact with Sophia via email. It is clear she has developed refeeding syndrome in Bali. She is weak and breathless, relying on hotel staff for mobility. Sophia is clearly aware that she may die. She has written a will and asked me to ensure her parents find it.

I have discussed Sophia's case with other eating disorder specialists. Sophia's most recent episode of treatment was highly coercive, life saving medical intervention was prolonged and challenging with extremely poor compliance from Sophia.

There is overall agreement that further such treatment is futile—the outcome has been very poor, with little time since discharge before life threatening deterioration. The costs of treatment to Sophia are huge—she describes her last episode of treatment as "damaging" to her and her family.

Sophia's parents feel that previous inpatient treatment has made very little difference and are ambivalent about further attempts at inpatient care. They do not wish for Sophia to be treated heavy-handedly anymore for fear of this leading to more harm than good. They accept that Sophia is not likely to live for long and have spoken to Sophia about making arrangements for her funeral.

Sophia is relieved but unsure when she will return to the UK. If she does survive during the time she is in Bali, there is high risk that she won't survive the flight back.

I have considered court of protection, but there is no disagreement within the treating team, or with patient and family about best interest and futility of compulsory treatment.

Sophia's Community Treatment Order has been revoked and we will offer her palliative care. Sophia's best prospect of surviving her illness is likely to be through supporting her own efforts and avoiding narcissistic wounding through battles of control.

Sophia has very severe and enduring anorexia nervosa. She has had many periods of inpatient treatment in different settings and treatment philosophies. She has had a long period of compulsory treatment with nasogastric feeding that has had a poor outcome. We know there is a high mortality from this condition and Sophia is at high risk of dying from her illness whatever we try to do. A good, peaceful death is far kinder and more appropriate than a death fighting coercive treatment in hospital. She may well survive longer without the threat or reality of coercive treatment. Sophia may surprise us and find a way to live.

I will surprise you all. I will find a way to live, or at least I will die trying.

From a withered tree, a flower blooms.

—*Gautama Buddha*

From first sight of me, the hotel manager knows I am not well. She doesn't push me for information but after a few days I confide in her. I feared they would chuck me out if I revealed my circumstances and degree of ill health. Instead, the staff help and nurture me.

After a few days of weakness that I thought would be the end of me, my condition begins to improve and my muscle strength returns to the point I can get about the hotel a bit. The pool boys even help me in and out of the pool. Whilst swimming, I keep a kaftan on to hide my skeletal body from the other guests. I learn to meditate and for the first time in as long as I can remember I feel relaxed. All anxiety and worry is washed away.

Most amazingly though, I have been able to eat. My bad habits are broken and I am managing small meals in the restaurant. I haven't sat down and eaten a meal since I was discharged from the unit and even then it was not out of choice. This is the first time I have willingly sat down to eat for as long as I can remember. My urges to binge are suppressed.

I stare out at the ocean, wondering if I would have the strength to enable me to swim in it. I can't remember the last time I swam in

the sea—many years. The people of Bali are genuinely kind. I wish to
thank them and ask what people in Bali buy as a thank you gift. The
young pool boy I speak to says "No presents. Just a big smile."

Email from Sophia:

Dear Dr. Cole and Dr. Fresher,

Would you kindly send written agreement that I will not be forced into compulsory treatment on return to the UK? I would like you to prepare documentation supporting a decision not to enforce treatment under the Mental Health Act in order for me to feel safe to return home.

I feel I must comment on the way this situation has been handled. My mother has informed me that there was a plan to take me against my will from my place of work. I am utterly disgusted that you would be prepared to humiliate me in such a way. To think how close I came to my life being totally devastated yet again under your care.

Treatment at your unit has done nothing but grind down my soul, battering my self-esteem and my sense of worth. I am so thankful that I made it to this safe haven to try and reverse the damaging treatment you put me through. Life here is such a contrast to being roughly manhandled and held down, tortured for months stuck in one room without any kind of therapeutic support and being stuffed with drugs and Ensure.

Gone are those days. You will never do that to me again. You came so close to destroying me, and I am so grateful that plane took off before you could drag me back into yet another round of pointless treatment. As the Balinese people have said to me,

379

my body was dead but my soul was still alive. They could see it in my eyes. That is something that my treatment under your care never acknowledged. I am learning to be strong so you can no longer degrade and control me. After such trauma, I deserve to live or die in peace.

In my history it is clear that compulsory treatment has shown to be ineffective in the long term and I think most people are in agreement on this point once they have actually engaged their brain and realised Interpol have better things to do than track down anorexics in Tenerife.

I feel I have perhaps expressed my feelings too strongly and I am certainly struggling to remain inoffensive—it is difficult when you have been through so much devastation. And currently drinking a margarita probably isn't helping either.

In the beauty of Bali, the horrors that I have been through under your care are almost forgotten, but sadly not completely. I know for however long I live, I shall always be tarnished. I will always have the nightmares, the scars, that familiar feeling of impending doom and suffering at the hands of your enforced regime. But I can still see the beauty in the world around me and for that I am incredibly grateful.

Best regards,
Sophia

Do not dwell in the past, do not dream of the future, concentrate the mind on the present moment.

—*Gautama Buddha*

For the first time in as long as I can remember, I wake up and look forward to the day ahead. Before breakfast, I go and sit by the ocean and listen to the gentle lapping of the waves. I spend the morning meditating and taking a swim in the pool when the pool boys are around to help me. At lunchtime, I wait until most of the guests have eaten and the restaurant is quiet. I feel so strange to be sitting and choosing to eat. The battles I have had with everyone over food have somewhat evaporated—I can do this, I can feed myself.

I have even chatted to some of the other guests. One lady approached me and said her daughter had been through anorexia nervosa but was now recovered. I explained my situation to her—it was bizarre that I felt able to open up to a complete stranger like that.

I am a different person to the one I left behind in the UK. I choose to eat my meals late when the bulk of the other guests are gone and I can have a bit of privacy. Although my struggles with eating have lessened greatly, I still feel self-conscious and unsure about what I am doing when I put food in my mouth. I fear people are watching me and judging what I am eating. On finishing my meal, I am full but

*the thoughts of revulsion are much more distant than they have been
for as long as I can remember.*

*I feel happy and empowered because this is the first time I have
actually felt I am successfully dealing with my eating disorder. However elated I feel, I can't ignore the worry about what things will be
like if I make it back to the UK. I have a horrible feeling anorexia
nervosa will be waiting for me at Heathrow airport and it won't take
long before I slip back into bad habits.*

Email to Sophia:

Dear Sophia,

We have given a lot of thought and discussion
regarding your care and we are agreed that compulsory treatment and nasogastric feeding are not
in your best interest.

I have absolutely no intention of imposing treatment. We would like to support you trying to find a
way to manage your illness yourself. I understand
that it was impossible to be honest and open when
you felt you had the threat of intervention hanging
over you, but perhaps without that, things could
feel different. You will not be on a Community
Treatment Order, and that is concrete evidence of a
changed approach.

I suggest that we include in your care plan a very
clear statement about compulsory treatment not
being in your best interest. The philosophy of care
will be about supporting you to have the best life
you can.

Best wishes,
Dr. Cole

We shall find peace. We shall hear the angels, we shall see the sky sparkling with diamonds.

—*Anton Chekhov*, Russian author

I can't change what has happened. I can't burn away the past. The bad memories will always be there and all I can do now is try to replace them with good memories. As much as possible, I want those that care about me to remember the good times more than the bad. If I can achieve that, it will be one victory in my battle against anorexia nervosa, even if I can't win the war.

As darkness comes over, I float on the surface of the hotel pool and stare up at the stars. There are so many and they twinkle brightly. The more you stare at the sky, the more appear. The moon looks so much bigger than I have ever seen before and it casts a beautiful shine down on the world.

I realise that this is the first time I have not been consumed with obsession and anxiety about times and rituals. I don't think about what I should be doing, what I need to do, when I will allow myself to eat, or any of the thoughts that usually plague my head.

All I think about is being in that moment, and just how beautiful the sky is.

Darkness cannot drive out darkness; only light can do that. Hate cannot drive out hate; only love can do that.

—Martin Luther King Jr.

Email from Sophia:

Dear Dr. Cole,

I know I was a very difficult patient and I can forgive most of the trauma because I know the majority of those treating me thought that what they were doing was in my best interests. However, being in Bali has enabled me to objectively reflect on my treatment and I would like to share my thoughts with you.

Unfortunately, mistakes were made pretty much from day one. Being dragged through the hospital against my will was extremely traumatic and a terrible start to relations with staff at the clinic.

A team of staff members invading my room to restrain and force feed me was certainly not the best way to handle me when I was struggling to eat. I accept at times I was too unwell to accept food orally, but there were certainly occasions where I could have been calmed down and persuaded to return to the dining room by one or two members of staff. This would have been far less traumatic for everyone involved. A team of staff jumping on you is terrifying and I think it is only human to feel attacked and defensive when put in such a situation.

There were many aspects of my treatment that reduced me to feeling like I wasn't seen as a person anymore. I was seen entirely as an anorexic monster. I can see that sometimes my behaviour justified this, but perhaps I would have felt less resistant if staff had tried to remind me that underneath the anorexia nervosa I was still "Sophia".

The decision to transfer me to Avery Lodge was regrettable. What they claimed their unit was set up for wasn't the case and you would have realised this if you had gone to inspect their set up before making the decision to transfer me. The lack of communication from Avery Lodge during the two weeks I was under their care meant that my situation became even more life threatening. If there had been communication earlier, I would have been transferred to a medical ward much quicker because it was clear that my condition was deteriorating rapidly.

As for my lengthy admission to the medical ward, I should not have been confined to a room for months without any kind of psychological support or even thought about my emotional well being. I know your response to this has been "but you were extremely unwell" but I really feel that is no excuse. I still had a brain and I still had to sit with the huge feelings of guilt, disgust and hatred with nothing but pharmaceuticals to alleviate some of my misery. With each syringe of Ensure, the only thought that would make any of it bearable was that one day I would be able to starve myself again. All of that brutality was totally pointless because in my head the anorexia nervosa just grew stronger and stronger. There was no outlet for my thoughts or feelings, nobody to help me through it, just a nurse sat flicking through one of the magazines my mum had brought me or moaning about their colleagues. It's ironic that although I had to have someone with me at all times, that episode of my life has been the loneliest I have ever felt. Even simple acts, such as doing crosswords with the staff observing me would have helped me feel less down. Tying my hands up in the way they were was excruciating and I still have nightmares where my hands are bound in such a way. A less barbaric approach would have been for the nurses assigned to be with me to hold my hands to prevent me from removing the nasogastric tube. If that had proved insufficient, it would have been kinder to sedate me to the point where I was unable to sabotage treatment. I understand the high level of risk when sedating someone as unwell as I was, but it is my view that taking such a risk would have been preferable to the trauma and barbarity of tying my hands up so tightly that I was sobbing in pain.

I think that my transfer back to your unit from being nasogastrically fed in the medical ward could have been handled differently. It was a chance for a fresh start, but instead we entered into the familiar combative approach, which has always shown to be fruitless in my long-term prognosis. My care plan was very much thrust upon me with no opportunity to discuss it or have any input in my treatment.

I had hoped that relationships with staff could be different, but instead it was just assumed I would fight the team. This was demonstrated in my organisation of the special "restrain and force feeding room" next to my room on the unit. When I was made aware of this, I immediately felt scared and defensive. All hope that things could be different was lost.

Although I find forgiveness very difficult and it has felt good to express the anger I feel towards my treatment under your care, I realise that blaming others just gives my power away and without power I cannot make change. I suffered many months of trauma and violations, but I understand you thought you were helping me.

I have found putting all this in writing very challenging and I am not sure how I feel now—maybe relieved and less angry about things. It's hard to articulate just how awful things got under your care in an assertive way because it does still plague me and most nights I have nightmares about it all happening again. One comfort is that, however low I feel when I wake up now, I can always remind myself how much more miserable I was during those dark times.

Best wishes,
Sophia

Beauty of whatever kind, in its supreme development, invariably excites the sensitive soul to tears.

—*Edgar Allan Poe*, author and poet

I wake up to the sound of rain. It's not just a light drizzle; it's rain like I have never heard rain before. I slide my hotel room door open and step out into the downpour. I walk out a few steps into the secluded grounds of the hotel and sit down on the grass.

It's early still and already light, but I am completely alone except for the frogs jumping around me. The hotel manager told me that frogs are a symbol of happiness in Bali and I reflect on this as I watch them spring up and down over the lawn. The more I watch them, the more I think they certainly do look like they are leaping with joy.

The torrential rain hits the surface of my skin and my pyjamas are completely saturated. I take a deep breath and close my eyes. I think of the past years and the journey I have travelled in that time.

The tears come slowly and then all at once. I am wracked with sorrow. I sob as the rain washes away my tears. It washes away the grief for everything I have lost. It washes away the anger and bitterness I feel. Alone in this cleansing downpour, it feels safe to be vulnerable and release these deep emotions.

After some time, the rain abruptly stops. I feel the prickling of sunshine on my skin replace the heavy raindrops. I exhale and open my eyes. I feel an overwhelming sense of relief and calm.

That was the first time it had rained in Bali for five months so, like for me, it was long overdue.

The secret of health for both mind and body is not to mourn for the past, nor to worry about the future, but to live the present moment wisely and earnestly.

—*Gautama Buddha*

Sophia's mother writes

If anyone had told me in the early years of her childhood, that my daughter Sophia would become chronically and incurably anorexic, I would have said, "Don't be ridiculous, she loves her food." She was quite chubby as a baby, but grew very tall, very fast and by the time she was at school, she was absolutely fine in terms of size and was never overweight. She did find separation difficult, and other mothers have since told me from her first school, that she was "always a little different". She was intimidated by large social gatherings and clung to me amongst people she didn't know. I was relieved therefore that she seemed to make a little group of friends at senior school. Initially I think she was terrified. She hated being conspicuously taller than the other girls in her year. She wanted to do well and was never satisfied if others did better than her. For me, one of the most painful aspects of our family life has been the breakdown of the relationship between Sophia and her sister.

Sophia's descent into chronic anorexia started gradually, and it was at least two years between the initial signs and her first admission to hospital. I felt a mixture of anger, hurt and bewilderment. Why was she behaving like this? It was baffling and desperately frustrating. It has taken me years to accept that she has an incurable mental illness. Now we have stopped trying to find an answer, a cure, we are finding life easier, but the process of grief continues. We grieve for the life she should have had. We know she will not live very long and we already grieve for her inevitable death. I failed as her mother to raise her to become a strong and healthy adult. No matter how many people tell me that it is not my fault, that fact remains. And it breaks my heart.

So fifteen years on, over half of which Sophia has spent as an inpatient in various units or on medical wards, we have reached the point where no more can be done to try to help her. So much has happened during those fifteen years, nearly all of it heart breaking, traumatising and just plain grindingly awful. There have been short bursts of hope and optimism. I will never forget the day she went back to (a new) school to start A levels. She walked through the door, so brave, shaking like a leaf. There was a period of about a year when we thought she might just make it. If I had to choose the worst times, it would be hard. There are so many. Like when she ran away from the eating disorder unit aged sixteen and we had to get her back, literally kicking and screaming. When she was discharged from a medical ward and sent home, far from well, to London to an empty flat while we were away on the other side of the world. When it was agreed she could go to a clinic abroad which we had been to visit, and felt very positive about, only to find that she had been falsifying her weight and was way below the required limit. When the police came to take her back to the unit where she was being treated under a mental health section order, after she had run away, and she was hiding in her cupboard in the bathroom. Seeing her in intensive care, unconscious from an overdose. Two months in an acute ward with terrible oedema creeping into her lungs and having to be drained off. Seeing her arrive at hospital on a stretcher, emaciated, wrapped in a foil blanket because her body temperature was so low. There are just too many other times to mention, after which we would get home absolutely drained emotionally and wretched with the misery of it all. We have however been very fortunate in having had wonderful support from family and friends.

I wish I could have handled it better, for the sake of the rest of the family who have been so badly affected by the years of worry and unhappiness. That my husband also had cancer twice and underwent a stem cell transplant didn't help! But although his illness was terrifying, I knew that there was nothing I could do except look after him as well as I could. It was up to the brilliant doctors, who immediately knew what course of action to take. And he has survived. With Sophia's illness, there was, until fairly recently, the feeling that I should be able to do something, that I could make a difference. But I was wrong. Nothing I did or tried to do made any difference at all. Loving her, my precious daughter, just wasn't enough. I no longer ask myself "What if we had done this or that?" I hope more than anything that one day they will discover a way of helping people who are addicted to starvation. Tragically it will be too late for Sophia.

Carefully I tiptoe over the hot black sand until my feet reach the cool rush of the ocean and I wade into the gentle waves. The hot sunshine prickles my skin, which is relieved as I slowly submerge my frail body into the sea. The water is so clear I can see the fish darting around beneath me. I lie on my back and just allow myself to let go. I close my eyes and drift. I am surrounded by nothing but tranquillity. This is the moment I thought I would never reach. This is the moment where all my thoughts and worries are gone. What has happened has passed and I am no longer trapped. This is the moment that the trauma and sadness is forgotten. The physical and emotional scars are washed away. This is the moment I am finally at peace.

EPILOGUE

Happiness comes when your words are of benefit to others.

—*Gautama Buddha*

Every sufferer in the horrendous world of eating disorders is different. As individuals, there will be no two pathways to recovery that are the same. Some sufferers will get well, and some unfortunately will not win their battle with this addiction. It takes a lot of courage and bravery, which I am doubtful I possess, to overcome the demon that takes over your head when in the grips of anorexia nervosa.

After experiencing a variety of different approaches to treatment, I have personally found imposed boundaries difficult to accept, but I can see they may need to be in place to support recovery. I have also found that the smaller the treatment group is, and the greater the staff to patient ratio is, the longer I have managed to stay relatively well. Sadly, in more and more situations, cuts to the costs of treatment have meant it is not financially viable for this form of treatment to be offered and admissions are becoming shorter and shorter, so there is a higher incidence of relapse. Sufferers of eating disorders are not getting quick enough referrals and the necessary funds for making a lasting change.

As a long-term chronic sufferer of anorexia nervosa, I think there is a much better chance of treatment being successful when there is as much recognition as possible of the identity of the person underneath the illness and all its associated behaviours. I have found efforts made to keep relating to me as "Sophia" and not "the anorexic" helpful. It reminds me that I am still a person beneath all the misery and that anorexia nervosa has not completely taken me over.

I very much hope that more trials and new approaches to treatment will develop to increase the chance of making a full recovery. Unfortunately, I think it is too late for that to happen whilst I am still alive, but I remain determined to get the best quality out of life whilst I still have it and I am in a place in my head now where I know I have to eat a certain amount to keep going. I don't have the life I wanted or assumed I would have, but I make the best of things and hope that there are more good days than bad. I do not wish to live for much longer—it is too hard to see friends and family enjoying life and being left alone and stuck in my behaviours.

I have so much admiration and envy for those that do have the strength to make a full recovery from this misunderstood and miserable condition. It is possible and it should always be the aim until treatment has repeatedly been deemed futile.

The reality of anorexia nervosa is that the longer you suffer, the harder it is to recover, so please recognise you need help and don't stick your head in the sand about what is happening before your life is completely destroyed. My biggest regret is that I did not accept help and face the anorexic demon when I still had a chance to live my life the way I would like to, instead of watching everyone else enjoying good times and moving on in their lives.

ACKNOWLEDGEMENTS

Thank you to my family and friends—I am sorry for the destruction that has been inflicted on your lives.

To all the staff and professionals that have tried their best to help me over the many years of treatment, thank you for trying and I am sorry for the times when I inflicted my foul temper and twisted behaviour on you.

My pet shop colleagues—you gave me a purpose again in life and I don't know what I would have done without you all.

Staff at SVT Bali—you came to my rescue in the nick of time.

And finally, Mia—my chocolate angel, you have made all of this worth it.